SUPERTRAINS

TRAINS

SOLUTIONS TO AMERICA'S TRANSPORTATION GRIDLOCK

JOSEPH VRANICH

FOREWORD BY TOM CLANCY

ST. MARTIN'S PRESS   NEW YORK

In Memory of My
Mother
Margaret Feola Vranich

Library of Congress Cataloging-in-Publication Data
Vranich, Joseph.
Supertrains : solutions to America's transportation gridlock.
p.   cm.
ISBN 0-312-06476-4
1. High speed trains—United States.   2. High speed trains—Europe.   3. High speed trains—
Japan.   4. Magnetic levitation vehicles—Research.   I. Title.
HE2741.V73   1991   385'.2—dc20   91-21176

FIRST EDITION: DECEMBER 1991
10 9 8 7 6 5 4 3

CONTENTS

FOREWORD

by

Tom Clancy

PEOPLE HAVE TO TRAVEL. WHETHER FOR BUSINESS
or pleasure, we all have to move from place to place. Sometimes
we're in a hurry, sometimes not, but more often the former. It
is, moreover, a truism that no one really likes to travel—we like
to *be* somewhere else, but the process of getting there is usually
boring and frequently uncomfortable. The privacy and flexibility
of our personal automobiles—America's most frequent mode of
transportation—must be balanced against the discomfort of its
seats and the often-denied fact that people get killed in large
numbers on our highways. Navigating into strange cities is always an adventure, and when you get there, where do you leave
the car? Still, being master of your fate is what America is all
about, and the car gives you that feeling of control over your
destiny. We hold on to that illusion even when we're crawling
along at 5 mph on an interstate that costs upwards of $50 million
per mile.

Air travel puts us in even less comfortable seats, but gives
us safety and speed. It adds the hassles of airport accessibility
(something of a joke in Washington, D.C., and many other cities),
delays, missing baggage, and TV-dinner food.

Both forms of travel are remarkably inefficient in terms of
energy consumption. One hyperbolic example is the *Concorde*,
which weighs 400,000 pounds when it lifts off in the United
States and 200,000 when it lands in England, having left *100
tons* of fuel in its supersonic wake. It doesn't require too great
an imagination to understand that it takes a lot of energy to lift
a 100-ton aircraft seven miles and then propel it at 600 miles
per hour. Less apparent is the fact that our airways, like our
highways, are growing more crowded. For instance, air traffic

control radar scopes must be run by the coolest professionals, since to the unschooled their job looks like organizing a street riot by remote control.

In short, while both modes of transportation have their advantages—some real, some psychological—both suffer from the same fundamental malady: the systems and spaces that support them are at the limit of their capacity. We can't make more airspace, and building additional highways is hugely expensive. In addition, both are vulnerable to fluctuations in our energy supply, and the oil they use is instantly converted into pollution, of which we have all too much already.

Yet Americans love to travel, and that isn't going to stop. What if someone were to invent a magical new mode of transportation that was safe, energy efficient, and environmentally benign?

Someone has. It's called the train.

There was a time when many Americans traveled by train, and in areas where such travel is available, many still do. Amtrak moves more people between Washington and New York than Donald Trump or Pan Am does with their shuttles (both of which, at this writing, are on the block to be sold). The Superliner trains operating out of Chicago are fully reserved months in advance. In fact, Amtrak turns away one customer for every one it serves, which is another way of saying that it could double its existing equipment and still be running at capacity.

What is really remarkable about this, however, is that Amtrak is 1930s technology at best. The Pennsylvania Railroad introduced its GG1 high-speed electric locomotives during the Great Depression, and the new Swedish-designed AEM-7 engines that operate on the same corridor today are little changed in speed. The same is true of diesel-powered engines on other routes.

Amtrak's fastest run is the *Metroliner Express*, which travels from Washington to New York at an average speed of 87 mph, and a top speed of 125 mph. For a distance of 225 miles, that is fast enough to out-perform airliners that travel six times as fast. Why? The *Metroliner* leaves from a city center and arrives at a city center. It's not affected by adverse weather or taxiway backup. The traffic control system under which it operates allows much closer spacing of trains, and the trains themselves can be increased in size to permit higher passenger loads. And that's 1930s technology.

Unfortunately, 1930 is about where American development of passenger trains ended. But not elsewhere.

In France there is the high-speed *Train à Grande Vitesse*, or the TGV. It cruises at about 200 mph, and has recently been tested at a top speed of well over 300 mph. A simple calculation reveals that at an average speed of 200 mph, these trains can compete with airline flights out to a range of about 500 miles. The majority of airline flights in America don't go any farther than that.

TGV has 10 times the energy efficiency of an airliner. It requires only a relatively straight right-of-way approximately 50 feet wide. It's electrically powered, and electrical generating plants, if they're properly run, don't have to pollute anything. And it makes money. TGV is showing better than a 15 percent profit over and above debt service. Transportation doesn't get much better than that.

Yet TGV is primitive technology also. An electrically powered locomotive driving a steel-wheel train over steel track isn't exactly a technological revolution. What France has done—and we have not—was select an efficient method of transportation as a national goal and use off-the-shelf tools to build it. Seems simple enough.

Another emerging technology is magnetic levitation. Invented here in the United States, maglevs float on a pulsing magnetic field and, while nobody really knows how fast they can go, 300 mph looks like a reasonably conservative figure. Already prototype trains are blazing along test tracks in Germany and Japan, but not in America.

It might have happened here. Railroads once had the prestige and financial capital to do nearly anything, but that changed for several reasons. Railroads matured as a technology more than 60 years ago. They were for a long time effectively a monopoly, and they rapidly developed the customary diseases of monopolies: first they charged too much for what they did; next they became arrogant; finally, they ossified. All three traits earned them the enmity of their own labor force, the public, and Congress. Even so, the result wasn't quite fair. Railroads, which had to build their own tracks and stations, and had to pay taxes on every bit of it, found themselves in competition against highways and airports built with public funds. At the same time, railroads were regulated by people who thought public service meant giving a hard time to the railroad industry.

Still, the railroads largely destroyed themselves as passenger carriers. Successful companies are run by providing the public with good service, and by taking proper care of employees. The record of railroad labor policies still echoes today in union disputes that are every bit as acrimonious and adversarial as the better-known disputes with air-traffic controllers. Even commercially successful railroads are still recovering from their own mismanagement.

FOREWORD

America could tolerate that so long as there were alternatives, but those alternatives are beginning to fade. There is not room in the sky for many more airplanes, nor is there room on the ground for many more highways. Our country will soon need a more efficient means of moving people rapidly, safely, and comfortably from place to place. History teaches that if transportation by rail is managed properly it will make money. After all, people will always need to travel.

Sooner or later there will be another energy crisis—perhaps sooner because oil-producing nations may limit our oil imports, or later because the oil may someday run dry. We ought to start thinking about that eventuality now. Rail travel will never replace cars and planes. We'll always need automobiles for their flexibility, and we'll always need aircraft for their speed. However, what high-speed rail travel can do is reduce the strain on both systems without polluting the sky or destroying much open ground. America needs a coherent national transportation policy now, before one is forced upon us. Joe Vranich examines one entirely reasonable answer to this coming dilemma. I think this is an important book.

SUPERTRAINS

ALL ABOARD, AMERICA!

"Make no little plans. They have
no magic to stir men's blood."
—Daniel H. Burnham, 1846–1912,
architect of Washington Union Station

PATRICK CLEARY IS YOUNG, DEDICATED, AND DE-
clares with a smile, "Labor is my life." He traveled from Washington, D.C., to several Pacific nations while working on labor issues for the Republican National Committee. Arriving in Japan, he went directly to Tokyo's Okura Hotel for an overnight rest before shuttling off to another city the next day.

"I asked the Toyota guy in Washington, 'Hey, I'm going to be in that end of the world—if I stop off through Japan, can you get me a tour of your plant?' " said Cleary. "He said, 'Fine. When you get there, in your hotel room will be a train ticket.' I figured, fine, you know, I'll be rumbling on this old rickety train for like 20 minutes."

Cleary didn't think about what was in store for him at the station, but there it was. Shimmering in the early light of a clear January morning sat the fabled Bullet Train. It was the first time Cleary had seen one. The bullet nose and slightly bulging sides of the blue and ivory train warranted a lingering look.

Realizing this was no local—this was a Supertrain—brightened his mood.

"It looked fast just sitting there—sleek and shiny, looked great." Cleary got aboard and then, well, "Then it took off, and I mean took off—*psssssh!*—it moves. It was so smooth and very quiet."

Cleary looked around and was impressed. The train was clean. The conductor saluted Cleary with a bow as he took the ticket. Attendants pushing carts came through selling trays of food and drink. Cleary passed on the selections, which included *unaju teishoku*, an entree of eel, and *makunouchi bento*, an assorted dish of smoked fish, pickled vegetables and rice. It was too early for *sake*.

How about the scenery?

The first true-blue high-speed trains were Japan's Bullet Trains, running since 1964. The speedsters have been popular since they went into service between Tokyo and Osaka. Their punctual operation has set the standard against which all other developers of high-speed trains, both steel-wheel and maglev, are judged. *(Japan National Tourist Organization)*

ALL ABOARD AMERICA!

"It goes right by Mount Fuji; it's visible from far away and that's really neat to pass," said Cleary. "I loved it—I can stare out the window with the best of them. And I just like the railroad, there's some fascination with the railroad."

His two-hour ride to the industrial city of Nagoya went without a hitch. Lights inside the cars came on automatically when the train entered tunnels. The smooth ride was deceptive, and he did not know he was traveling at more than two miles a minute. His arrival in Nagoya: on time.

Cleary is not a railroad buff, but he has a railroad heritage.

"I took a train to high school every day for four years in the cradle of civilization, New Jersey," he said. "I rode the Erie-Lackawanna, which is now New Jersey Transit, from Mountain View and got off in Hoboken." Railroads, however, go further back in his family—both of his grandfathers rode trains to court the women who would become his grandmothers. "The train was the cornerstone of both my grandfathers' courtships."

French TGV is the fastest train in the world.
(French National Railways)

Today, his interest in railroads is professional. President George Bush appointed Cleary, a lawyer, to the National Mediation Board, where he is one of three members who handles disputes arising out of the Railway Labor Act. In official Washington, Cleary is a very important person. But Cleary also is a very excited person—excited about Bullet Trains. "I mentioned it to everybody," Cleary said. "In the course of going to Toyota, something that otherwise could have been forgotten—the mode of

ALL ABOARD AMERICA!

transportation—wasn't. I always mentioned to people '... *and* I took the Bullet Train.' If the people I'm talking to have ridden it, they say, 'Isn't it great?' If they haven't, they say, 'Wow! What's it like?' There's a real fascination out there about trains."

When asked how the trips aboard the Bullets—he's been aboard twice since—affected Cleary's views about trains, he paused, then said, "I know exactly how. It's expanded my horizons, if you will, like the difference between seeing a Model T and a Porsche. If we were still riding in Model Ts, you'd say, 'I'm really sick of this.' Then, all of a sudden you'd get in a Porsche and say, 'I love cars!' The Bullet Trains showed me the potential of rail travel."

With building enthusiasm, Cleary added, "The more people who travel to Europe, who travel to Japan, who use the high-speed trains, the better our chances for getting it over here. Having seen it in action, it just opened a whole new realm of possibilities. Having seen Paris, if you will, it's hard to stay down on the farm. It's terrific. We should be building a good high-speed rail system for ourselves."

The trend is on Cleary's side. For example, "Eurailpass sales exploded in 1990," reported Stephen F. Forsyth, president of the Forsyth Travel Library in Shawnee Mission, Kansas. "Eurail actually ran out of passes in the early summer" because so many Americans opted to travel on Europe's train system.

Cleary will live to see Supertrains—trains that travel between 150 and 300 mph—running in America. Dazzling projects are being planned, reflecting the shift in the public's attitude about high-speed trains from a position of mere curiosity to one of interest and even demand.

The advanced European rail systems are in operation and have proven records. At least one magnetic levitation, or maglev, system is "ready to go." Public enthusiasm for the trains is growing, especially as highway and air travel gridlock shows no signs of easing.

"Coming back from Chicago recently I was delayed over an hour, not because of air traffic control problems, but simply because we have too many flights and not enough runways," said Transportation Secretary Sam Skinner. "The fact is the roads, bridges, and runways of America are wearing out, while the demand for mobility continues to grow. As our economy expands, as our citizens' aspirations expand, transportation demand will continue to grow. So the congestion, delays, and discomforts will only get worse unless we do something to prepare for tomorrow's transportation demand."

Will there be a place for Supertrains? "There's no question that there are some very, very knowledgeable people throughout the world who believe that high-speed rail is an effective way to move people, specifically on what I call shorter routes," said Secretary Skinner.

The largest intercity travel market in the United States is made up of people traveling 600 miles or less. True, there are plenty of coast-to-coast air schedules. But for every New York–Los Angeles flight, there are dozens of flights over shorter distances like New York–Boston, Cleveland–Cincinnati, Los Angeles–Las Vegas.

The Supertrains will operate on all-new tracks or guideways for most or all of their routes. Most systems will not physically intermingle with existing rail lines, whose physical structure and engineering are designed for heavy freight trains—and thus are unable to support true high-speed passenger train operations.

Super-speed trains will run in America—trains that are

ALL ABOARD AMERICA!

already running or are at least successfully tested. Scheduled to start running in this decade, they will whisk us between major cities at speeds never imagined before, and millions of travelers will flock to them.

Magnetic levitation trains will cruise as high as 300 mph. Maglev trains have been tested for many years, have carried thousands of riders on demonstration runs in Germany and Japan, and will be put in place here. America's first Supertrain will begin service in Florida, where a maglev demonstration line will be built. The United States, in an effort to catch up with the technology, has finally started a maglev research program.

Some trains will be maglev while others will be steel-wheel versions. "I believe that just as each family has a choice, because of their pocketbook, or where they live, they can choose a Cadillac, or a small truck, or a Volkswagen, there's a vehicle for them," said Robert J. Casey, executive director of the Pittsburgh-based High Speed Rail Association. "The same exists in the field of high-speed trains—one type may be more appropriate in one area, and another technology elsewhere."

Casey ought to know. He was named by Ohio in 1979 to direct that state's Supertrain agency, becoming the first employee anywhere in the nation whose duties were dedicated full time to developing a Supertrain system. He went on to direct a similar agency in Pennsylvania.

Throughout the 1980s, studies have been completed in one state after another, finding that America has a pent-up demand for fast train service. In the West, the southern California–Las Vegas line is expected to serve almost eight million people in the year 2000. Who would opt for the five-hour endurance drive through the desert when a Supertrain can get travelers from the Los Angeles area to Las Vegas in 1¼ hours?

Considered together with the lines planned for Florida, Texas, Ohio and Pennsylvania, Supertrains can take more than 40 million travelers annually out of the skies and off the highways, easing America's mobility problems. The issue is warming up in Minnesota, Wisconsin, Illinois, the Northeast, and elsewhere. Canadians, too, are active, discussing a Supertrain line for the Windsor–Toronto–Ottawa–Montreal–Quebec corridor.

Travelers will find they can relax more easily on trains, which are safer and more comfortable than either airplanes or autos. Thanks go to the Europeans and Japanese for removing the technical barriers. The French have their very high speed *Train à Grande Vitesse*, or TGV; the Germans the Intercity Express, or ICE; and the Japanese the famed Bullet Trains.

It's time for these trains in America.

Airport congestion is causing a growing number of travelers to despise flying. One example of that phenomenon is that many people enrolled in airline frequent-flier programs do not want to take free airplane trips on their vacations. William Jackman, a vice-president of the Air Transport Association, said, "Some frequent fliers are not interested in a postman's holiday. They would welcome the opportunity to get merchandise" like clothing and appliances. So many Americans sell their frequent-flier benefits that nearly 50 coupon brokers do a brisk business throughout the nation.

That so many are eager to sell their coupons is understandable. The public is fed up with late airplanes, computer-generated fares that result in wildly different ticket prices for identical trips, and overcrowded "cattle car" conditions. Then there are the forgotten travelers, the 25 million Americans—about one out of every seven adults—who are afraid to fly, as estimated by a Boeing study.

Transport demand continues to grow. The population of the United States now stands at about 250 million. Although the rate of population growth is expected to slow, the total is still expected to rise by 47 million persons between 1990 and 2020, an increase of nearly 20 percent. The 1990 census figures show that more than half of the nation's population lives in urban areas of at least a million people. It is the first time the nation's population has been so concentrated, and the pattern improves the market for high-volume, high-speed train systems.

Record numbers of women in the workplace continue to increase the value that society attaches to time and convenience. William Johnston, a vice-president at the Hudson Institute said that people in two-income families report a dramatically declining number of leisure hours.

"We see a premium being placed upon time by all kinds of people in our society and it's increasingly affected every kind of decision, ranging from where to shop, where to live, what sort of transportation system is desired," says Johnston. "Time, measured from initial departure to final arrival has become the single most important aspect of a satisfactory transportation system. The important questions have become, 'How long does it take to get to work?' 'How long does it take to get in and out of the parking lot?' 'How long does it take to travel from Los Angeles to Chicago or to the beach or to the mountains?'"

The American Association of State Highway and Transportation Officials reports that surface travel demand is expected to at least double by the year 2020. If this nation is to attempt to keep up with the anticipated growth—while at the same time providing faster transportation—then it must begin to turn to new train technologies.

German Intercity Express (ICE). *(German Rail)*

The arrival of Supertrains will instill fear in some and hope in others. Southwest Airlines, based in Dallas, already has become panic-stricken and lobbied the state legislature against the trains. Others, however, support them as a way to relieve congested airports. USAir Chairman Edwin I. Colodny, in a Washington, D.C., news conference, told surprised reporters that

ALL ABOARD AMERICA!

removing short-distance flights from critical airports, and building Supertrain systems instead, might be more efficient than trying to build new airports.

Europe has learned to connect services in a way that eases travel. Passengers can transfer between trains and airplanes inside the terminal at a number of major European airports. Many Americans will be lured to Western Europe in 1992 when the Continent celebrates the 500th anniversary of the Old World's discovery of the New World. These tourists will witness the ease with which they can change from one system to another.

Perhaps more than anything else, Americans will experience a *bona fide* cultural change—a fundamental shift in the way we think about transportation. Few in the United States appreciate the benefits of a good rail system. We just don't have that many *superior* trains anymore.

Some Amtrak trains are indeed time-competitive with air travel, particularly between New York, Philadelphia, and Washington. Amtrak has trains that are fun to ride, like the long-distance trains that thread the narrow canyons of the Rockies or glide through our national parks. Nevertheless, the North American continent has no trains like the fast trains in Europe and Japan. Additionally, the federal government, until now so overwhelmingly skewed to improving air and highway systems, has cast a shadow over the virtues of trains. The result is that the American public poorly understands the progress that has been made in rail service.

Washington has lavished billions of dollars on highways and airports, but says that because of the national debt—which exceeds a whopping $3.2 trillion—it can't afford to invest in trains. Indeed, that debt is big: it forces the government to spend more than 20 percent of the entire federal budget on interest pay-

Italian ETR-500. *(Breda Transportation Inc.)*

ments, about $236 billion per year. In 1990, the federal government spent six times more on interest on the national debt than on transportation.

Washington has been pitiful in its paltry research program for train technology. Yet, that same federal government has been generous in its funding for aviation, which rose 125 percent from the last budget submitted by President Jimmy Carter to the last budget by President Ronald Reagan. Highway funding, already into the billions of dollars, is up 28 percent in that period. President Bush generously increased road and aviation budgets still more, with highway funds reaching an all-time record high in the 1991 budget.

Ironically, since both air and highway travel use energy inefficiently, both programs foster increased reliance on foreign

ALL ABOARD AMERICA!

oil. It's as if the country has not learned its lessons from two previous energy crises during the 1970s. Some conservationists, alarmed at surging oil imports, have long pointed to America's vulnerability to Mideast oil flow disruptions, the very kind that occurred in the aftermath of the 1990 Iraqi invasion of Kuwait.

The federal government has made a remarkably small commitment to developing domestic Supertrain technologies. Washington foolishly killed its advanced train program in 1975, and America is 20 years behind European and Japanese Supertrain developments. And compared to subsidies for airports and highways, the amounts to Amtrak are tiny. Small wonder that trains overseas are so much better than ours.

America certainly has a significant amount of catching up to do. High-speed advocate Robert Casey says of America: "It happens that the United States is a Third World country as far as high-speed rail is concerned—it's a disgrace."

American railroads have known for years what it takes to run speedy trains. The New York Central broke all records when, on the tenth of May, 1893, steam locomotive *No. 999* pulled the *Empire State Express* at the then breathtaking speed of 112½ mph between Batavia and Buffalo. The engineer, Charles H. Hogan, and *No. 999* became world famous. Legend has it that after the trip Charlie Hogan's hair changed from deep brown to snowy white. By the 1930s, several American railroads regularly scheduled passenger trains for 100 mph runs.

Our railroad ancestors would be unhappy with the condition of passenger trains in America today. However, so would some aviation pioneers. Robert Goddard, the "Father of American Rocketry," might take one look at gridlock today and recommend new trains.

In the November 1909 issue of *Scientific American*, Goddard wrote of magnetic levitation trains. He suggested that a tunnel could be built from New York to Boston, and, "The cars might be held in suspension by the repulsion of opposing magnets. . . . When thus isolated, they could be propelled by the magic power of magnetism." Sounds better than driving the New Jersey Turnpike.

An example of today's much needed new thinking is found in Pennsylvania where a state legislator, Richard A. Geist, has successfully attacked myths about super-speed trains.

Geist represents Altoona, a community with a rich railroad heritage, but more importantly he has served as chairman of the Pennsylvania Intercity High Speed Rail Passenger Commission. In comments at the National Press Club in Washington, D.C., he said it is a myth that Americans are too wedded to their autos to be lured to trains. Geist offered evidence of Amtrak's success between Los Angeles and San Diego. There, Amtrak traffic has grown to more than 1.7 million people per year, setting records, and that service is not even considered high speed.

The experience proved that Americans, even in auto-dominated southern California, will turn to trains. Of course, Amtrak trains there for the most part are frequent, comfortable, and on time. That counts for a lot.

Another myth is that the United States is not populated densely enough for Supertrains to work here. Geist pointed out that the popular French TGV on its Paris–Lyon route actually serves a sparse intermediate area. Ohio wants to link Cleveland with Columbus, Dayton, and Cincinnati by Supertrains. That corridor, for one, has a greater population density than the TGV Paris–Lyon route.

ALL ABOARD AMERICA!

Geist and his allies can refute many other myths about Supertrains. They'll have to keep at it to overcome the vacuum in leadership that America has suffered on this issue.

One often-asked question is whether trains operating at such speeds are safe. Paul H. Reistrup, a former Amtrak president, praised the Japanese and French safety records before a Transportation Department policy study group.

"The Japanese *Shinkansen* has never had a passenger killed in 25 years of operations. During that time, the system has carried almost three billion passengers." Reistrup reports that his audiences are always surprised to hear that. In the same quarter-century, more than a million Americans died on highways. The French TGV also has a perfect passenger safety record.

We are quite unlike our overseas neighbors. The industrial powerhouses of Japan and Germany have been joined by Spain, Great Britain, Belgium, Netherlands, Portugal, Switzerland, and Austria in what is becoming a common quest—building new Supertrains instead of more highways and airports.

Their central governments have learned so much about the art and science of such systems. Most Japanese Bullet Trains have operated at a profit for years. Ridership on the French TGV was so high at first that the railroad found itself in immediate need of 13 more trainsets—the original 87 trains simply could not handle the demand. These governments made a sustaining commitment to build the new systems.

With borders so close, cooperation among the Europeans is absolutely necessary and joint efforts are thriving. The long-sought-for Channel Tunnel between England and France is under construction, with completion due by mid-1993. The tunnel, first proposed in 1802, will allow the 31-mile trip between the French and English coasts to take just 33 minutes, at a maximum speed of 99 mph. Thus, not only do the Europeans build new trains, they build new tracks, new routes, new stations, and even new tunnels—an entire infrastructure—to do the job right.

Daring projects that test the skills of railroad engineering staffs are under way in the Soviet Union, according to Eugeney A. Sotnikov, deputy director of the Railway Research Institute in Russia. He has spoken of passenger services planned for 180 mph, building tunnels 30 miles long under seas and through mountains, and railroad construction in regions of permafrost and deserts. Again, the trains and the infrastructure would be built as one package.

Essentially, the French look to Paris and the Japanese to Tokyo for a vision of what their future holds. The British, Spanish, Italians, and Germans look to the experts in their capitals, too.

In the United States, it's been quite different. Here, the action has come from the states. Floridians look to Tallahassee and Texans to Austin for leadership on this issue. In tourist-dependent areas—Las Vegas and Orlando are but two examples —the spark has come from local leaders. An official National Governors' Association policy statement urges consideration of Supertrains "in heavily traveled transportation corridors."

State highway departments have always been strong advocates of paving over America. Now, highway bottlenecks are so costly to correct that even they have had a change of heart. In a report issued in July 1989, the American Association of State Highway and Transportation Officials said it "believes that the federal government should support and participate in a public-private partnership to develop high-speed rail in those selected corridors in which it will relieve highway and airport congestion, and improve intercity travel efficiency."

That? From the highway lobby?

Even state aviation officials are stirring. A California aviation plan said that new train technologies "could either supplement or supplant air travel for trips of 300 to 500 miles or could provide links between outlying airports and the urban centers."

However, until the late 1980s, it's been nearly impossible to plan Supertrains in America.

What happened to the spirit our federal government used to show in pioneering advances in transportation? We have yet to see a transportation secretary call for a network of Supertrains in America. Had the federal government neglected highways and aviation the way it has Supertrain development, we would be driving on two-lane roads and flying on DC-3s into one-runway backwater airports.

An exception to negative thinking in Washington is a small agency named the Federal Railroad Administration, a part of the Department of Transportation, which is due some credit for helping to fund Supertrain studies in several states. Although the effort has been puny by aviation or highway standards, without it America would be further behind.

The Congress has begun to stir. In a 1989 report the Senate Maglev Technology Advisory Committee recommended start of a program costing $750 million over a seven-year period to design a domestic maglev train. Another pro-Supertrain report was issued that year, this one by the Argonne National Laboratory. Funded by the United States Department of Energy, it concluded that maglev trains could replace airplanes in many trips of 600 miles or less. The study suggested building a 2,000-mile network, running alongside interstate highways and stopping at both airports and downtown train stations. The study leader, Larry Johnson, says by reducing air traffic congestion, trains could eliminate the need for sprawling new airports.

"Airports are so costly and difficult to build that nobody wants one," said Johnson. He said the project could be funded by the federal government or by the airlines.

Is the United States really going to have Supertrains? Haven't these proposals failed in the past? The answer to both questions is, yes.

Today's Supertrain developments are a far cry from the early 1980s when residents of southern California communities resisted a Bullet Train proposed to link Los Angeles with San Diego. Then, the organizers of the American High Speed Rail Corporation made several mistakes.

In a misguided attempt to cut red tape, they petitioned the legislature in Sacramento for an exemption from all environmental requirements. That was a terrible move, for it turned environmentalists from being strong allies into real foes.

Another serious blow was a set of faulty ridership estimates. The Los Angeles–San Diego program's credibility suffered because planners said 11 million passengers a year would use the line. Critics said the projections were too high, and Wall Street agreed.

Also, the public's allegations of noise problems never were adequately addressed. The planners failed to do simple things, like return phone calls from the media, and as a result failed to convey how the new generation of Japanese Bullet Trains proposed for the line were much quieter than the first ones built a quarter of a century ago.

As the *San Diego Union* said in an editorial, the California

German magnetic levitation Transrapid train.   *(Transrapid International)*

failure was "less the fault of the idea than it was the maladroit manner of its presentation." Result: one project killed.

Those lessons were not lost on Supertrain planners today. The emerging industry, through the High Speed Rail Association, created tough guidelines by which ridership estimates are prepared—a non-controversial method that will stand up to close public scrutiny. A number of states have used it in their new studies; criticism is absent, and Wall Street is interested.

Perhaps most importantly, today's Supertrain planners, unlike the promoters of the ill-fated California project, strive to involve the communities that are to be served through public hearings and other efforts.

The Supertrains of the future are a response to the travel boom that is expected to continue. An all-time United States travel record was set in 1988 when the number of intercity "passenger-miles," the equivalent of one passenger traveling one mile, totaled 1.968 trillion. That means that total domestic travel more than doubled since 1966. All predictions point to more of the same. Inbound tourism, too, is on the upswing. In 1990 the United States expected to attract 42.5 million foreign visitors, and that could double by the year 2000, according to the Department of Commerce. New systems are needed to handle all this traffic.

Advocates of Supertrains think of what rail travel can be, not what it has been. "I wish we would get on the stick and move forward on this," said Bullet Train rider Patrick Cleary. "Whatever it takes, either a combination of funding from the feds to underwrite the bonds, the cursed gas tax, or private-sector monies or guarantees here and there, whatever it takes."

Cleary and others wonder how to pay to build Supertrains. There are answers, with private interests willing to help finance the new trains in some cases. This is a case of history repeating itself. The first railroad here, the Baltimore & Ohio, was funded partially with foreign money. Funds were raised in Great Britain by B&O President Louis McLane to allow construction of the line west to the Ohio River in the 1840s.

In the 1980s, Americans have invested in the French TGV line, as well as the English Channel rail tunnel, and are enjoying the returns from the former. Such investment can happen here, but first the government will have to overhaul some short-sighted and unfair policies.

Financial experts here can consider investment-grade ridership studies that predict farebox revenue will exceed operating costs on some high-density routes. In many instances, however, some public funding will be necessary if Supertrains are to compete effectively with subsidized aviation and highway systems. A mixture of public and private financing to build Supertrains is warranted because the social benefits and greatly reduced congestion and pollution are well worth the cost.

However, a national plan for a Supertrain network is lacking. Federal officials barely blink an eye when it comes to financing aviation—one government estimate is that nearly $117 billion in tax dollars will be spent for new air traffic control systems and airports by the year 2000. If that's what America wants, fine. But let's bring the facts out in the open. Let's quit pretending that aviation is "private enterprise" at work when in fact airlines operate through an infrastructure that receives billions in subsidies annually, expenditures that far exceed the user fees collected.

Highways aren't cheap, either. In 1989, Seattle opened seven miles of an interstate highway at a cost of $1.46 billion. Admittedly, the project on I-90 involved building a bridge across Lake Washington, but was it worth spending nearly $208.6 million *per mile* on the highway? Many think not.

Estimates say the total investment needed in our transportation infrastructure by the year 2010 will be as much as $3 trillion. Should that money be available, will we spend it wisely? One answer: cost comparisons show that Supertrains running in densely traveled corridors would reduce the need for new airports and actually save the government money.

"In this decade, we will have two or three high-speed rail corridors and one or two maglev systems," said Gilbert E. Carmichael, head of the Federal Railroad Administration. The evidence suggests his prediction is correct.

Initiation of service on just one line will stir demand elsewhere in the nation. The day a conductor collects the first Supertrain ticket is the day remaining doubts will be swept away. Then, America will rejoice in the realization that fast trains are a practical way to travel.

As Pennsylvania's Rick Geist says, "The right elements exist for a 'typically American' program. Americans like speed, Americans like high technology, and Americans like comfort. High-speed trains have all of that, and can offer capacity expansion in a less environmentally destructive manner than any other mode."

We can build upon our rich railroad heritage. The New York Central Railroad began operating the most famous train in the United States, *The 20th Century Limited*, on June 15, 1902. It was faster, better, sleeker than anything before it and became an instant hit on the New York–Chicago route. History is repeating itself. New types of trains are about to help usher in the next century.

Perhaps one of the new Supertrains will be named *The 21st Century Limited*. That would signal a new era in common-sense use of advanced technology to solve travel problems. Another name might be *The Sunshine Express*—apt, because every time a passenger hops on a Supertrain instead of driving, our air stays a bit cleaner.

Within just a few years, Patrick Cleary and millions of other American travelers will be using the phrase "meet me at the train station" in conjunction with their domestic trips. No longer will it be necessary to fly across oceans to sample a Supertrain ride.

OVERSEAS RACE ON RAILS

"Passenger traffic growth is continuing and we are making substantial profits from TGV traffic."
—Jacques Fournier, Chairman,
French National Railways

EVER SINCE THE AMBITIOUS JAPANESE BURST ON the scene with the Bullet Trains in 1964, planners worldwide have talked about fast trains. Unfortunately, "talk" was just about the limit of their activity in many countries, especially the United States. But the French and a few others did something about high-speed trains—they built them.

The French trains are remarkable. Every day in a busy Paris terminal, polished trains depart on time, sail west through the French countryside, and deliver contented passengers to points on the Atlantic coast. In another bustling Paris station, trains leave in a different direction, flashing their bright orange

color as they dash to destinations as far away as Switzerland and the Riviera.

They are the TGVs, the fastest regularly scheduled trains in the world. On the Atlantic Line, these Supertrains operate at a top speed of 186.4 mph. Even at that pace, the wine doesn't spill.

The day they began running in September 1989, the *New York Times* noted: "Paralleling the superhighway at some points, the train easily left behind France's speeding drivers, who often drive at 110 miles per hour." Those same TGVs, in a special run

Ground transport records and ridership projections have been broken in France with the TGVs, the world's fastest regularly scheduled trains. This version, the *Atlantique*, connects points on the Atlantic Coast with Paris. Demand is building in the United States and Canada for TGV-type Supertrain service.
(French National Railways)

in western France on May 18, 1990, set a speed record of 320.2 mph. The news was big enough to make the American television networks. Not only was the TGV the fastest train in the world, the record marked the third time in a month that the TGV had bettered all previous speed records. Also, crossing of two trains at a relative speed of 483 mph was tested without problems.

Officials of the French National Railways, known as *Société Nationale des Chemins de Fer Français*, or SNCF, hope to keep increasing the maximum speed on each of the new TGV lines it opens. SNCF plans to run London-bound TGVs at 198 mph beginning in 1993. The new line to the Riviera, due to enter service in 1997, will see TGV trains break records by running at 217 mph in regular service.

On the TGV Southeast and *Atlantique* lines, the trains run about 10 minutes apart in peak periods and they have on-time performance records of about 98 percent. Both have something else in common: French President François Mitterrand attended the Atlantic Line commissioning in May 1989 and the Southeast Line opening in September 1981. He lavished praise on railway officials and industry leaders for the bold thinking that characterizes the Supertrain program.

TGVs are so successful—carrying 24 million customers in 1989—they are spreading to other parts of Europe. Hoping for an international network of TGVs, the French have sold the high-technology trains to Spain and are pursuing opportunities in Belgium, Holland, the United Kingdom, and Germany. Overseas, their marketing efforts include the United States, Canada, South Korea, and Brazil.

A ride on a TGV is better than any auto or air trip. No matter how much the train picks up speed, the ride *stays* smooth. TGV Conductor Christian Chaintreau, when asked what it feels

Whoosh! This French TGV was setting a new world's speed record of 320.2 mph at the time this photo was taken on May 18, 1990. The event made news around the world, including coverage on American television and radio networks.

(French National Railways)

OVERSEAS RACE ON RAILS

like to ride a train at nearly 190 mph, said, "Oh, it's not so scary. I don't really get the impression that we're moving at such speed."

The trains ride over continuous welded rails, eliminating the "clickety-clack" sound of the old days. Except on approaches to a few stations, the trains do not meet on the same level with highway crossings. Tracks are built above or below roads, eliminating safety hazards associated with motor vehicles at grade crossings.

Reservations are required so all passengers are guaranteed seats. Travelers can also reserve meal service in first class, where a choice of hot or cold food is brought to a passenger's seat with French aplomb.

This Supertrain is reasonably priced, with the basic fare no different than other trains. Gerard Mathieu, director of the International Department of the French National Railway, said, "A series of supplements levied on certain TGV trains at particular times of day, or at busy periods, has enabled daily or weekly traffic peaks to be evened off." Travelers can avoid the supplement charged on peak-hour TGVs by switching to earlier or later trains, and Americans traveling on the Eurailpass are excused from paying a supplement.

The railroad uses a calendar coded in red, white, and blue, the colors in the French national flag, to set out the price for travel on each day of the year. On blue days, some 250 off-peak days annually, all fare reductions apply. On white, or standard, days, only certain lower fares are available. On days marked in red, the peak travel days in France, the fares are highest, preventing a massive influx of passengers that it would not be able to handle. The railway also has devised season tickets for regular TGV users.

Evolution continues as the French upgrade each generation of TGV trains. The blurrier train above is the original TGV that runs from Paris to Lyon at a top speed of 168 mph. The train below is the newer, lighter *Atlantique* version that operates at 186.4 mph. *(French National Railways)*

OVERSEAS RACE ON RAILS

Americans tend to be familiar with super-saver fares offered by airlines, but such tickets impose more restrictions than does the French railroad.

The newest generation TGV trains are 10 cars long, with a power car at each end. One set can carry 485 passengers each trip, but at busy times two trains will operate coupled together with a total capacity of nearly 1,000 riders. That is about the capacity of two jumbo jets, but passengers ride in far greater comfort than they would cramped into smaller airplane seats.

On the new Atlantic Line, the train's exterior color scheme is blue and silver, evoking, the French say, the sun, the sand, and the sea. Compartments, a meeting room for eight, and first-class accommodations pamper business travelers. In second class, the seats are priced equivalent to coach class in the United States. Special spaces are set aside—a play area for small children, a nursery for babies, and a video lounge. Doors between cars have been eliminated, making it easier to move through the train while carrying luggage. A bar car provides telephone service.

The French are excited about their TGVs and are quickly building new lines. The proposal to build the Atlantic Line was made in 1983 and work began in February 1985. In late 1989, the TGV began linking Paris with numerous cities along the Atlantic seaboard, cutting travel times by about one-third. Only a little more than 4½ years was required to complete the first section to Brittany.

The Atlantic TGV operates over new tracks of a 177-mile trunk line linking Paris to Courtalain. There it branches, forming a Y-shape. One new line heads west to Le Mans where it connects with existing trackage, over which TGVs continue on to Brest and other points. The other part of the Y heads south to Tours, the main city of the Loire Valley. There it connects with existing lines to Bordeaux and Lourdes that have been upgraded to allow a maximum TGV speed of 136 mph, meaning their existing-but-improved lines are faster than anything in America.

The time savings are substantial. A 125-mile trip between Paris and Le Mans, for example, dropped from 1 hour 40 minutes to a mere 55 minutes. About an hour was cut off the schedules to Rennes and Nantes. Bordeaux, deep in wine-producing country, became a mere 2 hour 58 minute trip from Paris. TGVs now reach the Spanish border at Hendaye, along the Bay of Biscay.

"This new infrastructure is compatible with the rest of the rail network, thus enabling TGV trains to penetrate right into city centers and provide wide-scale territorial coverage," said Gerard Mathieu. That is one of the great virtues of the trains —their ability to approach existing train stations by using conventional tracks. In the open countryside, TGVs switch over to passenger-only super-speed tracks.

"Elimination of freight trains simplifies problems with safety and limits the cost of track maintenance," said Jack L. Duchemin, a transport expert in the Brussels-based Commission of the European Communities. "That is why the French National Railway, after nine years of experience, claims that TGV high-speed lines are less expensive to maintain than traditional mixed freight and passenger lines."

For the Atlantic line, the French prepared to meet demand by placing orders for 95 trains from Alsthom-Francorail at a cost of nearly $1.4 billion. Almost $1.9 billion more was allocated for line construction and upgrading existing tracks. Thus, the total cost of the Atlantic TGV program was almost $3.3 billion. What will the investment reap? By 1993, the Atlantic TGV is expected

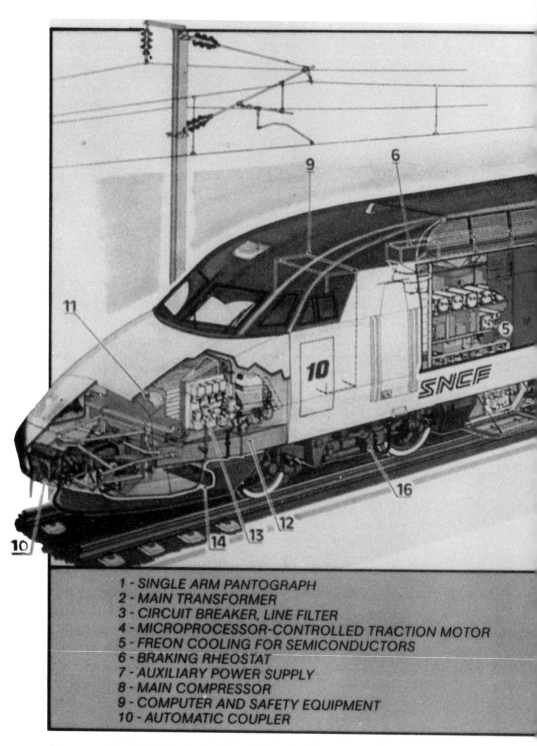

1 - SINGLE ARM PANTOGRAPH
2 - MAIN TRANSFORMER
3 - CIRCUIT BREAKER, LINE FILTER
4 - MICROPROCESSOR-CONTROLLED TRACTION MOTOR
5 - FREON COOLING FOR SEMICONDUCTORS
6 - BRAKING RHEOSTAT
7 - AUXILIARY POWER SUPPLY
8 - MAIN COMPRESSOR
9 - COMPUTER AND SAFETY EQUIPMENT
10 - AUTOMATIC COUPLER

Advances in solid-state technology and motors have reduced the size and weight of the TGV's propulsion equipment. This cutaway shows the compact nature of the equipment that propels the TGV and provides electrical power to the rest of the train.

(GEC Alsthom)

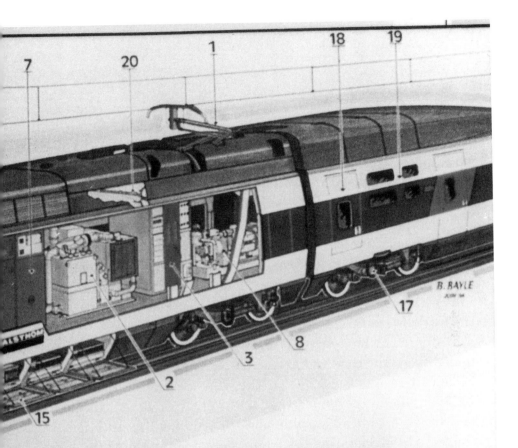

TGV 24000
25 kV, 50 Hz/1.5 kV d.c. dual-current power car.
Synchronous motors. Rated output: 4,400 kW.

1 - IMPACT SHIELD
2 - BODYFRAME MADE OF HIGH YIELD POINT STEEL
3 - BRAKING CONTROLS
4 - TRACK CIRCUIT CODE SENSORS
5 - EQUIPMENT HOUSING
6 - TYPE Y230 A POWER TRUCK
7 - TYPE Y237 AB TRAILING TRUCK
8 - BAGGAGE COMPARTMENT
9 - PASSENGER SEATING
20 - LIGHT ALLOY ROOF PANELS

to serve 25 million passengers a year, of which 25 percent will have transferred from other forms of transportation.

To handle the traffic, the French remodeled three dozen terminals served by the Atlantic TGV. Paris has several stations, but the one used by these new trains is *Gare Montparnasse*, which has been remodeled using pink granite. The work also included installing a new signal system to expand the station's train capacity. By the middle of the 1990s, *Gare Montparnasse* will handle 60 million passengers a year and become the busiest rail terminal in France. However, it isn't the first time a station in Paris was refurbished: when the TGV Southeast Line opened, the *Gare de Lyon* was similarly spruced up.

Americans have trouble understanding that railroads can, under the right conditions, earn a profit carrying passengers. Financial results for 1987 on the TGV Southeast Line were $737.5 million in revenues, and $291 million in direct expenses, leaving an operating surplus of $446.5 million. In addition to the full cost of operating the trainsets and maintaining the new line, the expenses include the portion of TGV costs for operating on the stretches it shares with other services.

The net surplus covers interest on the debt that funded the project, depreciation of the trains, future track renewal, and a contribution to French National Railways overhead costs. The remaining surplus is used to pay back the principal on loans. Full debt repayment is expected to be completed less than 10 years after full service began, several years ahead of schedule. What all of this means is that the French National Railways is enjoying a rate of return of 15 percent on the investment—a pretty good deal.

By any standard, the Southeast TGV is an economic success. The TGV Atlantic has started out that way too. Its capital costs are expected to be fully paid back by the year 2000 with a rate of return of more than 12 percent.

The TGV Southeast Line was built without government subsidies. Railway spokesmen point out that they covered the $1.6 billion cost from internally generated funds and by borrowing in the private capital markets. However, the loans were guaranteed by the French government just as the United States Government has backed loans to Lockheed Aircraft, Chrysler, and to purchasers of commercial aircraft.

In testimony before the United States Congress, Dagobert Scher, a vice-president of the French National Railways, said of the Southeast Line: "Contrary to what many people in this country seem to think, this project was entirely financed by the French national railroads without any government subsidy or any money coming from the taxpayer." He said loans were floated in France and in the United States. The TGV Atlantic line, however, came about with the government putting up 30 percent of the construction costs. First-year results are good: About 10 million people used Atlantic line trains in 1990 and rail travel from Rennes and Nantes to Paris was up by 35 percent.

Bob Blanchette, a former Federal Railroad Administrator, has represented TGV in the United States, trying to market the French technology here. He told Congress that the economics of the Southeast Line were noteworthy:

"Capital costs were about $1.6 billion using 1983 dollars and exchange rates. Cost overruns were negligible for a project of this size—about 1 percent over the original estimate for fixed facilities and 4 percent for rolling stock. The train is remarkably economical. At a 65 percent load factor, the entire cost of a TGV train running between Paris and Lyon, including interest and depreciation, is less than the cost of jet fuel alone on an Airbus

OVERSEAS RACE ON RAILS

[aircraft]. The TGV is truly a case of the right technology in the right place at the right time."

On the Southeast Line, where the top speed for the first-generation TGV trains is 168 mph, the service is so popular that it has carried more than 100 million passengers in its first nine years of operation. In 1988, it served 47,000 riders daily, a 74 percent gain in ridership over the pre-TGV level along the same routes in 1980. Customers include former airline and automobile travelers.

"A comparison of trends for airline traffic on radial routes to and from southeast France and the rest of the country shows that the airlines' upward trend was reversed right from the time the TGV went into partial service in 1981," said Mathieu. "It was estimated that in 1984, after the first year of full-scale TGV operations, the airlines lost two million passengers, representing one-third of the new traffic acquired by the railroad as a result of the TGV."

The amount of traffic gained by the TGV from former automobile travelers is not precise, but researchers estimate one to 1½ million passengers for the same year.

As many as three million new riders were generated by the TGV itself. That is, they belong to a new market of passengers who would not have traveled if the TGV had not existed. The specialists have a name for this phenomenon—"induced ridership"—and it has been a matter of some debate on Supertrain systems proposed for America.

The heaviest TGV Southeast patronage is between Paris and Lyon, but the French say the benefits of Supertrain travel are felt over a far wider area as a result of extending the trains off the new lines and onto upgraded existing tracks. The TGVs leaving Lyon travel as far south as Marseilles and Nice on the Mediterranean. They also sweep into Switzerland, serving Bern, the capital, as well as Geneva and Lausanne. With demand rising steadily, the French have found it necessary to add trains to the timetable.

"On each occasion when services have been enhanced, ridership has increased almost immediately, which shows how rapid passenger reaction can be," said Mathieu. The success of the Southeast Line has prompted plans to extend high-speed tracks to Valence, about 75 miles south of Lyon, by 1994 and to Marseille by 1997.

The TGV line to Marseille has sparked opposition by farmers, small-town mayors, and some radicals in Provence who claim it will be disruptive and bring in too many tourists. In August 1990, "human barricades to protest the TGV project stopped 44 trains between Avignon and Marseilles, delaying 20,000 passengers," reported William Drozdiak of the *Washington Post*. "But the French national rail company has fought back by marshaling the arguments of consumer and environmental groups. . . . The TGV, according to Jean Sivaldiere of the Rhone-Alps Federation for the Protection of Nature, 'would reduce noise, save space and energy and avoid the expansion of airports and auto routes that are worse' for the environment."

A bold link called the "interconnection line" is being built. "Bypassing Paris, it will connect the TGV North, the Southeast and the Atlantic routes, via 65 miles of new line which will serve two stations—Charles de Gaulle International Airport and Euro-Disneyland. This line will enable fast through services to be offered between cities in the provinces," said Mathieu. "The project costs $1 billion, and involves 11 million passengers, and the expected rate of return is about 10 percent."

The first TGV project was conceived in the late 1960s, when

Freedom from cramped airline seats is a bonus to TGV passengers. Clockwise, passengers snack in the bar car; coach seating offers room to stretch; first-class seating is more luxurious; the lounge area is equipped with plush seats and video equipment. Other Supertrains designed by the Germans, Japanese, Swedish, and Italians offer similar comfort. *(French National Railways)*

OVERSEAS RACE ON RAILS

lines between Paris and Lyon became saturated with traffic. The Southeast Line was approved by the government in May 1974; work began two years later, and the first segments opened for service in 1981. One unexpected result was that some Parisians began taking occasional trips to Lyon, a city known for culinary excellence, simply to sample the restaurants.

All the new sections were opened by September 1983, coinciding with the delivery of the last of 87 trainsets initially ordered. With later traffic gains, the number of trains in the Southeast fleet increased to 109, plus two trains with windowless cars used solely by the French Post Office for carrying mail.

The TGV Southeast trains were a leap forward in technology, reflecting several decades of research and development. Two special French test trains in 1955 hit a speed of 205 mph, demonstrating a quest for rail research at a time when, in the United States, President Dwight Eisenhower was preparing to sign the interstate highway act that would help bring down the American passenger train.

To design the TGV Atlantic trains for even higher speeds required more attention to wind resistance than had been the case with earlier trains. Thus, intense aerodynamic research was undertaken. Wind-tunnel testing produced a new streamlined profile that reduced drag by 10 percent over that of the first TGVs. New electric motors are an astonishing 54 percent more powerful than those used on the TGV Southeast. Wheel assemblies, suspension and brakes were redesigned to allow for even smoother rides. Computer microprocessors control all of the motors.

The design of the TGV Atlantic incorporates all the lessons learned from operating the first TGV trains. It doesn't hurt that the French manufacturer of the TGV trainsets,

Alsthom Incorporated, founded in 1928, is a world leader in its field.

All of this is a bit difficult for Americans to understand. Dagobert Scher testified before the United States Congress that the TGV technology is widely available, as he explained to Representative Dan Glickman of Kansas:

> **Mr. Glickman: "You have basically said that there is really no exotic technology involved in this railroad."**
> **Mr. Scher: "Correct."**
> **Mr. Glickman: "That is, everything that you used is technology that is available to anybody in the world?"**
> **Mr. Scher: "Correct."**
> **Mr. Glickman: "No exotic materials used?"**
> **Mr. Scher: "None whatsoever . . ."**
> **Mr. Glickman: "Then you were being ingenuous with existing technology?"**
> **Mr. Scher: "Exactly."**

Design advancements continue. Prototype double-deck passenger cars have passed tests and 100 trainsets have been ordered, and consideration is being given to designing TGV sleeping cars for use on longer routes. On May 31, 1990, Transport Minister Michel Delebarre signed an agreement with French National Railways and GEC Alsthom providing for a four-year program to develop a Super-TGV. The $96 million development effort will study a tilting TGV, adapting the TGV to different electrical power supply systems, further improving aerodynamics, and decreasing energy requirements.

OVERSEAS RACE ON RAILS

More and more, Europeans are cooperating with each other. Trade barriers are down. Workers more easily find jobs in neighboring countries. Complex agreements help keep the Airbus consortium in the business of building commercial jetliners. This "Europe as one family" attitude also is evident on the railroads.

Belgium, France, the Netherlands, and Germany have agreed to "express the common will" to build a Supertrain system on a Paris–Lille–Brussels routing. At Brussels, the line will split, with one branch running to Amsterdam and another to Cologne, Germany, crossing several borders and shortening journey times between Europe's largest cities.

The industrial city of Lille is expecting a burst of economic growth as a result of the TGV bringing it closer to other cities. "Lille will ride into its post-industrial future on steel rails," said the *New York Times*. Its TGV rail station will be built near the heart of town, near a new $500 million international business and commercial center.

The TGV also will lure auto travelers off some of Europe's most congested roads. Motorways in the Netherlands, Amsterdam especially, are notorious for bumper-to-bumper traffic. Environmentalists are welcoming local mass transit improvements and opposing highway expansion that harms the tiny nation's fragile ecosystem.

"It's been shown time and again that improved roads attract more traffic, which in turn necessitates more roads—it's a vicious circle," says Willem-Jan van Grondelle of the Dutch Nature and Environment Foundation.

This international line, named the TGV North, will shorten travel time between Paris and Brussels from 2 hours 25 minutes to 1 hour 30 minutes. Paris–Cologne schedules will be two hours quicker than the current 4 hours 50 minutes. The routing of the

TGV North corridor was announced in October 1987, and it will include a link to the new Channel Tunnel to allow direct service into London from both Paris and Brussels. Altogether, 210 miles of new line will be constructed.

The newest Supertrains are expected to carry about 17 million passengers between France and Great Britain and about 12 million between France and Belgium. The cost has been estimated as high as $5 billion, and the expected rate of return is 13 percent. Parts of the TGV North should be in service in 1993, meaning that train travel in that region will never be the same again.

In a new French National Railways master plan, designed to make Paris the center of a European high-speed network, about $33 billion would be spent to build a 2,000-mile network of 14 new high-speed lines by 2015. Eventually, 160 million passengers annually would use that system, with still more riding France's many other intercity and local trains.

As spectacular as the TGVs are, however, they are about to be partially upstaged by, of all things, a tunnel.

——— ——— ———

Dozens of schemes have come forward over the centuries on ways to build tunnels or bridges across the English Channel between the British Isles and mainland Europe. Tunneling was started twice, in 1882 and again in 1974, but both projects were abandoned.

Now, it's a different story—British and French workers digging the Eurotunnel met under the English Channel on December 1, 1990. Using jackhammers, Graham Fagg of Great Britain and Phillippe Cozette of France knocked out a tunnel passage large enough to walk through. To workmen's cheers, the pair clasped hands, embraced, and exchanged national flags. Unlike the others, this tunnel would be finished.

"The first serious proposal came from French mining engineer Albert Mathieu, whose tunnel design Napoleon received with great enthusiasm in 1802," wrote Richard Alm of the *Dallas Morning News*. "Within a year, however, the two nations were at war, with the French dictator eyeing the channel as a route for an invasion, not a tunnel."

The Eurotunnel was made official when, early in 1986, then-British Prime Minister Margaret Thatcher and French President François Mitterrand signed an agreement to permit a consortium to build the rail-only facility.

It is the largest privately financed engineering project in history.

"Perhaps the single most historic travel development of the entire decade will be the opening, set for 1993, of the 'Chunnel'—the tunnel under the English Channel linking Britain and France," said *Travel Weekly*, an American publication specializing in tourism issues. Supertrains using the tunnel eventually will link Paris with London in 3 hours, rather than 7½, and with Brussels in 2 hours 45 minutes.

Traffic across the channel is booming. In 1985 about 48 million passengers traveled between Britain and mainland Europe in airplanes or on ferries, and that is expected to double by 2003. The Channel Tunnel provides a major opportunity for Great Britain to improve its links to other countries in the European Community, its largest single export market. Big economic benefits will result simply through shortened journey times.

The Eurotunnel is expected to be only six years in construction. The tunnel's capacity will allow it to handle almost as many

After centuries of anticipation the British Isles are connected to the Continent. The breakthrough in the Channel Tunnel occurred on December 1, 1990; construction should be completed in mid-1993. *(Eurotunnel)*

OVERSEAS RACE ON RAILS

passengers as pass through Heathrow Airport *and* more freight than passes through the Port of Dover. Its planners hope to carry 33 million passengers a year on trains and to grow to nearly 45 million annually by 2003, which would make it the most heavily used rail line in the world.

The tunnel will extend for 31 miles, 24 of which are under the sea. Actually, there are three tunnels—two main tunnels, which will contain a single track each, and a smaller service tunnel between them for ventilation and access by maintenance workers.

A version of the TGV, called the *Transmanche Super Train* (TMST), has been purchased to operate through the tunnel. Each TMST will consist of 18 passenger cars, able to carry 794 passengers. They are expected to be as highly reliable as other TGVs, which have never once failed to arrive at their destination in all the years of operation.

Another service besides Supertrains will be provided by Eurotunnel—shuttles where passengers and their autos will travel on enclosed double-deck trains, crossing the channel in some 30 minutes from terminals near Folkestone in Britain and at Coquelles, near Calais, in France.

Passengers won't have to wait very long, since Eurotunnel shuttles will leave approximately every 12 minutes in peak periods, with no need to book in advance. Trains will travel at 100 mph, nearly double the speed limit on most United States highways. At their destination, drivers will head straight off the shuttles and out of the terminal, as British and French customs formalities will have been carried out earlier. The trains will move as many as 8,000 road vehicles per hour.

The Anglo-French group building the facility has multi-year rights to operate the tunnel. The concession period is due to last for 55 years, until 2042, and Eurotunnel is free to operate the tunnel according to its own policies. Moreover, the governments will not help anyone else build a second link before the year 2020.

The project is financed through private capital, and a return of as much as 19 percent was projected to the partners, Britain's Channel Tunnel Group Limited and France Manche SA. Eurotunnel will earn its money from charges paid by the railways to run their trains through the tunnels and fares paid for vehicles using the shuttle service.

The consortium raised $10.2 billion to cover the project. More than 200 banks, primarily in London, Paris, New York, and Tokyo, agreed to $8.3 billion of the underwriting. Eurotunnel raised the rest in an equity offering, which resulted in half a

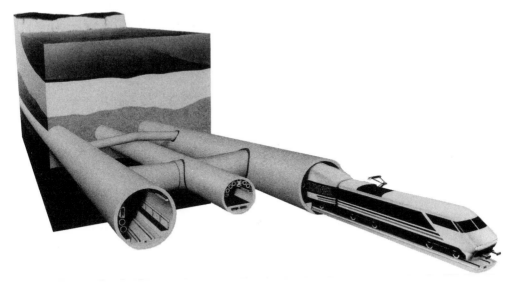

The Eurotunnel system will incorporate two rail tunnels and a service tunnel to provide ventilation and allow routine maintenance. *(Eurotunnel)*

OVERSEAS RACE ON RAILS

million people signing on as shareholders. Later, costs rose to $14 billion, with contractors blaming the increase on inflation, design changes, construction problems, and higher costs for rail cars.

Charges and countercharges have flown between the parties working on the tunnel. As explained by William Grimes of the *New York Times*, "the project has been a page-one tabloid story, with Eurotunnel and Transmanche Link (the contractors) slugging it out before an enthralled public. Eurotunnel accused Transmanche Link of dragging its feet and running up the bill, protected by the lenient cost-overrun terms the consortium had written for itself. Transmanche Link saw Eurotunnel demanding an ever more complex and expensive project without being prepared to pay for it."

Despite problems, Eurotunnel chairman Andre Benard, chief executive Alastair Morton, and John Neerhout, a Bechtel executive working on the project, have discussed future construction of a second set of tunnels on another routing between Great Britain and the continent.

Forbes magazine examined the Channel Tunnel and was optimistic, saying, "If the revenue projections are even close and if there are no bad construction delays, the investors may have gotten themselves a pretty good deal. With operating costs expected to come to only 19 percent of revenues after its planned opening in 1993, Eurotunnel should become a giant cash machine once up and running. . . . Watching the situation unfold, an American is struck with a thought: if the Europeans can harness private enterprise to improve their infrastructure, why can't the United States?"

England was considering building an entirely new 70-mile high-speed line to accommodate trains between London and the

Channel Tunnel. But the Thatcher government wouldn't help fund that link, meaning the London–Paris travel time will be about three hours—30 minutes longer with the slower running in England.

Work is underway on a new terminal adjacent to London's Waterloo Station for the TMSTs. Between London and Dover on the Kent Coast, British Rail work gangs are upgrading existing rail lines, modernizing signals, laying new rails, and renewing bridges to prepare for 1993's Channel Tunnel traffic. One stretch of this track will become the busiest in Great Britain.

The British debate whether the upgrading is sufficient. "The traffic will now speed through as far as our side of the tunnel, and then the men with red flags will lead it on to London," complained Keith Speed, a Conservative Member of Parliament, to the *Wall Street Journal*'s Barbara Toman. Agreeing was the Labour Party's transport spokesman, John Prescott: "Britain will enter the 21st century with an inadequate 19th-century railway link."

Optimists believe people will tire of endless political infighting and that the line will be constructed, but perhaps not until 1998. Regardless of when higher-speed British tracks are built, the tunnel will be financially viable.

While the tunnel and Supertrains are sure to divert passengers from airlines, a majority of ferry riders also will transfer to the train system. So much so that British Rail has sold its ferry division, Sealink.

British Rail passenger traffic continues to rise, especially on routes served by the 125-mph High Speed Train (HST) and Intercity-225, services that have cut travel times on key corridors such as London–Newcastle.

Starting in 1967, British Rail began drawing former airline

OVERSEAS RACE ON RAILS

One artist's view of the *Transmanche* Super Trains, a version of the TGV, operating through Eurotunnel. *(Eurotunnel)*

patrons. Then British European Airways traffic into and out of Manchester Ringway airport dropped by more than 20 percent a year as passengers were attracted to the railway's speeded-up London–Manchester service.

Time will be lopped off East Coast main line schedules as British Rail completes upgrading and electrifying the trunk route between London and Glasgow. Then trains like the *Cornish Scot* and *Sussex Scot*, outfitted with the new British IC-225 train, will run at 140 mph speeds. The British keep researching high-speed train technologies, including a new IC-250 train capable of 155 mph that may link London with Glasgow by 1994. Also contemplated is a 186-mph train to compete with the French TGV. The question is, will Britain ever build the tracks to run such a train?

— — —

While high-speed rail is developing north of France, it has also spread to the south. Spain has taken decisive steps to bring the Supertrain era to its national railroad, the *Red Nacional de los Ferrocarriles Españoles*, or RENFE. The railroad will put its red and white colors on new TGVs assembled in Spain. Officials have altered the TGV name to AVE, for *Alta Velocidad Español*.

In a bold move, the Spanish railroad is building three new lines for 155-mph operations while double-tracking and upgrading existing lines to 125-mph standards, all for the AVEs.

But the Spanish want to do even more. A major nationwide program to change the track gauge (distance between the rails) from a "broad gauge" of five feet to the European "standard gauge" of 4 feet, 8½ inches is in the planning stage. Such a bold reconfirmation of the importance of their rail system would startle many Americans.

OVERSEAS RACE ON RAILS

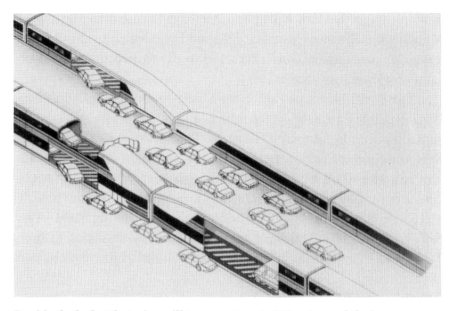

Double-deck shuttle trains will transport up to 200 autos and their passengers through the tunnels at 100 mph. New terminals in France and England will allow travelers to transfer rapidly from approach roads to the shuttles.

(Eurotunnel)

Entry into Spain from France has required either a change of train or a change of wheel assemblies under the cars. This means that all trains have to stop at the border, losing as much as 45 minutes, which is incompatible with the Supertrain concept. Changing the track gauge will improve services internationally as well as to every corner of Spain. Manuel Diaz del Rio, director for international affairs of the Spanish Railways, explained:

"This conversion would begin with the new high-speed lines under construction and then extend progressively to the rest of the network. . . . The change of track gauge creates no problems

British Rail is introducing the Intercity-225 on its East Coast Main Line that links London with Leeds and Edinburgh. Thirty-one of these trains are under construction. Rail planner David Rollin said this train is kinder to the track at 140 mph than a heavier diesel train is at 125 mph. Designers are even now working on a faster successor, the Intercity-250, expected to be ready for assembly in 1994. *(British Rail Intercity)*

OVERSEAS RACE ON RAILS

for new high-speed lines under construction, particularly the Madrid–Seville line whose infrastructure is already at an advanced stage of construction." Spain wants its tracks compatible with those of the rest of Europe for the same reason that Great Britain wants the rail-tunnel link—to become a more vigorous player in the Common Market.

"On April 30, 1987, the government proposed a rail transport plan and one year later on April 28, 1988, it was passed," said Diaz del Rio. "The plan is the most ambitious project to be undertaken in Spain since the start of the construction of the railway in the last century, and its major aim is to modernize the lines and introduce high-speed trains."

The Spanish National Railways has ordered 24 AVE trains from Alsthom at a cost of about $745 million, marking the first time the TGV had been sold outside of France. Deadline for the equipment: have it ready in time for the celebration of the 500th Anniversary of Columbus' discovery of America, the World Expo in Seville, and the Olympic Games in Barcelona—all planned for 1992.

Spain's AVEs will operate over new high-speed lines linking Madrid and Seville via Cordoba and between Madrid and Barcelona. The new Madrid–Seville line represents an investment of an estimated $250 million for track construction. More than twice as fast as existing service, trains leaving Madrid will reach Cordoba in under two hours and Seville in less than three hours. The overall annual ridership is expected to increase to 2¼ million, about a million more than now ride, and to expand the railroad's share of the market.

Eventually, Spanish AVEs will serve a new link connecting Barcelona with the French border. Spanish Transport Minister José Barrionuevo said construction could start in 1993. Within

The *Alta Velocidad Español*, or AVE as shown in this model, is the Spanish version of the TGV. Soon, trains in Spain will be faster than any in North America. *(RENFE)*

four years, passenger trains could be operating over the line at more than 200 mph. An AVE station may be built at the Gerona Airport, which is located in Spain about halfway between Barcelona and Perpignan, France.

In the early 1990s, Spain will have better trains than anything operating in the United States. With pride, the Spanish point out that the next century may see another development—construction of a rail tunnel under the Straits of Gibraltar. Spain and Morocco have been discussing the link between Europe and Africa for a number of years.

— — —

OVERSEAS RACE ON RAILS

The TGV may be a raging success for the French, but the Germans have been crafting their own technology. Called the ICE train, meaning Intercity Express, the new technology operates on super-speed tracks. Officials of the *Deutsche Bundesbahn*, the German Federal Railways, say the trains are luring highway and air travelers to rail service with their 180-mph operations.

"Our strategy is to go twice the speed of the car and half the speed of the plane," said Reiner Gohlke, the railroad's chairman. "Above all, we need more high-speed lines."

The ICE trains offer first- and second-class seating, lounge space, and a conference area. Passengers have an audio system at their seat, and a few seats have video entertainment. Because the trains are somewhat larger in size than TGVs, an already generous level of comfort is further increased. The ICE is electrically powered and runs with as many as 14 cars per train.

Germany's research and development program includes this super-speed Intercity Express designed to compete with the TGV. The trains will be used on high-speed lines, including a new line into Berlin from the west.

(German Rail)

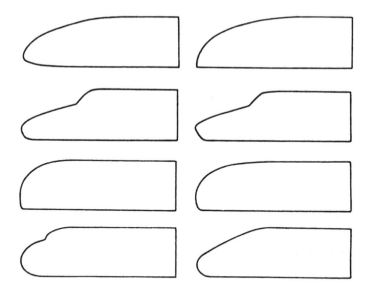

Nose designs tested

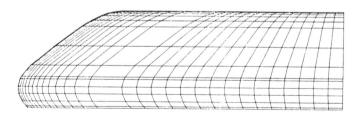

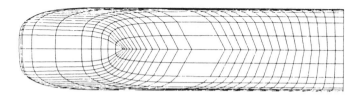

Ideal nose design

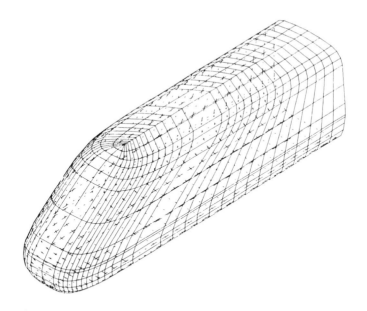

Ideal nose design with pivotal breakdown

"The Leap into the Future" is what German railroad officials call the ICE train. Its aerodynamic design reduces wind resistance, allowing greater energy efficiency at high speeds. *(German Rail)*

New technical ground has been broken and the trains include an onboard diagnostic system to allow fast corrections of malfunctions. The innovations are an example of how Europeans transfer know-how from aerospace to ground transport systems.

Nearly 20 years of development have gone into the ICE train, with backing from the Federal Ministry of Research and Technology along with the railroad and a supplier consortium. Companies involved are Siemens, Krupp, and MBB, which is more formally known as Messerschmitt-Bolkow-Blohm. Experts say these companies have sponsored a burst of engineering developments in the last decade.

OVERSEAS RACE ON RAILS

German officials have been building all-new, high-speed routes, one between Hannover and Wurzburg, 203 miles, and the other linking Mannheim with Stuttgart, a 61-mile segment. These are the start of bigger plans to build four new lines and upgrade a dozen others, resulting in 1,670 miles of routes served by high-speed track.

The Hamburg–Munich line saw the first ICE train service, which went into service on June 2, 1991. Other big corridors to be served include Frankfurt–Stuttgart–Munich and a new route between Cologne and Frankfurt by 1995.

To put the program in perspective, if Germany's web of upgraded and new super-speed routes were linked in one line in the United States, trains could travel from Portland, Maine, all the way to Miami at speeds as high as 180 mph, which illustrates the extent of Germany's commitment to its railroads; the United States so far has done nothing like it.

The Germans lagged behind the French, even though both plotted their new routes at about the same time, because the German lines traverse tougher geography and both passenger and freight trains will use them. Thus, tunnels have been built in mountainous areas to avoid steep climbs for freight trains. Also, German law permits more time-consuming appeals by dissatisfied citizens than does French law.

In a special run in May 1988, a prototype ICE trainset set a speed record of 252 mph, the fastest steel-wheel train in the world until the title was regained later by the TGV.

The ICE trains have entered the ranks of the fastest in the world. On new lines, the maximum is 186 mph. On existing lines being upgraded, the speeds will rise to 137 mph. Another result is sharply reduced travel times for the longer-distance trains, too. For example, a trip between Hamburg and Wurzburg takes only 2 hours 45 minutes compared to 5 hours 18 minutes previously.

Priority has been given to routes that serve traffic heading in a north-south direction. The German Federal Railways inherited a network that dates to the 19th century. Then, east-west traffic predominated and the rails were laid out accordingly. After the post-World War II division of the country, most traffic in West Germany flowed north-south, and projects in this decade will finally help to better serve those markets.

The reunification of Germany has caused a surge in travel between its formerly divided parts. To handle demand, trains like the Frankfurt–Leipzig *Johann Sebastian Bach* have been restored. Now more than 200 daily trains run between the two parts of Germany, compared to 37 before the opening of the Berlin wall. Existing rail links are being upgraded while nine cross-border connections ripped up after World War II will be restored.

Officials early in 1990 decided to increase some train speeds in then-East Germany from 65 mph to 100 mph, and later to 125 mph. But bigger projects are ahead as the transport minister plans to build a Hannover–Berlin high-speed line along the existing route. Peter Haefner of the German Federal Railways said construction will begin in 1992, with operation scheduled for 1997. Some time in the next century, the line could well reach Warsaw and Moscow.

A major marketing change was made a decade ago when the railway in West Germany introduced the "Intercity System," which attracted passengers in great numbers and offered service "every hour, every direction." Passengers who had to transfer from one train to another at an interchange station found that the connecting trains arrived at the opposite sides of the same platform at the same time. The lessons learned from this experience have become the basis for the Supertrain program in Germany.

The German Federal Railways has ordered 60 ICE trains, at a cost exceeding $1 billion. The total program cost for the rail construction and upgrading projects, ICE equipment, station work, and related efforts will be $5 billion. The funding is coming from the German government because of the program's benefits.

Wolfgang Henn, director of the high-speed office in the German Federal Railways, said, "High-speed rail is protecting the landscape. It's clean. It's saving energy. No means of transport is more ecologically beneficial than a high-speed rail system. An efficient rail system is, therefore, not only for the customers, but everybody."

—— —— ——

Italy has been enamored of high-speed trains for decades. After recovering from World War I, but before suffering the ravages of World War II, Italy had built a high-speed line between Rome and Naples where, in 1938, a three-car train achieved 125 mph on a test run.

For the 1990s, Italy has big plans. They call it the *Alta Velocità*, or high speed, project. It is a $15 billion forward-looking investment, which some experts predict will pay for itself in 15 years.

Pierluigi De Marinis of the Italian State Railways, *Ente Ferrovie delo Stato*, or FS, says the high-speed project started in January 1986 with a feasibility study. According to the Italian General Transport Plan, the lines will form a "T" shape with one line in a north-south heading between Milan and Naples. The second high-speed line, or top of the "T," will cross east-west

Years of top engineering talent have gone into this new Italian speedster, capable of 187.5 mph. It began its trial runs in 1990, and eventually will connect Rome with a number of Italian cities. *(Breda Transportation Inc.)*

on a Torino–Milan–Venice routing. Massive new construction will be needed.

On the north-south axis, the portion between Florence and Rome called the *direttissima* has been open for a dozen years. Italian engineers made remarkable achievements in building great viaducts and long tunnels to overcome difficult topography on the line. Nearly one-third of the 160 miles from Florence to Rome is tunneled through terrain that has been compared to Pennsylvania's Allegheny Mountains.

Construction is under way on the new Rome–Naples portion. Expansion plans call for high-speed lines to serve southwestern Italy, or the "toe" part of the "boot," with a further extension to Sicily via a bridge over the Messina Straits.

"The most spectacular and meaningful aspects of the new project are running time and frequency. For instance, 3¼ hours between Milan and Rome ... with a train every 20 minutes during rush hours," said De Marinis. That schedule will be possible starting in 1992 and will be an improvement over the current Rome–Milan time of 5 hours 10 minutes.

In addition to the *Alta Velocità* project, a public-private venture wants to build a high-speed line between Milan and Genoa in northern Italy. Investors include the Italian Railways and CIV, a company owned by the Genoa Airport Authority, toll-highway operators, and others.

The Italians have been using the ETR-450 train, or *Pendolino*, a tilting train built by Fiat Ferroviaria, which carries travelers at 155 mph. The company is considering design of a model named the *Avril*, with a speed approaching 200 mph. Another new passenger train, the ETR-500, already exists and can run as fast as 186 mph. The prototype was completed in April 1988.

"The trains are going to be the fleet of the 90s," said De Marinis. "We foresee about 100 trains." Their first use of the ETR-500 will be between Milan and Rome in 1992. These trains are manufactured by a consortium led by Breda Costruzioni Ferroviarie S.p.A., of Pistoia, Italy. The company has been constructing cars and locomotives for more than a century.

The first Italian financing, about $4 billion, came from public funds under a law passed in 1987 and is committed to the route between Rome, Naples, and Battipaglia. In the future, a mixture of public-private funding may be arranged since the Italian Railways are now permitted to raise money in commercial markets.

Other nations have quietly gone about the task of improving their rail networks. Trains of the Swiss Federal Railways hardly need upgrading—timekeeping is so tight that passengers are guaranteed connections in as close as two minutes.

Nevertheless, Switzerland's residents approved the Rail 2000 referendum, a $2.6 billion program that will improve services by making connections easier at key stations, build new sections of track, and upgrade much of the system. The studies have recommended a program named "New Railway Across the Alps," a project costing as much as $7.3 billion to build two tunnels to Italy.

In Austria, the *Neue Bahn*, or new railroad, project includes two new lines to permit speeds of 155 mph. One would connect Vienna with Amstetten to the west, while the other line would be built from Vienna south to Graz. Both new segments are rather short, but would allow routes to be straightened and travel times cut to many destinations.

Denmark plans to raise speeds to 110 mph on its main east-west line between Copenhagen and Fredericia. In 1993, when a combined bridge and tunnel replaces ferries across the Great Belt between the two halves of Denmark, a one-hour ferry trip will take 12 minutes by train at speeds up to 125 mph. The region's governments are discussing a 10-mile rail tunnel from Copenhagen north to the Swedish port of Malmo and another tunnel south to Germany. The projects could cut Malmo–Hamburg train times from 10 hours to three.

Areas sometimes thought of as "Europe's far corners" are active, too. Portugal is considering new line sections and improvements to existing north-south tracks on the Porto–Lisbon–Faro route. The planners for the railway, which is officially known as *Caminhuos de Ferro Portugueses*, or CP, are willing to change tracks to standard gauge to ease a linkup with Spain's high-speed tracks.

The Turkish State Railways is pondering a $2 billion investment in a 150-mph Ankara–Istanbul line. Greece will give priority through 1997 to building several new sections on the Athens–Thessaloniki–Idomeni line to Yugoslavia enabling 125-mph operations. Ireland envisages faster trains between Dublin and Cork, as well as quicker Dublin–Belfast schedules.

— — —

An economic revolution is occurring in Europe where, by the end of 1992, a dozen countries will virtually dismantle their trade barriers to form a single market. Some have called it the "United States of Europe," a market with 320 million consumers and $4 trillion in economic activity each year. The free flow of trade will inevitably trigger a surge in travel demand.

The Community of European Railways has focused on these developments and has proposed a larger high-speed rail network. It has urged each nation to do its part to "dismantle economic frontiers" by building Supertrain links between existing high-speed lines. The group has quite a plan in mind.

Throughout the 1980s when Europe's high-speed lines were planned, each country's domestic travel was larger than international traffic. To maximize profits, as well as for political purposes, Supertrains were designed to serve domestic traffic. Now, the idea is to interconnect them into an international web, disregarding borders and serving population corridors that have the heaviest traffic flows, such as Scotland–Marseilles, through two countries, or Hamburg–Zurich–Rome, which traverses three nations. These are intense traffic corridors where boundaries mean less than ever.

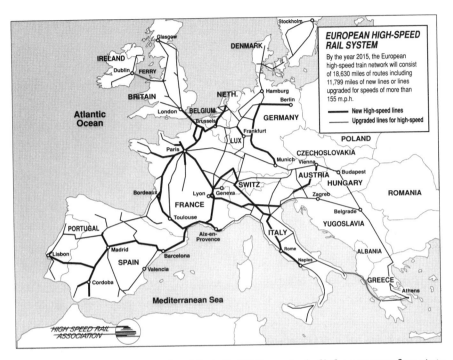

The United States lacks leadership to build Supertrain links across a few state lines, while Europe plans to spend more than $100 billion on a Supertrain network that crosses national boundaries. The contrast proves that obstacles to good train service between populated American cities are political and institutional, not technological.

Most international traffic growth has gone to the airlines, particularly from the north to Spain, Portugal, and Italy, whose mountains have made it difficult for railroads to compete. Europe, like the United States, has its hub airports in major cities, such as London, Paris, and Frankfurt, and all suffer from congestion. The frequency of highway traffic jams has increased as well, along with a rise in auto ownership, all of which prompted the Community of European Railways to say: "High-speed trains are fully able to provide a viable alternative, even in the face of fierce price competition. This has been demonstrated by the success of the Southeast TGV despite particularly cheap air fares over the same route."

The Channel Tunnel's construction means that a key link will be in place to serve a particularly high volume of traffic. The projects in Spain and Denmark also help to internationalize the rail system. Other gaps are gradually being closed. A Franco-German task force is looking at forging better links from Paris to Frankfurt and Paris to Stuttgart.

Europeans say they will no longer let natural barriers get in the way of the Supertrains. Two tunnels across the Sund between Copenhagen and Malmo, which Denmark and Sweden are negotiating, would create a direct route between Sweden and Germany. For years, trains have been put on ferries to cross this channel. Another tunnel, this one south of Copenhagen across the Fehmarn Belt, has been proposed, which would link Rodby, Denmark, and Puttgarden, Germany. The Community of European Railways suggests these be completed by 2010, but some experts say it will be 2020 before the more difficult projects come to fruition.

"Time savings are enormous, journey times being cut by half or more," said France's Gerard Mathieu. "By day, distances of 600 or 800 miles can be covered in four or five hours. For longer distances, research is in hand into high-speed rolling stock for night travel so that 900 to 1,500 miles could be traveled in eight or 12 hours overnight."

These programs do not come cheap and the sources of funding vary widely between countries. Some nations believe infrastructure development is the responsibility of the state, especially Germany, Italy, and Spain. Others hold the view that a private operator should be responsible for all construction, financing, and operations, with the Channel Tunnel being the best example. The French National Railways and British Rail stand somewhere between these two extremes, carrying out projects with a mixture of public-private financing.

Europe's Supertrain network could eventually require laying 4,600 miles of track and improving 12,000 more. Mathieu said the investment needed could reach $105 billion, of which $18 billion has already been spent. "But," he noted, "between now and the year 2010, this only represents $10 per inhabitant per year." While some of these projects will be completed, others are uncertain because national concerns can still outweigh European interests.

Even the design of new equipment is international in scope. A Swedish-Swiss company based in Zurich, ASEA Brown Boveri, is developing the Fastrain for speeds as high as 150 mph. Each Fastrain set will hold about 600 passengers. Experts expect the company to develop a top-of-the-line train, and its sales force is spreading throughout the world in search of orders.

The design is based on the X-2000 train, which has been ordered by the Swedish State Railways for delivery through 1994. The X-2000, capable of running 130 mph, has cut travel times in the Nordic countries. Sweden uses the train between Stockholm, Malmo, and Gothenburg while the X-2000 is being discussed for use on Norway's Oslo–Bergen route and Finland's Helsinki–Tampere line.

Eastern European countries are stirring, too, and cooperating with the West. Poland and Czechoslovakia say they have plans for high-speed trains. Their railroad leaders have met with counterparts in Hungary, Yugoslavia, Romania, and Bulgaria to consider ways to implement a set of internationalized high-speed services over the next 20 years. The Polish showed their intent by signing a five-year accord under which the French National Railways will provide advice on developing a high-speed network. Yugoslav and French interests may upgrade portions of the Budapest–Belgrade–Sofia route to allow speeds as high as those found on the Paris–Lyon TGV line. Even Yugoslavia's feuding Croatians and Serbians seem to agree on the need for advanced train services.

Different European nationalities are cooperating in the design of a truly international system, committed to Supertrains in the same way the United States has been committed to highways and airports.

The Swedish and Swiss collaborated on the X-2000, designed for high-speed service on rail lines in the Nordic countries, shown here on a test run. A version of this equipment, named the Fastrain, has been proposed to run at 150 mph in Florida from Orlando to Tampa and Miami. *(ABB Traction Inc.)*

The Soviet Union is revolutionizing its railroads as well. Late in 1989, the privatization of the state-operated railways began; since, the Soviets have spun off 32 regional railroads into autonomous units, expecting them to become self-sustaining. One small money-losing railroad in the Yaroslavl Region has actually been sold. According to *Railway Age*, the Dekor Cooperative, its new owner, cut management staff from 52 to five, improved the physical plant, sought new small shippers, and now operates at a profit.

The Soviet Union has a big rail system, the largest in the world. It also has big ideas about high-speed.

In an electrifying moment at a convention in San Antonio in May 1990, three high-level representatives of the Soviet Union revealed their plans. Attending from Moscow were Gennady M. Fadeev, first vice-minister of railways; Eugeney A. Sotnikov, deputy director, Railways Research Institute; and Boris E. Lukov, senior expert for international relations for the Minister of Railways.

When they spoke, people listened.

Sotnikov: "Our new line to be built from Moscow to Leningrad will allow travel times to be reduced from six hours to three hours. The government has approved this project. We plan to put it in operation in 1998."

Fadeev: "One benefit is conversion of factories that make military equipment. The people who run these factories say they do not want to make pots and pans; they want to build more complex civilian products like high-speed trains."

Sotnikov revealed to members of the High Speed Rail Association, organizers of the conference, that relying on the government's treasury was not the only way to pay for the project: "Under consideration is the possibility of unconventional fi-

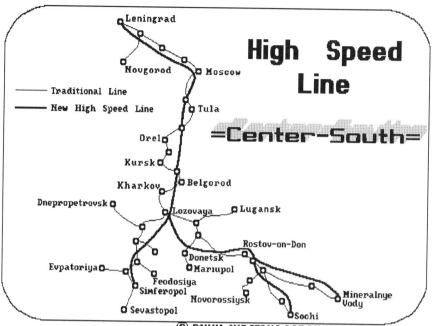

Soviet railway officials flashed this map on a screen at a 1990 meeting of the High Speed Rail Association, startling participants by saying this ambitious plan may be partly financed though the sale of stock to the public. The Leningrad–Moscow portion would be built first, with later extensions to points on the Black Sea.   *(Soviet Railways Research Institute)*

nancing, such as getting money from the public through share-holders and cooperative banks, issuing long-term loans with payment from the operating revenues, as well as participation of foreign firms in the project financing." Shareholders? Less than two months after Sotnikov's comments, Soviet President Mikhail Gorbachev authorized creation of public companies with the right to issue bonds and sell shares both to Soviet citizens and foreigners.

Meanwhile, the Soviet Union does have one high-speed train

between Moscow and Leningrad—the ER-200, which entered service in the mid-1980s. A 14-car electric train with a design speed of 125 mph, it is viewed skeptically since it operates only once a week in each direction. Clearly, the Soviets hope to do better the next time around.

Australia has been watching the successful high-speed train programs of the Continent closely. Australia is a large country, but most of its population is centered between Sydney and Melbourne, and a consortium is evaluating a $3.9 billion Supertrain link between the cities. An electrified VFT, or very fast train, could vie for the honor of becoming the world's fastest train, running at about 220 mph. Involved in VFT, an unincorporated joint venture, is Australia's largest company, Broken Hill Pro-

Australian trains at 220 mph are proposed for the Sydney–Melbourne link. Reasons given to build the VFT (Very Fast Train) parallel those in the United States and Europe: airport congestion and worries about mobility.   (VFT)

OVERSEAS RACE ON RAILS

prietary Company, a transport giant named TNT, and the Japanese engineering firm Kumagai Gumi.

"The VFT project was born not from a dream, but from a nightmare—the nightmare that Australia would enter the 21st century with an archaic train system more suited to the 19th century," said Dr. Paul Wild, founder of the VFT project. A related concern is that Sydney's Kingsford Smith Airport has begun to experience traffic delays, and the VFT may link with one or more of the region's airports to divert short-distance passengers away from air travel.

The current circuitous train routing links Sydney with Melbourne in about 12 hours. Trains over the new line would take a mere three hours, including time for a stop in Canberra, the nation's capital, and would carry 10 million passengers a year. Alan Castleman, chief executive of VFT, said approvals for the public-private project must come from the federal, New South Wales, Australian Capital Territory, and Victorian governments. A full feasibility study should be completed by the end of 1992, and the line could be fully operational in December 1997.

The project would surpass Australia's experience thus far in upgrading rail service. The State Rail Authority of New South Wales in 1982 introduced the 100-mph XPT passenger trains, which now operate on five routes out of Sydney.

Korea is engineering a Supertrain system between Seoul and Pusan, cutting the four-hour travel time between the cities by more than half. Tremendous economic growth, typical of the Pacific Rim, has sparked intense travel between the two busy cities. Transport Minister Sohn Soo-ik has said he is certain the $8.3 billion project will be completed in 1998. Korea may build four more high-speed lines in the early part of the next century, including a Taeju–Mokpo link.

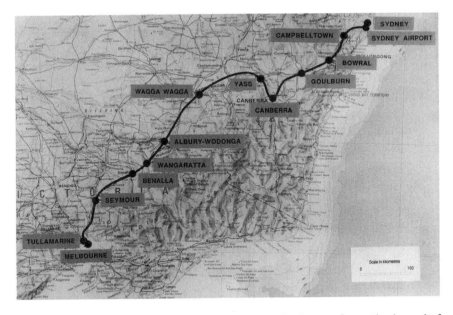

The VFT would link Sydney and Melbourne via Canberra, the nation's capital, on an inland route. Travel time would be three hours, end-to-end. After studies, planners found this line to be superior to a less-populated coastal route.

(VFT)

Taiwan, through the Republic of China Transportation Institute, is planning a high-speed system to connect its main cities, Taipei and Kaohsiung, in a 200-mile corridor. It's expected that journey time between the two cities will be cut from four hours to 1 hour 45 minutes. The government wants to open the line by 1996. "The total cost of the project is estimated at between $12 billion and $15 billion," reported the *International Railway Journal.* "Between 50 million and 60 million passengers a year are expected to use the new service."

South America has entered the scene, with Brazil considering a super-speed line between Rio de Janeiro and Sao Paulo. An unresolved question is how this country, with its massive

OVERSEAS RACE ON RAILS

debt problems, plans to pay for the line. Brazil is Latin America's largest debtor, owing foreigners $110 billion, and it has fallen short of fulfilling obligations to its creditor banks.

"The financing is up in the air, but we're studying solutions," said Raul V. Bravo, a Washington consultant working on the Brazilian project as well as on proposals in Europe and the United States. "If there is a market in the world, that's it. Sao Paulo and Rio each have a population in the millions, and there's a good-sized intermediate population. They're looking at a system to connect the cities between two and three hours. That means trains operating between 100 and 150 mph."

———   ———   ———

The Japanese started it all with sleek blue and ivory speedsters that were dubbed the Bullet Trains. The stylish trains, originally running only between Tokyo and Osaka, caught the attention of their countrymen and also impressed the world with their comfort, punctuality, and 125-mph speed. They've been around awhile: in 1989, the Japanese recognized the Bullet Train's 25th anniversary.

Starting with a contest to name the trains, which drew an avalanche of 700,000 entries, the Bullets have become part of Japan's culture. Advertisements for Japanese consumer products like cigarettes have featured smartly uniformed Bullet Train engineers instead of airline pilots or race-car drivers.

After decades of discussion, the Japanese decided in 1958 to build high-speed rail lines. In 1959, only a week after approval by the Parliament, the ceremonial spade of dirt was turned. In an astonishing feat, the line was completed and opened just 5½ years later on October 1, 1964, in time for the Olympic games in Tokyo. Travel in Japan hasn't been the same since.

Known throughout the world, the Japanese Bullet Train revolutionized think-ing about high-speed ground transportation. Their on-time performance re-cord: 99 percent. *(Japanese National Tourist Organization)*

The Bullet Train's stunning ridership levels earned world-wide attention. Koji Takahashi, senior vice-president for engi-neering of the old Japanese National Railways, tells the story: "The *Shinkansen*, or new trunk line, has captured at least 80 percent of the market between Tokyo and Osaka, 320 miles apart. That led us to believe that our *Shinkansen* is competitive with other modes of transportation in medium-length of 100- to 500-mile intercity corridors. The increase in ridership in the Toyko–Osaka corridor for 1970, after five years of operation, was more than 1½ times our optimistic estimate. The actual daily ridership grew by 300 percent in those first five years." By the late 1980s, more than 135 million passengers a year rode the Bullet Trains.

OVERSEAS RACE ON RAILS

Fresh Bullet Train designs include this Series 100 *Shinkansen*. The nose is lower than on the original model, and the train comes with double-deck cars, which allow the railroad to increase capacity without sacrificing comfort. French TGV designers also are planning such cars.

(Japanese National Tourist Organization)

The first line, an engineering marvel, was built on a completely grade-separated and exclusive right-of-way. The route, set back from the coast to conserve valuable land, borders mountains which required building 66 tunnels and more than 3,100 bridges. The total mileage of such structures accounts for more than one-third of the entire route.

The Japanese experience was so successful that the Bullet Trains have been expanded, section by section, during the past

OVERSEAS RACE ON RAILS

two decades. Out of Tokyo, the *Shinkansen* was brought south to the Island of Kyushu. Later, a line north to Niigata and another to Morioka were completed. Japan has almost 1,300 miles of high-speed passenger lines. If strung together in the United States, the route would stretch from Seattle to San Diego or New York to Kansas City. The Japanese plan to build more Bullet Train routes, from Morioka to Aomori, and later to Sapporo on Hokkaido Island; from Takasaki to Komatsu, and from Hakata to both Kagoshima and Nagasaki.

The trains boosted mobility within Japan's crowded heartland, an area where existing rail lines were saturated. The world's first true high-speed service, the Bullets represented a shining example of what could be accomplished using existing technology to the limit. The trains, built by Hitachi, have become an integral part of the Japanese transport network, and have served as a paragon for the emerging high-speed rail movement throughout the world. Not having high-speed rail service in Japan would be unthinkable.

Superlatives abound. The *Shinkansen* runs every day without a hitch, racking up an enviable on-time record of 99 percent. Hiroumi Soejima of the Central Japan Railway Company reports that in 1989, when a train was late, it was late an average of only *28 seconds*. About 260 Bullet Trains are operated daily, covering a distance equal to circling the globe three times. The system serves 400,000 passengers a day and does so at speeds as high as 170 mph.

Some Bullet Trains earn a profit, some don't.

The 320-mile route between Tokyo and Osaka cost $640 million to build, but within 18 months of its opening it became the only Japanese rail line—passenger or freight—to operate at a profit. Every year since 1975 the Tokyo–Osaka *Shinkansen*

Still more designs in Japan, as illustrated by this prototype Series 300 *Shinkansen*. Much of the work on this train was inspired by France's success with the TGV. This new model is quieter than other Bullet Trains. Known also as the *Super Hikari*, the prototype is expected to connect Tokyo and Osaka in about 2 hours 30 minutes, while hitting a top speed of 167.8 mph. In February 1991, the *Super Hikari* set a Bullet Train speed record of 202 mph.

(JR Tokai)

has yielded handsome profits, and paid off its World Bank construction loan in the 1970s.

Koji Takahashi, in testimony to the United States Congress, said of the first line: "The government provided a subsidy only during the construction period. The government subsidized a part of the interest we had to pay on loans during construction. After the *Shinkansen* started operating, the government ceased to subsidize it." The Osaka–Fukuoka Bullet Train route, known as the Sanyo line, also earns a profit.

OVERSEAS RACE ON RAILS

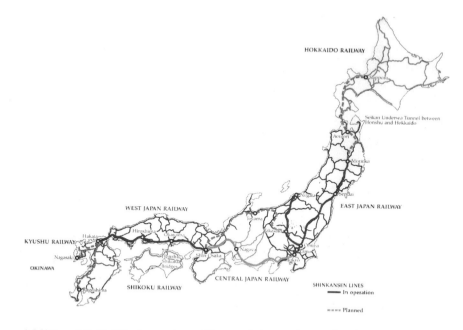

Additional Bullet Train routes will come into service under Japan's "National High-Speed Railways Construction Act." Rising oil prices as a result of the Persian Gulf War have intensified Japanese demands for a more extensive energy efficient Supertrain network. (Shinkansen *Holding Corporation*)

Other Bullet Train routes serve smaller cities and have been subsidized by the government. An example is the planned service to Hokkaido, Japan's northernmost island. Rural Hokkaido is what the Japanese call their "last frontier." The upcoming Bullet Train line will not earn a profit soon because it will serve a sparsely populated area and is viewed as a tool to encourage economic development.

The subsidies are a good investment. Japan has no petroleum reserves. Its trains help the country to keep purchases of overseas oil under control, which directly benefits its economy.

Japan's international balance of payments isn't as healthy as it is just because the Japanese export so many finished products; Japan also relies heavily on its railroads to limit what would be extravagant oil imports. Gas-guzzling America has a lot to learn.

Bullet Trains will eventually get to Hokkaido through an engineering masterpiece. In 1988, railway officials opened the 32.3-mile Seikan Tunnel, a $5.6 billion link with Japan's main island, Honshu. The tunnel's construction lagged behind schedule, taking a total of *24 years* to build because of unexpected difficulties with the soils. Until the Bullets arrive, conventional trains alone will run through the tunnel.

According to Douglas W. Polinder writing in *Trains* magazine, the structure contains the world's deepest railroad station, "Tappi Undersea Station, located inside the world's lowest railroad tunnel." The station is available for emergencies, but visitors on tours notice that it is outfitted with vending machines. The undersea tube will lose its title as the world's longest when the Eurotunnel under the English Channel opens.

The new rail link is essential for Bullet Trains to reach Hokkaido, but is vital for other reasons. The tunnel eliminated a four-hour ferry trip between Aomori and Hakodate. That ferry passage, known for its treacherous stormy weather, has been the site of some of the worst sea disasters the world has known. In a 1954 ferry tragedy, the *Toya Maru* sank in the Tsugaru Strait, killing more than 1,000 passengers.

The Bullets are in their third generation of research and production. *Railway Gazette International* reported that new trains, the *Super Hikari*, are distinguished by a low body profile and a streamlined front end without the characteristic bullet nose. These trains began rolling out of the factory in March 1990.

OVERSEAS RACE ON RAILS

In 1964, Bullet Trains started running between Tokyo and Osaka in four hours. Over the years, time was trimmed to 2 hours, 52 minutes. The *Super Hikari* trains are more powerful, offer about a 25 percent weight saving, and will cover that distance faster still—in 2 hours 30 minutes. Business continues to grow. Railway officials plan to run 76 trains *per hour* on the line by the end of this decade, compared to 61 per hour today.

Meanwhile, Kawasaki is testing a prototype *Series 400 Shinkansen* on the Fukushima–Yamagata line. The unit, often called a mini-*Shinkansen*, is designed to offer Bullet Train performance on routes converted from narrow to standard gauge.

At Tokyo's central station is a monument to Shinji Sogo, president of the Japanese National Railways, recognizing him as the father of the Bullet Trains. Perhaps it should say that he sparked Supertrain plans around the world.

— — —

The Japanese and French Supertrains have something even more important than speed in common—an absolutely perfect safety record. As commentator Andy Rooney of CBS' "60 Minutes" television program said, "If the maintenance on the engine of a train isn't good, you may get stuck out in the country in the middle of nowhere, but the train doesn't fall to the ground, killing everyone on board."

"The most important human factor in transportation is safety, and the safety record of high-speed rail is perfect," said Paul H. Reistrup, a former Amtrak president and proponent of Supertrains in America. "If 100 percent safety is desirable as one factor in travel, then high-speed trains are the answer."

He pointed to the safety records of the world's true high-speed systems as examples. The Japanese Bullet Train has never had a passenger injured or killed in all of the years it has operated, and during that time it has carried nearly three billion passengers—equal to more than half the world's population. Meanwhile, in the United States, more than half of the country's accidental deaths occur in the transportation sector, and more than 90 percent of those are on the highways.

Foreign nations are at work on their super-speed steel-wheel train systems, while America is just waking up. Could these technologies be transferred to the United States and used here? Other nations learn from each other—a technology exchange is in effect for the mutual benefit of the Japanese and the French. The Bullet Train makers want the French TGV's noise-reduction and vibration-control techniques. In turn, the TGV operator wants the Japanese train control software to better organize frequent train schedules.

"Using overseas technology in the United States wouldn't be difficult at all," said Robert J. Casey, an expert with two decades of experience in rail technology. "It would be reinventing the wheel to do otherwise. Excellent trains already exist in other countries. Some adaptations would be necessary because of regulations by the federal government, but we should do it," he said.

Versions of these Supertrains will be running in the United States by the turn of the century.

GREEN LIGHT FOR FLOATING TRAINS

"We may perhaps learn to deprive large masses of their gravity and give them absolute levity, for the sake of easy transport."
—Benjamin Franklin

MAGLEV TRAINS WILL BECOME A COMMON sight in some of the most populated areas of the world.

In 1989, a United States Energy Department study recommended spending $30 billion to link 50 of the nation's largest urban areas with a network of magnetically levitated Supertrains. The study, done by the Argonne National Laboratory, said the new trains are quiet, smooth, super-fast, and affordable.

The response? Calls for action in states suffering from traffic congestion. Requests for further studies of the maglev trains from, of all people, some aerospace leaders. Those who have

been promoting high-speed trains said, simply, "It's about time."

Magnetic levitation trains work. A transit-type maglev system is in use in Birmingham, England, and has been demonstrated in Hamburg and Berlin. The first super-speed maglev

Magnetic levitation trains are able to sprint at 312 mph. Under German research, development, and testing for 20 years, this Transrapid will be America's first maglev train, set to run between the Orlando Airport and a tourist complex near Disney World. Proposed is a Transrapid line between Anaheim and Las Vegas, and a network with Pittsburgh as a hub.   *(Transrapid International)*

line is to be built in the United States in Orlando, with the opening set for the fall of 1995. In the West, a commission is considering a maglev Supertrain that can operate at 300 mph between Las Vegas and Anaheim. Such systems will also be built to link cities within Japan and Germany.

"The concept of a high-speed train supported by a magnetic cushion and driven by a non-contact linear motor had a fanciful introduction to public consciousness through comic books in the 1940s and 1950s—long before such ideas became technically viable," said Tony Eastham, a Canadian researcher. "However, it is said that what one generation dreams, the next generation does. Such is the progress in technology development that maglev is now being seriously considered as an option for high-speed service in many North American corridors."

Children have played with magnets for years. Put two magnets together in the way they "attract" and they clamp together. When magnets are "repulsing" each other, trying to push them together is futile. Those same forces can be multiplied thousands of times with large electrically powered magnets. Find an efficient way to harness those magnetic waves and the result is enough power to lift and move trains—very fast trains.

Maglev trains, the world's newest mode of transportation, "fly" without wings, and they have one conspicuously missing feature—there's no engine. Instead, powerful magnets in the vehicle and also in the guideway create forces that lift, guide, and propel the trains. When maglev trains move, they have no physical contact with the guideway and suffer no friction except wind resistance. This means that even higher speeds are theoretically possible than with steel-wheel trains.

"Maglev provides a contact-less, friction-free system," Federal Railroad Administrator Gilbert Carmichael told Congress.

"Some of the engineers have told me that this system once in motion could go up to 1,700 miles an hour, but the human being may not be very comfortable in it."

Although discussed for many years, maglev is just now graduating from research, development, and testing. Because they use only a fraction of the energy required for aircraft, maglev trains will be cheaper to operate than any jetliner. Proponents claim guideways for maglev trains can be less costly than rail lines because the lack of contact with the vehicle reduces maintenance costs.

Different versions of the Transrapid run repeatedly at high speeds, but quietly. Making only the sound of an aerodynamic whoosh, less than the noise generated by one automobile on an interstate, means that farmers working below the guideway are not disturbed. Cows don't even look up.
(Transrapid International)

GREEN LIGHT FOR FLOATING TRAINS

Two basic types of maglev systems have been designed, and they rely on different philosophies. The electromagnetic system has "attractive" physical principles at work. Trains using the attractive system include the German Transrapid and *M-Bahn* systems, the British system in Birmingham, England, and the Japanese High Speed Surface Transport (HSST) system. In the Transrapid train, magnets located on the underside of a guideway pull upward on the train's wrap-around section, and the vehicle floats about three-eighths of an inch above the top guideway surface.

A competing technology is the electrodynamic or "repulsive" system. In it, the magnets are located on the upper side of the guideway and they push the train upward into a floating position. When operating, the distance between the train and its guideway is about six inches. It is this type, designed by the Japanese National Railways and now in the care of the Railway Technical Research Institute, that experts say would most benefit from superconducting magnets.

Those explanations best describe how the trains float. But how do they move? Imagine a magnet on the floor. Hold another magnet in front and move the magnet on the floor by "pulling" it through "attractive" magnetic force. Place still another behind in a "push," or repulsion, position, and the magnet on the floor will move faster. Now imagine that a series of magnets are lined up, rapidly changing "push" and "pull" polarities. That, combined with their great power, creates "propulsion" strong enough to move as well as float a train.

Discussions of maglev systems often contain references to superconductivity. Richard Uher, director of Carnegie Mellon's High Speed Ground Transportation Center in Pittsburgh, explained what it is: "In layman's terms, superconductivity refers to the ability of a material to carry electricity without electrical resistance. It is the electrical form of nearly perpetual motion."

Superconductors, almost unknown to the average person until recently, could help maglev systems by reducing the amounts of electrical power they will need to operate. They can also reduce the weight of magnets aboard the vehicles, in turn cutting the cost to build guideways, although experts can get into heated arguments about the extent of cost and weight savings.

Superconductivity can have a beneficial effect on what already is an energy-stingy transport system. Some say, however, that superconductivity is not necessary to usher in the maglev era. The director of the Argonne National Laboratory's Center for Transportation Research, Larry R. Johnson, said, "We looked at the high temperature superconductor technology and . . . concluded it was enhancing, not enabling." Incidentally, all trains powered by electricity, including Amtrak's New York–Washington *Metroliners*, could enjoy enhanced efficiency through superconductivity.

The Argonne Laboratory report, issued in June 1989, found that 300-mph maglev Supertrains could alleviate growing aviation gridlock by serving busy airports. For instance, operating at that speed, passengers can travel from Philadelphia to Pittsburgh in a few minutes under two hours. Airlines could operate trains as part of their systems.

"The maglev trains could substitute for 100- to 600-mile flights, thereby substantially reducing air traffic congestion," said the report. "Over the next 20 years, more than 2,000 miles of maglev system networks, radiating from major airports, could be built for the equivalent cost to airlines and their passengers of current air traffic delays estimated by the Federal Aviation

Prior to unification, the West German government studied these routes for Transrapid service. The lines between Bonn and Cologne, and Dusseldorf and Essen are high on the government's list. Most schemes call for these maglev Supertrains to be integrated with that nation's busy air system.

(Transrapid International)

Administration at $5 billion annually. . . . If maglev systems were integrated into major hub airports, they could become economical in many high-density United States corridors."

The report continued: "Maglev vehicles could operate from the terminals of existing airports, just as Lufthansa operates a train system between its Frankfurt airport and Dusseldorf. The systems could be built along existing interstate highways or abandoned railroad rights-of-way, a significant advantage in urban centers. Even though maglev systems can be used as airline technology to connect airports, they can also connect downtowns and major suburban developments as part of intercity travel."

A double-track system could cost about $15–20 million per mile, and that would include terminals, vehicles, and construction of the guideway. By comparison, interstate highway segments often cost much more than that and new airports, if they can be built over public objections, are expected to cost as much as $5 billion each. If the nation builds the 15 to 20 major airports the airlines say are needed, the costs would greatly exceed the price tag of a maglev system.

Argonne's staff recommended building a 2,000-mile, $30 billion network that would serve many of the busiest airports. Senator Harry Reid of Nevada said spending that money doesn't worry him. To build two aircraft carriers would cost $38 billion, he said, adding, "With a fraction of the money that it would take to build one aircraft carrier we could revolutionize what takes place in this country today."

The Argonne plan included maglev service in the Boston–New York–Washington corridor, Philadelphia–Pittsburgh, and lines in the Midwest out of Chicago to Minneapolis, St. Louis, Cincinnati, Detroit, and Cleveland. Western routes with heavy traffic, such as San Diego–San Francisco, were also included.

GREEN LIGHT FOR FLOATING TRAINS

"Every study before ours has looked at magnetic levitation as railroad technology," said Larry Johnson. "Ours is the first to integrate it into airline and airport operations."

Rail labor has been urging Supertrain service to airports for several years. William Lindner of the Transportation Workers Union of America, in a Philadelphia speech, said: "I would certainly hope that if we look at high-speed trains as a new development, that we will provide for the kind of airport connections that some of our friends overseas have done. . . . It seems to me that, if we are going to be effective in hauling passengers comfortably and quickly and cheaply, we have got to provide connections that have been ignored up to now."

His view has been supported by four other rail unions—the Transportation and Communications Workers Union, which represents both airline and railroad employees, and labor organizations representing the locomotive engineers, signalmen, and the maintenance-of-way workers.

A few months after the Argonne report was issued, another government study strongly endorsed maglev networks. It was issued by an advisory committee to the Senate Committee on Environment and Public Works, chaired by Daniel Patrick Moynihan of New York. Among its findings:

"High speed maglev systems can be built to run beside existing interstate highways at acceptable cost and without significantly interfering with normal highway operation. A maglev guideway will encounter many overpasses and interchanges along its route. Since it is probably not acceptable to relocate or modify most of the bridges and ramps on the interstates, there are only two options."

One way would be to elevate the maglev guideway to a height of about 40 feet, allowing it to pass over existing structures. This guideway could run either alongside the interstate or in the median. The other option would be to run the guideway at grade level, passing under existing bridges. However, this is suitable only in rural areas, where medians are wider.

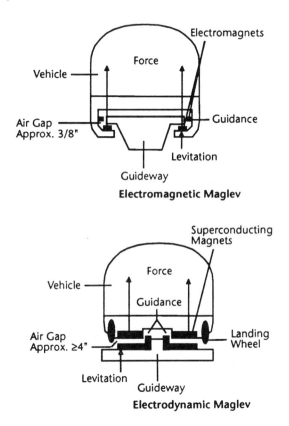

Electromagnetic Maglev

Electrodynamic Maglev

How maglev trains float: the bottom diagram illustrates how magnets on the top of the guideway *push away* the magnets on the bottom of the train. This is called the "repulsive" system and is used in one Japanese system. The top diagram shows how magnets on the low wrap-around arms of the Transrapid train are *pulled up* to magnets under the guideway. This is called the "attractive" system. Superconductivity is not necessary for the Transrapid to work, although it would allow that train, as well as electrically powered steel-wheel trains, to run more efficiently. *(Federal Railroad Administration)*

GREEN LIGHT FOR FLOATING TRAINS

While maglev trains in open country could cruise at 300 mph, speeds would be lower in urban areas. Curves on urban interstates are tighter, rights-of-way are narrower, and the surrounding areas built up, bringing the practical maglev speed down to 100 to 150 mph. However, that is not as much of a sacrifice as it might first appear. After all, in certain cities stations will be relatively close together, as they are on commuter railroads, and often it will not be feasible to run at higher speeds. That does not mean that maglev trains will be inordinately slowed because of numerous stations as they enter cities.

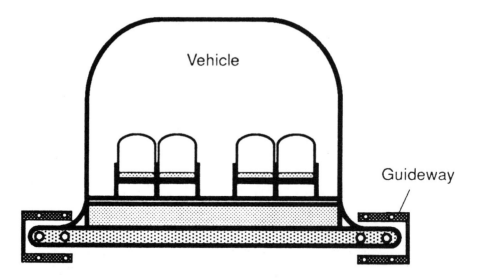

U.S. maglev pioneers Gordon Danby and Jim Powell have proposed using the "null-flux" concept on a maglev vehicle. Here, vehicle-mounted superconducting magnets are centered between track-mounted normally conducting coils. The resulting suspension of the train would be extremely stable—an external force much larger than the weight of the train would be required to make it contact the guideway. The principle of this system has brought much acclaim to its designers. *(Argonne National Laboratory)*

"It is not necessary or desirable that maglev vehicles stop at every station in urban regions," the Argonne report said, "By using off-line loading, maglev vehicles will be able to stop at selected stations and bypass others."

Inhabitants along the maglev lines won't have to worry about noise because the trains are quiet. Maglev vehicles carry no power source and do not contact the guideway. The only sound is the aerodynamic whoosh of wind from the vehicle body. From 50 feet away, a maglev running on an elevated guideway registers a noise level of only 70 decibels. This is well below normal auto and truck traffic noise.

There are three types of maglev systems: metropolitan feeder, intercity corridor, and multi-state networks.

Feeder systems would connect outlying reaches of a metropolitan area with its core. Interstate 495, the Long Island Expressway, is also known as "the world's largest parking lot." A Long Island–New York City maglev system along I-495 was examined in detail by the Senate advisory committee. "Overall length is about 100 miles, with an average spacing between stations of approximately 15 miles," stated the report. Operating speed would be 100 to 150 miles per hour. New York, along with Washington, D.C., Los Angeles, and Chicago, could increase mobility using maglev feeders along the interstates.

The researchers said intercity corridors also appear to be promising. They examined a San Francisco–Los Angeles–San Diego maglev along busy I-5 and concluded that the route, with "branches" along other highways such as I-10, would serve almost all of the population of California.

The Senate report concluded that maximum benefits would result from multi-state interconnected maglev networks, such as an Eastern system connecting with another in the Midwest.

GREEN LIGHT FOR FLOATING TRAINS

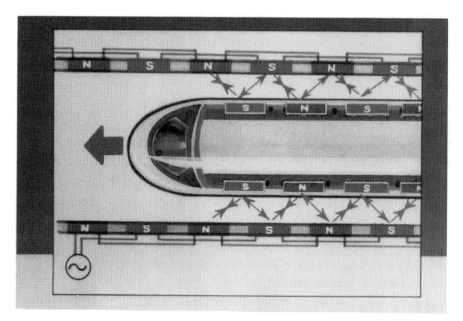

How maglev trains move: this particular vehicle, the Japanese MLU-002, is equipped with magnets on each side. The powerful push and pull of magnets embedded in the sides of the guideway create forces that propel the train.
(Japan Railway Technical Research Institute)

Long-term planners say a New York–Chicago maglev line is not out of the question.

While the United States talks and studies, Germany and Japan undertake serious research and test hardware. The most advanced super-speed maglev technology currently available is from Transrapid International, a joint venture of three German companies—Krauss Maffei, MBB, and Thyssen Henschel.

This maglev Supertrain is not just a futurist's dream. A full-scale system has been up and running at the Transrapid test facility in Emsland, Germany, since 1983. There, trains sweep by so quietly at high speeds on an overhead structure that cattle

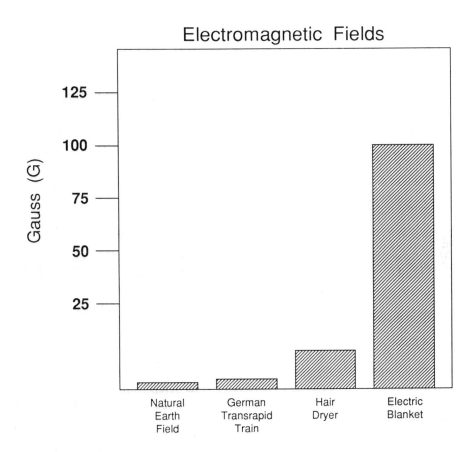

Electromagnetic Fields

Gauss (G)

Natural Earth Field · German Transrapid Train · Hair Dryer · Electric Blanket

Researchers concluded that the Transrapid would not generate magnetic fields strong enough to harm human beings. The train's field as expressed in gauss is trivial when compared to what is found in common household appliances. Some researchers point to a different concern—exposure to cosmic radiation while flying, which can be a significant health risk. A few hours in a jetliner is equal to one chest x-ray.

grazing below do not even lift their heads. One German farmer was asked by a visiting California mayor, Peter Buffa of Costa Mesa, how he felt about having the train running across his farmland. His response: "We don't even know it's there."

GREEN LIGHT FOR FLOATING TRAINS

Argonne's Larry Johnson and Donald Rote were near the German track when the Transrapid maglev zoomed by. "The noise from the Transrapid-06 was less than that from two crows flying near the train," Rote said. "They were both at essentially the same distance away from me, probably a kilometer."

The test center is operated by a group that includes the German Federal Railways and Lufthansa German Airlines. The consortium's commitment is due partially to the $1 billion research and development investment made by the Federal Ministry of Research and Technology, according to Werner Menden, deputy minister of science and technology. The private companies like MBB have invested additional funds.

William W. Dickhart III is the Transrapid representative in the United States. With years of experience in rail systems, he has represented both rail and maglev technologies to industry and government. He says Transrapid's maglev "is essentially ready for revenue operation."

One successful Transrapid test has followed another since the program started with Transrapid-01, which operated at 55 mph in 1970. That vehicle has earned its place as an exhibit in the *Deutsches Museum* in Munich, Germany. Designers were greatly encouraged when Transrapid-04 reached 157 mph in 1973. Continuing the program with another vehicle, Transrapid-05 shuttled more than 50,000 passengers at Hamburg's International Traffic and Transport Exhibition in 1979.

The next generation train, the Transrapid-06, has been exhaustively tested, traveling 100,000 miles on its track. In January 1988 it set a world record for a maglev operating with passengers aboard when it reached 256.4 mph. Later that year Transrapid-06 made 358 consecutive public demonstration runs and carried 16,600 passengers at speeds as high as 250 mph, making eight-minute trips around a 25-mile track. The Germans' demanding program of running 18-hour-day endurance tests on maglev equipment in all types of weather has paid off.

The newest and fastest version, Transrapid-07, named *Europa*, incorporates still more improvements. One way of enhancing performance was to make the vehicle lighter. Compared with the Transrapid-06, each section of the 07 contains 28 magnets instead of the previous 32, reducing the vehicle weight by 20 percent. That, along with a better aerodynamic shape and improved controls, allowed the design speed to be raised to 312 mph. During one test run, this model was struck by lightning. The Transrapid is similar to an automobile in that it acts as a faraday cage, dispersing current from the lightning strike along the outside of the vehicle. No damage to the vehicle could be observed.

The Transrapid-07 set a new world speed record by running at 271 mph on December 18, 1989, making it the fastest maglev to operate while carrying people.

This Supertrain floats above its guideway about three-eighths of an inch, and the separation is maintained by a sophisticated on-board automatic control system. Officials say Transrapid-07 can climb grades as steep as 10 percent and negotiate curves at speeds as high as 250 mph. This performance could cut construction costs by reducing the need for tunnels or circuitous route alignments—the single greatest expense in building Supertrain routes.

The manufacturer says complete safety is assured: "There's just no way it can come off the track because the vehicle actually wraps around it," said Dickhart. "Collisions also are impossible

GREEN LIGHT FOR FLOATING TRAINS

because the propulsion system prevents two trains from approaching head-on or one from overtaking the other from the rear."

Dickhart said the Transrapid monitors its track on a near-continuous basis: "Every time it runs, it does its own track geometry. If there's any change from the previous run, it's detected."

One fear occasionally expressed is that the magnetic waves, or electromagnetic field (EMF), from either the vehicle or guideway will harm passengers or neighbors along the line. "There is very little magnetism actually in the Transrapid passenger compartment," said Dickhart. The magnetic "leakage" from the guideway to surrounding areas is considerably less than from electromagnetic fields associated with overhead power lines, for several reasons: one is that the types of magnetic fields are different; another is that power lines are continuously charged, while the maglev guideway is energized only at the moment when a train is passing.

Researchers from the Canadian Institute of Guided Ground Transport examined the German system and concluded that fears were unjustified. They found that the Transrapid vehicle would not generate magnetic fields strong enough to harm either human beings or sensitive equipment such as a wristwatch or heart pacemaker.

"The magnetic flux density in the cabin of the vehicle is about 1 gauss," said Dickhart. To laymen that means the magnetic field inside the train is trivial, quite close to the 0.5–1.0 gauss, or magnetic flux per square centimeter, for the Earth's natural magnetic field to which all people are continuously exposed. That is less than the 7.3 gauss for an electric drill or 9.7

gauss for a hand-held hair dryer. The Transrapid certainly is far below the 100 gauss found in electric blankets.

Senators were told by Gil Carmichael of the Federal Railroad Administration, "As the agency responsible for the safety of intercity high-speed rail and maglev systems, we have initiated a major research effort to provide the basis for safety standards. . . . Research on the German maglev system will be accelerated to insure that unresolved concerns with safety do not slow implementation."

"One report given to the Federal Railroad Administration says that the Transrapid is the safest transportation system ever designed," said Dickhart.

Transrapid, in conjunction with Maglev Transit, plans to help build the line in Orlando, and along with the Bechtel Corporation, the Las Vegas–Anaheim route. A Pennsylvania agency recommended a Transrapid system for a Pittsburgh–Philadelphia link. Robert J. Casey, former executive director of that state's rail commission, said, "Here, we have a mountain range to cross. Using a steel-wheel technology may require numerous tunnels at great expense. Using magnetic levitation, there would be a need for no tunnels whatsoever, saving in construction costs and time."

The Cologne-Bonn and Dusseldorf airport officials have proposed that those two airports be linked with a Transrapid maglev, a recommendation that Lufthansa Airlines applauds, which would also extend to Essen's Central station. "This will be the first one built in Europe," said Rolf Kretzschmar, president of Transrapid International. "The government has approved the line. Construction could begin in 1993 and it could be in operation by 1996."

GREEN LIGHT FOR FLOATING TRAINS

Another proposal calls for the Transrapid to be built between the seven major airports in Germany, and a study shows that these could come about entirely with private funds. Others propose to build a 600-mile system linking Munich with Stuttgart, Hamburg, and a number of other cities.

Countries nearby are active. The fabled cities of Vienna and Budapest, both planning World's Fairs for 1995, have discussed a maglev Supertrain link. A maglev ride of about an hour could easily cover the 140-mile distance between the cities, which were once tied politically and culturally.

The Germans are taking a practical approach to building a Transrapid maglev in the United States by teaming with Bechtel, an engineering firm with decades of worldwide experience in major construction projects. To Bechtel's credits are San Francisco's Bay Area Rapid Transit System, Washington's Metro subway, Boulder Dam, and other challenging construction projects.

In 1954, President Eisenhower named Steve Bechtel to the prestigious National Highway Committee. That group presented a blueprint for the National Interstate and Defense Highway System, which Eisenhower officially brought into being in 1956.

"Bechtel started in transportation because it was Warren Bechtel who was building railroads across the west—parts of the Rock Island Line, the Southern Pacific, and the Santa Fe," said Gerry Spencer, who heads Bechtel's New York office. "That started the company."

While Transrapid is enjoying world acclaim, the maglev at Birmingham, England, has been operating as a "people-mover" system licensed by Transrapid since 1984. It glides along at 30 mph, connecting the city's train station with the airport on a route only a quarter of a mile long. The system reliably carries as many as 1,500 passengers per hour.

A transit-type maglev called the *M-Bahn* was operated as a demonstration line in Berlin. Maximum speed was between 25 and 50 mph, depending on the distances between stations. Trains ran about every three minutes and could carry a maximum of 7,000 passengers per hour. A permanent *M-Bahn* will be built at the Frankfurt airport.

The potential to use maglev in city transit systems is incalculable. It is now reasonable to suggest that by the year 2025, New York and other cities may well be converting subway lines to whisper-quiet, vibrationless maglev trains. Such projects, while massive in scope for the transit industry, will provide so much rider satisfaction and cost savings that the public will eventually demand them.

Sound far-fetched? Wilfred T. Ussery, a board member of the Bay Area Rapid Transit (BART) has proposed that the agency designate maglev technology as the "mode of preference" for future BART lines. The technology could be used to retrofit existing BART lines as well as transit systems in Washington, Atlanta, and in other cities.

There is competition for these transit markets. The Japanese recognize the promise of maglev technology, which is characteristic of their long-standing concern for mobility. Japan, not to be outdone by Germany, has invested more than $1 billion in government funds in maglev research and development since the early 1960s.

The HSST has been developed by the Japanese for use in domestic and overseas markets. Some predictions are that this train will be wildly successful throughout the world. Editors and reporters at the *Wall Street Journal* handpicked the HSST Corporation as one of a highly select group of companies who will "lead business into the '90s."

GREEN LIGHT FOR FLOATING TRAINS

Its vehicle was long a project of Japan Air Lines, and the airline heritage shows in the advanced aerospace technologies that are built into it. The HSST is lightweight and designed to achieve aerodynamic efficiency for energy conservation. The product of research that began in 1971, HSST uses the "attraction" magnetic levitation method. Yokohama, Japan, will build the HSST for transit use there.

The program set new records year after year. The first version, HSST-01, achieved a speed of 191 mph in a 1978 test. The HSST-03 operated for six months at an exposition in the Japanese city of Tsukuba, where it made 13,220 runs and achieved a reliability factor of an amazing 99.96 percent. System downtime totaled only 49 minutes as a result of five minor incidents requiring repairs. The HSST also carried passengers at Expo '86 in Vancouver, British Columbia.

"I remember that ride in Vancouver," wrote Tom Turner of the Tucson *Arizona Daily Star*. "It was short, only a quarter mile of track, and slow, 25 mph, because of the short distance. But it was so smooth, silent, almost motionless. You could have been standing still while stagehands rolled scenery past the windows."

A newer model, the HSST-04, ran at the Saitama Expo in 1988 near Tokyo. To date, HSST has carried more than 1½ million paying passengers at such events. Among some of its most famous passengers are Japanese Crown Prince Akihito,

More than 1½ million paying passengers rode this HSST-5 (High Speed Surface Transport) maglev train from March 25 through October 1, 1989, at an exhibition in Yokohama, Japan. This train uses some technology patented by the developers of the German Transrapid. *(HSST Corporation)*

The HSST-100 is designed for duty within city limits. Its small turning radius enables the line to be routed through winding, hitherto restrictive downtown areas. Noiseless, even at its top speed of 62.2 mph, it can pass within close proximity of quiet zones such as hospitals and schools. Look for other versions of this train to appear in future years, one able to speed along at more than 180 mph. *(HSST Corporation)*

former Prime Minister Nakasone, and Britain's Prince Charles and Princess Diana.

Different HSST models are being promoted, ranging from an intercity 205-mph Supertrain shuttle to a 62-mph local transit system. Technological achievements of HSST are so significant that the first two vehicles are enshrined in Japan's National Science Museum, next to the oldest airplane built in Japan and the famous Mazda rotary engine.

Japanese experts have proposed that the first HSST line in the United States be built in Las Vegas, to link downtown with the airport. This particular HSST wouldn't operate very fast because the transit-type version would be built. Seventeen Japanese companies have agreed to invest in the $67 million project, including auto giant Mitsubishi. Late in 1990, the Nevada Public Service Commission granted a certificate allowing HSST to become the first licensed maglev system in the United States.

Researchers at Japan's Railway Transportation Research Institute have been busy with another government-funded effort. The group has been working on a super-speed maglev train that uses superconductors. Their vehicle, the MLU-001, also known as the "Linear Motor Car," uses the "repulsive force" method, where the magnetic field in the guideway repels coils of the same polarity in the car's underside. The opposing forces levitate the train between four and six inches off the guideway.

"Superconducting levitation is not effective at low speeds," said Hisashi Tanaka, chief engineer for the project, "so the vehicle is supported and guided by pneumatic-tired wheels at starting." The wheels retract when the train reaches about 100 mph, and in that regard it's been likened to an airplane because it needs a rolling start before it can "fly."

The MLU-001 in a two-car configuration has reached a speed of 250 mph. Tests of an updated version, MLU-002, began in 1987. Eventually, it will consist of a train 14 cars long. On a four-mile long test track in Miyazaki, on Japan's southernmost large island, a predecessor vehicle shattered the record books in December 1979. Then, the ML-500, which did not carry crew or passengers at the time, achieved a world record speed of 323 mph.

Was that super-speed record what the Japanese expected? Koji Takahashi, a Japanese railway expert, told a committee of the United States Congress, "we attained a speed of 323 miles per hour. That was exactly the same result we predicted from

Openness and lots of light are striking features of interior of HSST prototype.
(HSST Corporation)

our theories. We knew then that magnetic levitation is not a dream anymore, it is a fact, something which is actually going to be realized on a commercial basis. We are sure that magnetic levitation will be a future ground transportation mode providing service at over 300 miles per hour."

Kenji Fujie, chief engineer in the maglev's laboratory, said, "We can run it beyond 1,000 kilometers per hour [620 mph], theoretically."

The MLU-002 Supertrain is not yet ready for paying passengers. "We feel confident that we have solved all the technological problems of magnetic levitation as a transportation mode," Takahashi said, "but we are currently testing or doing research in the areas of safety, stability, dependability, and efficiency. . . . For these reasons, I think it will require more time before we can put that type of system into commercial service."

The Japanese continue to experience component failures with the MLU-002, but Tanaka doesn't worry. "It's supposed to break down," he told *Business Tokyo*, "otherwise we couldn't fix its faults." The vehicle also has problems with strong electromagnetic fields, and until they are resolved researchers say the train will not be offered for sale.

Meanwhile, the Japanese Ministry of Transport, in a show of confidence, doubled its funding of the superconducting maglev development program in the late 1980s. Hisashi Tanaka said, "We have finally reached a manufacturing stage of a prototype vehicle that is one generation before those for revenue service."

The Miyazaki maglev won't reach full operational readiness until 1996, and not until more trial runs are made. The Transport Ministry is building a new $2.7 billion test track near the city of Kofu in Yamanashi Prefecture, on the inland side of Mt. Fuji in mountainous central Japan.

This decision allows full-scale operational testing, and officials have a double duty in mind for the track—when testing is over in 1997, it could be extended for future commercial use between Tokyo and Osaka. Consideration is being given to building a maglev line that by 2005 would link those cities in about one hour. A new maglev service would relieve pressure on the Bullet Trains, which routinely carry full loads. But Hirouki Kasai, a vice-president with JR Central, part of the old Japan National Railways, said if the Miyazaki vehicle fails to live up to expectations, they could adapt the new *Super Hikari* Bullet Trains for operation over the new inland route.

Japanese officials say they want to build a 27-mile maglev link on Hokkaido Island, between Sapporo and the Chitose Airport at a cost of $1 billion, which could become the world's first commercial superconducting maglev service. No date has been set for construction or operation.

Also under study are maglev systems for city transit purposes in Tokyo and Osaka. Certainly by the year 2000, Japan will have several maglev lines operating. Considering how well the Bullet Trains were engineered and marketed, it will be no surprise if the Japanese again win world honors for building premier passenger-carrying systems.

While the Japanese did not participate in the bidding for the Los Angeles–Las Vegas route, they are behind the project in Florida to build the Orlando maglev system. The Japanese think that *any* maglev put in service in the United States will spark demand for more lines, and in future years they'll be able to compete.

Since the early 1970s, the Canadians have worked on a system similar to the Miyazaki maglev in that it also uses superconductors and retractable wheels. Their desire is to develop a high-speed ground link for the Toronto–Ottawa–Montreal corridor. Emphasis now is on a two-car train with a 280-mph cruising ability.

A Russian joke is that the country had a maglev back in the Stalin era, but it provided service only in one direction: "It would take people to Siberia, return empty, and take more away."

Yuri Sokolov, deputy general director of the Soviet Union's maglev program, said research and testing have been under way since 1978. Maglev was included in the government's priority technology program in 1989. At work in Rameskije, near Moscow, the Soviets are planning for a minimum Supertrain speed of 155 mph.

"In Armenia, the construction of the first 3.2-kilometer Yerevan–Abovian pilot section began in 1986 and will end in

1992," said Sokolov. "Maglev lines for the Crimea and the Baltic region are being contemplated and their completion dates will be fixed later."

The Soviet Union admits that Moscow has an airport access problem. The newspaper *Isvestia* reported interest in maglev for airport access because "about 33 million passengers are serviced by Moscow airports, and they take about 1½–2 hours to travel from the city to the airport when traveling on roads."

To solve today's traffic problems, the first maglev trains to run in the Soviet Union will most likely be of Japanese origin. Plans are to build an HSST maglev line linking downtown Moscow with Sheremetyevo International Airport. Akira Hayashi, president of HSST Corporation, and Evgeny Orlov, a Soviet deputy minister, signed a letter of intent to build the maglev line by 1996. The 185-mph maglev system, estimated to cost $607 million, will whisk travelers to the Soviet capital in 15 minutes.

Even Romania, which has been the most repressed country in Eastern Europe, has gotten into maglevs. Stalinist President Nicolae Ceausescu controlled the country with an iron hand from 1965 to 1989, when he was executed by a new government. Under his regime the country may have been backward, but since 1976 it has conducted maglev studies based on the "attractive" mode. Romania's Polytechnic Institute spearheaded the effort and one vehicle, Magnibus-01, was developed and put through static testing. A Magnibus-02 was to have been built for 250-mph performance. Two test tracks have been proposed, but neither has been built. The most recent entrant is the Korea Electrotechnology Research Institute, which has unveiled an experimental maglev vehicle named Komag-01. Ahn Woo-hee, the Institute's president, said that a 125-mph vehicle could be ready by 1997 and a 310-mph version by 2001.

GREEN LIGHT FOR FLOATING TRAINS

Japan's superconductive maglev vehicle is the MLU-002. An earlier version ran unmanned at 321.3 mph on a test track on December 21, 1979. The Japanese admit this system needs more development and testing before it will be put on the market.   *(Japan Railway Technical Research Institute)*

Interest in maglev is nothing new. The concept of high-speed ground transport using magnetic forces was discussed as early as 1907. The first "repulsive" maglev was conceived by Emile Bachelet, a French engineer working in America, in 1912. He actually levitated and propelled a model vehicle, but it required high levels of power, and the project lay dormant. In the 1930s, the concept of electromagnetic levitation was developed by German scientist Hermann Kemper, and he demonstrated that by using magnetic fields the advantages of a train could be combined with those of flying.

The United States once had a maglev research program, but abandoned it. More and more, it appears that a major mistake was made.

The superconducting type of maglev, a brilliant breakthrough, was invented in the United States in the 1960s by James Powell, a nuclear engineer, and Gordon Danby, a physicist, of the Brookhaven National Laboratory. Powell likes to tell the story of how, while driving from New York to Boston one Friday afternoon in 1961, he was hopelessly immobilized in traffic and began thinking of maglev trains. He talked the idea over with Danby and they went on to develop a train system, for which they obtained a patent, that would levitate six inches and travel at 300 mph. Their concepts were later adapted by the Canadians and Japanese.

After that, others examined maglev. Stanford Research Institute and North American Rockwell, with the support of Sandia National Laboratories, experimented with superconducting magnetic suspensions. The auto industry, both Ford Motor Company and General Motors, got interested in the 1970s, as did some aerospace researchers, notably Rohr Industries, Mitre Corporation and TRW Systems Incorporated.

GREEN LIGHT FOR FLOATING TRAINS

These traditional members of the automotive and aviation industries were uncommitted, and soon dropped out of maglev research. American behavior was quite a contrast to Japanese and German perseverence and commitment, which was generously encouraged by government financial aid.

The Massachusetts Institute of Technology and the National Science Foundation developed a maglev vehicle with a practical top speed of about 220 mph. In 1970 researchers Henry Kolm and Richard Thornton began work on this technology, named the Magneplane, which relied on superconducting coils. The MIT system differed from other concepts in that the vehicles, which looked like the fuselage of a small jet, moved through a trough guideway and were free to bank when negotiating curves.

The project fell apart in 1975, however, when President Gerald R. Ford's administration terminated all funding for high-speed ground transportation research. Thus, programs to build a maglev test track at China Lake in California and to speed Amtrak trains ended. Just a few years earlier, however, Gerald Ford as Congressman led a campaign for subsidies to the aerospace industry to construct a prototype of the Supersonic Transport.

Not one dime was available for high-speed train research and development. The reason given for termination was that growth in transport demand appeared to be slowing and the United States had adequate air and highway capacity to handle increases in travel. Those claims were false, as proved by the government's continual increases in tax-financed highway and aviation programs.

Perhaps the stage for the cutback was set when President Richard M. Nixon did away with the White House Chief Scientist position, meaning that many technical policies were crafted by non-technical persons. Things got worse under President Jimmy Carter, whose Transportation Secretary, Brock Adams, abolished the post of Assistant Secretary for Systems Engineering and Technology, which meant that the people who considered future technological directions for transportation were budget personnel and political appointees.

Robert Parsons ran the research function in the Federal Railroad Administration at the time the high-speed development program was abandoned. He later told Congress that DOT thinks in short-range terms and follows "yo-yo technology policies" from one administration to the next.

"I found it obscene for the Department of Transportation, a department so dependent on technology, not to have an assistant secretary for technology. Lawyers, economists, and accountants, no matter how good they are, must have qualified technology input to transportation policy, regulations, and programs," said Parsons. "I basically left federal service because I couldn't support policies that said we would be second best in transportation and let the foreign countries develop systems that we could implement. Budget people actually counted our savings from such policies!"

Years later, Parsons, a consultant, was retained by the City of Las Vegas and managed a complex two-year study of building a Supertrain system between that city and southern California. The city had to undertake the forward-looking study because Washington was not equipped to do so.

Meanwhile, a private effort has been underway in San Francisco to develop the Knolle Magnetrans or the K-Mag system. It is the brainchild of Ernst G. Knolle, who has consulted with the world's foremost scientists in magnetics. He has worked at his project over many years, having built the first K-Mag working

GREEN LIGHT FOR FLOATING TRAINS

Influence of Japan Air Lines is evident in the design of the MLU-002, made of a composite material to achieve light weight. Japan may spend $3 billion more than the $1 billion already invested in the MLU-002 technology. Plans suggest the one-car vehicle could grow into a high-capacity train 14 cars long.

(Japan Railway Technical Research Institute)

model in 1961, and he holds several maglev patents. The K-Mag system would use small two-passenger vehicles that could operate at 200 mph. In March 1989, a full-sized K-Mag was exhibited at a conference in Miami sponsored by the American Society of Civil Engineers.

A low-speed maglev for transit named ROMAG was developed by Rohr Industries in 1970 and later acquired by Boeing. The research program was helped by funds from DOT's Urban Mass Transportation Administration until that program was killed in the Reagan Administration. Because Boeing refused to continue the work with its own funds, the technology was licensed to the High Speed Ground Transportation Center organized by Pittsburgh's Carnegie Mellon University.

None of this is enough for Senator Daniel Patrick Moynihan, who wants a domestic maglev program to be revived in a big way. He wouldn't mind it, either, if much of the research were done at the Brookhaven National Laboratory on Long Island so that Brookhaven will be known as the Kitty Hawk of maglev. If Long Island aerospace contractor Grumman Corporation were to share in maglev work, that would be all the better.

U.S. News & World Report said the program was like reawakening Rip Van Winkle after a 15-year sleep, and suggested that the nation lacked the vision to implement an effective maglev program. That view isn't surprising, considering the government's failures in research and development.

Linda R. Cohen and Roger G. Noll, authors of *The Technology Pork Barrel,* a wide-ranging book published by the Brookings Institution, wrote that the history of federal research and development commercialization programs "is hardly a happy story of success," citing as "almost unqualified failures" the SST, the Clinch River Breeder Reactor, the Space Shuttle, and the synthetic fuels program. "The case studies obviously justify considerable skepticism about the wisdom of government programs that seek to bring new technologies to commercial practice," wrote the authors. These programs have cost the taxpayers dearly.

It doesn't have to be that way, argues Senator Moynihan, who states that maglev might be another technology like video cassette recorders, which were invented here but manufactured and marketed by overseas firms. That has been the fate of numerous technologies, and every time that happens the United States pays in lost jobs and deficits in international trade.

Senator Moynihan sponsored legislation to establish a federal maglev research program and permit the use of interstate

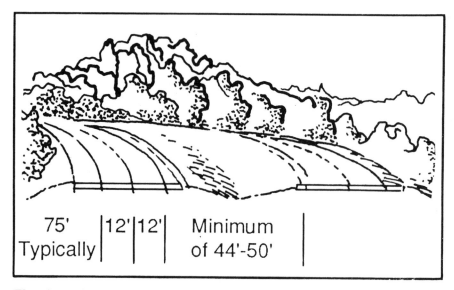

| 75'
Typically | 12' | 12' | Minimum
of 44'-50' | |

There's ample clearance on rural interstates for maglev construction along the median or the sides of the rights-of-way.

rights-of-way by maglev systems. The senator, a ranking member of the Committee on Environment and Public Works, established the Maglev Technology Advisory Committee, whose members include James Powell and Gordon Danby.

"We will have magnetically levitated high-speed transportation. We invented it. The only question is whether we will manufacture it and sell it to others, or whether others will manufacture it and sell it to us," said Senator Moynihan. "We should not minimize the scientific and engineering challenge. Rather we should welcome it."

Danby says, "It's stupid not to get into the game. It's so early it's like looking at airplanes in 1920 and saying, 'Oh my God, we're behind Germany and the British' and then giving up. That would be about equally intelligent."

The Advisory Committee report issued in mid-1989 said it

favors domestic development of a second-generation maglev that can be installed along the interstates. It also favors the superconducting approach because of its larger clearance between vehicles and guideways. About a billion dollars over seven years would be required to develop, test, and demonstrate several prototypes of maglev technologies.

The work by Senator Moynihan—as well as Senators Ernest F. Hollings of South Carolina and J. James Exon of Nebraska—has begun to pay off. President Bush has thus far called for $33 million in expenditures to begin developing a domestic maglev Supertrain. For those who think that is a lot of money, look at the budget for 1990 alone—$69.8 billion for research and development programs. Interestingly, the bulk of that research money is spent by three departments: Defense, NASA, and Energy.

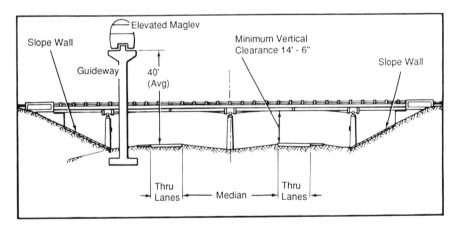

If maglev trains use interstate highways, the guideway would be elevated in some portions to pass over existing bridges. Maglev systems would be less expensive than building still more highways along new rights-of-way, and would result in a cleaner environment. Sketch is from a 1989 study advocated by Senator Daniel Patrick Moynihan of New York.

(Senate Committee on Environment and Public Works)

GREEN LIGHT FOR FLOATING TRAINS

The Department of Transportation was moving too slowly on maglev issues to suit Moynihan, so the Senator has involved the Army Corps of Engineers in plans to develop a maglev technology. The Corps presented a plan to Congress in July 1990 spelling out options the government can use to help industry develop a next-generation maglev by the year 2000.

In one option, Washington would establish a "fast-track" competition by industry teams to design and develop an American maglev, leading to a full-scale prototype system; however, unskilled federal employees would be involved in developing the technical characteristics, which could be a drawback. Another option is to encourage domestic industries to team with state and local interests in developing several different maglev designs, then determining which system is superior. In the report's final option, the federal government would not try to "reinvent the wheel" but would encourage private sector firms to adapt foreign maglev systems for domestic transportation needs.

Although maglev scientists Danby and Powell are distraught that the Army's involvement will result in more paperwork and less in the way of an actual product, Moynihan is supported by others. Early in 1991, Representative Charles E. Schumer, a New York Democrat, introduced a bill to authorize the use of highway rights-of-way for maglev trains. Representative Bob Mrazek, a Long Island Democrat, would spend $750 million to develop a prototype domestic design. While Mrazek's ideas have merit, his methods have sorely rankled others who have been promoting Supertrains for a decade or more.

In a Congressional hearing in June 1990, Mrazek complained about existing state-inspired high-speed rail projects. He suggested the state plans be "held up" because they would use foreign technologies like TGV and Transrapid trains. At some unknown later date, he would force the states to build an unknown domestic design throughout the land.

In other words, Mrazek wanted Supertrains running in America, but only *his kind* of Supertrains. Also, he claimed that a new domestic maglev could be designed and ready in the short period of three years. Experience demonstrates that the Congressman's three-year claim was totally unrealistic. Examples abound:

Steel-wheel trains. The first *Metroliners*, whose construction was rushed during Lyndon Johnson's administration, had design flaws that caused them to stall in snowstorms. The new trains suffered the indignity of being rescued by locomotives built in the 1930s, which easily operated through swirling snow. The *Metroliners* never did operate at 160 mph, the original goal.

Airplanes. Donald W. Douglas, when president of Douglas Aircraft Company, said, "There is no such thing as quick and easy development of a new transport carrier; to ignore this truism is to court disaster."

Transit buses. For much of the 1970s, the government tried to develop Transbus, a vehicle supposed to make transit more accessible to handicapped riders. After millions in tax funds were spent, it was an abject failure, an embarrassment to the transit community, and never put into production.

Republican Congressman Tom Lewis of Florida countered Mrazek by saying that his state had no intention of delaying its Supertrain plans. He said Washington had not been a good partner in high-speed rail, that it ran hot and cold over the years.

The chairman of the High Speed Rail Association, Paul Reistrup, later qualified his organization's support of the Mrazek bill "so long as current high speed efforts are not obstructed." Because he had sneered at state plans to build existing maglev and steel-wheel technologies, Congressman Mrazek's support weakened.

In another mistaken notion, Mrazek thought that prohibiting foreign-designed Supertrains from using highway rights-of-way was a good idea. However, by wrecking the market for the proven Supertrains, he would make it nearly impossible for American firms to co-produce such trains. He was in danger of prohibiting internationalization of Supertrains. Yet, that would be setting up a double standard because internationalization of aircraft is allowed. For example, there is no such thing as an "all-American" airplane anymore. Many sizable portions of Boeing airplanes are made in France, Italy, Brazil, Japan, and other countries, shipped here, and assembled into a jetliner. It is little known, but Boeing is a bigger contractor in France for jet engines than is its top competitor, the European Airbus consortium. Boeing has a higher percentage of its aircraft components and structures coming from overseas suppliers than it ever has in its history.

Indeed, more such internationalization should be expected. Three Japanese companies—Fuji, Kawasaki, and Mitsubishi—are joint-development partners in the new Boeing 777, with their share in the project reaching as much as 23 percent. The Energy Department, looking for a way to defray part of the $10 billion cost of the superconductor supercollider to be built near Dallas, tried to enlist Japanese and Korean partners. Domestic automakers have established profitable joint ventures with foreign firms, such as Chrysler's relationships since 1971 with Japanese companies. "Nearly nine percent of the cars sold under the Chrysler logo actually were made by Mitsubishi in Japan or at the [jointly owned] Diamond-Star plant in Normal, Illinois," wrote Paul Blustein and Warren Brown in the *Washington Post*. "The seemingly all-American Dodge Raider off-road vehicle is a Mitsubishi Montero. The only difference is the nameplate."

By July 1991, Congressman Mrazek had moderated his position. He again introduced a bill to establish a domestic maglev program, but this time he would permit foreign-designed Supertrains to use highway rights-of-way.

The Moynihan effort wasn't the first time Congress has tried to move the federal establishment into maglev research. A committee chaired by Kansas Representative Dan Glickman, in a 1982 report, said the United States ought to design a maglev research program utilizing the expertise and facilities at NASA's Lewis Laboratory.

Perhaps one reason why no action resulted is that NASA officials are guilty of some of the worst cost overruns in the history of the United States government. For example, the estimate for the space station Freedom has soared from $8 billion to $38 billion. "It seems to be the only thing in NASA that consistently goes up," wrote Robert L. Park of the American Physical Society in the *Washington Post*. "Indeed, scientists bristle at listing the space station among 'big science' programs. It's not really a science program at all, they insist; it's an orbiting pork barrel whose only purpose is to prop up the aerospace industry."

NASA also has been so enamored of aviation that it has scoffed privately at American attempts to develop Supertrains. After all, the aerospace industry flirted with trains in the 1970s and the results were unmitigated disasters. Three companies with major failures were Boeing, Rohr Industries, and United Technologies.

GREEN LIGHT FOR FLOATING TRAINS

Boeing struck out twice. For Boston, it built light rail vehicles that wouldn't work. "The cars failed to meet such crucial civilian design criteria as simplicity and durability," wrote Michael Renner of the Worldwatch Institute. "They proved so unreliable and required such costly repairs and modifications that most were taken out of service after only a few years." The city canceled most of the order.

Railway suppliers, who had warned against buying from aerospace firms inexperienced in transit, took great satisfaction at seeing Boeing bleed. Boston's Boeing fleet was replaced a mere 10 years later with far superior Japanese-designed cars. But the company's reputation continues to suffer. In mid-1990, the acting general manager of the San Francisco Municipal Railway, Johnny Stein, said the city's problem-plagued Boeing-built cars were "monsters," while the *San Francisco Examiner* labeled them the worst in the world.

Boeing also was a contractor on a controversial small train "people-mover" in Morgantown, West Virginia, and its system failed often and cost too much. The short, 2.2-mile line was originally priced at $20 million, but actually cost more than twice that, or $42.5 million.

As part of the government's high-speed ground transportation program of the 1960s, United Technologies tried its hand in designing the Turbotrain. A sleek, eye-catching unit, the train was capable of 160 mph but operated poorly. It swayed excessively on curves, racked up higher maintenance expenses than any train in the nation, and was a fuel guzzler. Amtrak scrapped the poor performers in favor of the French Turboliner.

Rohr built subway cars for San Francisco and Washington, D.C.; in both cases transit managers had to wrestle with doors that would not close and trains that would not operate properly.

One aerospace company had better luck: Grumman. The company is renowned for building the Navy's "Top Gun" F-14A all-weather fighter, the Tomcat, and other high-performance aircraft. As part of the government's high-speed ground program, Grumman completed a $3.5-million federal contract for a tracked air-cushion research vehicle. The train was impractical, but it worked.

However, Grumman, too, failed when it purchased the Flxible Bus Company of Ohio from Rohr Industries. The Model 870 was designed by Rohr and given the stamp of approval by Grumman's aerospace engineers during the company's purchase. Later, to Grumman's horror, the Model 870 suffered fleetwide structural failures.

It was Grumman, not Rohr, that endured the humiliation of bus breakdowns, critical media coverage, loss in market share when New York City refused to buy any more of its buses, and unexpected costs to retrofit every bus with a redesigned undercarriage. To its great credit, Grumman assumed the costs of repairing the buses in every city. Grumman finally sold Flxible, but not until its losses had surpassed more than $200 million.

After these repeated failures, managers in ground transportation are less than thrilled when an aerospace engineer knocks on the door. However, despite past disappointments, Grumman's interest in high-speed trains is serious—so much so that it helped Senator Moynihan and the Senate's Maglev Technology Advisory Committee with its work.

Grumman is in position to influence Washington. Its director for federal programs, George Prytula, is regarded by staffers at the Transportation Department as perhaps the most credible of the representatives who prowl the nation's capital. Unlike other aerospace industry officials, Prytula is known by key fig-

ures in the transit industry and in the growing Supertrain community because of his prior transit experience.

Aerospace expertise might help restore the lead that America had in one area—superconductivity. James Powell told Congress: "We published the first work in 1966 . . . and pioneered a couple of inventions which are now used in the Japanese national railway system. We were granted the first original patent on superconducting magnetically levitated trains. There is a funny story in that regard. We got the patent in the United States, and the patent attorney said, 'Well, do you want to acquire the Japanese rights for another five hundred dollars?'

Pittsburgh wants to Americanize the German Transrapid maglev train and under license manufacture it for use on a regional system as well as sell it elsewhere in the United States. Public agencies and private companies have formed Maglev Incorporated to reach such goals.
(Transrapid International)

We looked at each other and said, no, it will never be built in Japan. So we passed it up."

Senator Moynihan responded jokingly, "Oh, the life of the theoretical physicist," to which Powell replied, "Right, not too practical."

Superconductivity has been known since 1911 when a Dutch physicist, Heike Kamerlingh Onnes, discovered the phenomenon by cooling mercury to −270 degrees centigrade. Since, it has been much discussed by the scientific community, as evidenced by papers presented at an Applied Superconductivity Conference held in 1972 and in numerous technical journals since.

New superconductors have been developed, made out of materials discovered by IBM in 1986, that conduct electricity without resistance at higher temperatures than previously expected. A consortium in Japan made up of 45 companies and the government is working on superconductors for commercial uses, while United States research has been geared to military purposes. It troubles the scientific community that in the race to commercialize superconductors, the United States is behind the Japanese, again.

Some Fortune 500 firms are backing superconductivity research, including Westinghouse Electric, IBM, Du Pont, and the American Telephone and Telegraph Company. Some smaller companies are involved, too. Intermagnetics General Corporation of New York, a spinoff from General Electric Company, has devoted itself to the technology. Newer companies include Conductus Incorporated of Palo Alto, California, and the American Superconductor Corporation of Cambridge, Massachusetts. A Texas Center on Superconductivity has been established, as has an Applied Superconductivity Center at the University of Wisconsin.

An effort has been made to better organize these interests by forming Maglev 2000, a spinoff of the Washington-based Council on Superconductivity for American Competitiveness. The group is aiming to demonstrate a full-scale working prototype of a maglev train by the end of 1999 as part of a National Maglev Initiative.

"That sounds great, but the first two years of the National Maglev Initiative are devoted, as has become the norm in the United States, to feasibility studies, market assessments, technology assessments, environmental analyses, and economic analyses, until it seems that the bureaucrats are doing assessments of assessments," wrote Lee Carlson, editor of *Superconductor Industry*. "Has America forgotten how to produce anything but reports? While the feasibility studiers are busy studying, Japan and Germany are busy building. . . ."

Danby and Powell say they could do it faster. "We can leapfrog to the forefront if we start now on a five-year construction program," said Danby. "Rather than study the problem to death, a new influx of future maglev engineers should learn on the job, on actual construction projects."

Overseas interests have rail and maglev technologies that could be running in the United States in a few short years. Should those projects be held up while a United States maglev is designed? There is a chorus of opinion that says we need to start building systems now.

Minnesota Transportation Commissioner John H. Riley foresaw this problem when he served as administrator of DOT's Federal Railroad Administration. He applauded any domestic research effort, but stressed that we can't fear the political consequences of importing technologies. Said Riley:

"Whenever I talk about this to people who haven't dealt with

GREEN LIGHT FOR FLOATING TRAINS

the issue before, the first question we get is 'Why should we put all this money into buying something from Japan or France, or Germany, or England, or Canada, or wherever?' The answer is, to go ahead and invest billions of dollars in duplicating them not only wastes money but wastes time. There is ample opportunity for American investment in new systems, but that money ought to be spent on adapting existing systems to the unique needs of our environment.

"Since the systems are going to be built here, it's evident that the jobs are going to be here. Have no fear of the issue of importing technologies. It's going to be raised politically, but it's a false issue. People want service; they want jobs. There's nothing in the importation of technologies that's inconsistent with either of those concepts," Riley said.

Paul Reistrup says the United States needs to do both. He wants to get on with installing technology available now while designing new systems: "I think research is fine and would add to the whole effort. They might get to superconductivity more quickly. But let's not delay service a couple of decades. You look how long ago the Transrapid effort started, and why do that all over again?"

Major interests in Pittsburgh subscribe to that view. In a unique public-private partnership, a new company has been formed, Maglev Incorporated, aimed at making Pittsburgh a manufacturing and distribution center for maglev trains. The organizers—which include several corporations, the Allegheny County government, the Duquesne Light Company, United Steelworkers of America, and the redevelopment authority—want the rights to manufacture Germany's Transrapid maglev.

The Pittsburgh group is looking at the potential for "Amer-

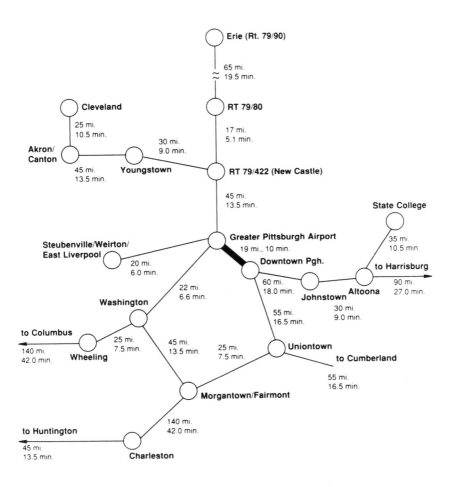

Erie (Rt. 79/90)

65 mi.
≈ 19.5 min.

RT 79/80

Cleveland

25 mi.
10.5 min.

30 mi.
9.0 min.

17 mi.
5.1 min.

Akron/
Canton

45 mi.
13.5 min.

Youngstown

RT 79/422 (New Castle)

45 mi.
13.5 min.

State College

Greater Pittsburgh Airport
19 mi., 10 min.

35 mi.
10.5 min.

Steubenville/Weirton/
East Liverpool

20 mi.
6.0 min.

Downtown Pgh.

to Harrisburg

22 mi.
6.6 min.

60 mi.
18.0 min.

Altoona

90 mi.
27.0 min.

Washington

Johnstown

30 mi.
9.0 min.

55 mi.
16.5 min.

to Columbus

25 mi.
7.5 min.

45 mi.
13.5 min.

25 mi.
7.5 min.

Uniontown

140 mi.
42.0 min.

Wheeling

to Cumberland

55 mi.
16.5 min.

Morgantown/Fairmont

140 mi.
42.0 min.

to Huntington

45 mi.
13.5 min.

Charleston

(NOT TO SCALE)

Maglev demonstration line to Pittsburgh's airport would be the first built under current proposals in Pennsylvania. System could be expanded in future years to provide service to suburban points as well as to Philadelphia, Cleveland, and Washington, D.C.   *(Maglev Inc.)*

GREEN LIGHT FOR FLOATING TRAINS

icanizing" the Transrapid maglev. "We believe that refinement of this technology for application to American conditions would generate nearly the same economic activity as an 'all-American' maglev, provide similar mobility and accomplish it 10–15 years earlier," said James C. Roddey, an advertising executive and acting president of Maglev Incorporated. "We have concluded that maglev represents a future potential market in the United States and in Canada in excess of $200 billion."

The effort, based on a proposal from Carnegie Mellon University, would also create a regional maglev system that might eventually link up with Washington, D.C. and Cleveland. To demonstrate maglev technology, the group has proposed a link from the city's downtown to the Greater Pittsburgh International Airport 19 miles away. The line, which could be operating by 1997, would eventually become part of a larger regional maglev system that could cost $29 billion over the next 30 years.

"Maglev represents an opportunity for large-scale replacement of manufacturing jobs we've lost in western Pennsylvania," said Roddey. "Service and high-tech jobs have been emphasized in our economic recovery, but we know that every manufacturing job creates two more jobs." Richard M. Cyert, former president of Carnegie Mellon, said it more simply: "Maglev is the future."

The effort was boosted by $250,000 from the New York Maglev Promotion Council, in reality a group of 25 Japanese companies. "The consortium has pooled $6 billion to help Pittsburgh and other United States cities construct maglev transit systems," wrote Don Hopey in the *Pittsburgh Press*. "The demonstration link would cost from $299 million to $648 million to design and build, depending on which route to the airport is selected and whether a single or double track system is built."

Senator Moynihan took a break from his drive to develop a United States maglev technology to ride on Transrapid's test track in Germany. He thought of the Transrapid line to be built in Florida and said, "I don't think we'll move in this country until we get a foreign one built."

Despite much good news, the specialists are arguing. Some claim the electrodynamic maglev system is better than the electromagnetic, or question the need for superconductors. Others argue the virtues of proven steel-wheel trains over maglev systems, noting that superconductivity also will benefit steel-wheel trains by improving their energy efficiency still more.

To the traveling public, these debates seem arcane and irrelevant—like rearranging deck chairs aboard the *Titanic* after it struck an iceberg. Americans want relief from monumental traffic woes suffered on the highways and in the air. At one public hearing after another around the nation, they say they want those fast trains *now*.

How about maglev trains linking different parts of the *world*, literally? Yoshihiro Kyotani, the retired head of Japan's maglev development program, thinks today's maglev trains are just a start. He believes that someday maglev vehicles will run in evacuated tubes at ultrahigh speeds—Mach 3—across and between entire continents.

At a maglev conference in Princeton, New Jersey, late in 1990, Kyotani showed an astounded audience maps of possible maglev routes. Trains could run from Tokyo to London in 3 hours 50 minutes; Montreal–New Orleans in 50 minutes; and Montreal–Buenos Aires in 5 hours 45 minutes. Other route possibilities include New York–Los Angeles.

American maglev pioneer James Powell supported Kyotani's

ideas, saying, "When you get down to it, this is probably a cheaper way of traveling than trying to develop a hypersonic plane."

Magnetic levitation will be used in other extremely interesting ways at sea, in the space program, and underground. Researchers at Argonne National Laboratory, in a new field of study called "magnetohydrodynamics," are looking at superconducting electromagnets as a way to move ships through water without the use of moving parts. The technology was the basis of the propulsion for the Soviet sub in Tom Clancy's best-selling book, later a movie, *The Hunt for Red October*. Again, the Japanese are past the mere study stage—the world's first electromagnetic-powered vessel, the *Yamato-1*, was christened in Japan by Mitsubishi Heavy Industries in July 1990.

In East Pittsburgh, Pennsylvania, Stephen B. Kuznetsov, president of PSM Technologies, said his company is designing an electromagnetic catapult powerful enough to launch 65,000-pound Grumman-built F-14 jets off Navy aircraft carriers. Required performance: accelerate the aircraft from zero to 128 mph in three seconds.

In another program, small satellites may be shot into orbit one day by an electromagnetic launcher designed by Sandia National Laboratories in New Mexico.

For mining applications, the German firms AEG and Ruhrkohle AG are developing a version of the *M-Bahn* maglev to transport persons and material. It will adapt with its small radii to sharp curves found underground, mount grades of up to 30 percent, be safely employed in explosive atmospheres, and operate automatically.

Two students, Makoto Mikita and Hiroshi Tsuzaki, at the Art Center College of Design, in Pasadena, California, have come up with a sleek, spokeless maglev bicycle. Pedal power energizes magnets that suspend and rotate the wheels. Hoping to head off a flood of inquiries, faculty member C. Martin Smith said, "The technology is not available now."

Magnetic levitation Supertrains, however, are ahead of all other applications—even bicycles. The products of pioneering research that has spanned decades, maglev train systems are ready now. New types, including American versions, will be on the market by the turn of the century. The determination of Congress is illustrated by Maryland Senator Barbara A. Mikulski's statement that "we are very good at making bullets, and I want to be equally as good at making bullet trains."

Will maglev trains serve travelers? That's no longer in doubt. The questions now are, when and where? Transportation progress never stops, and the inevitability of high-speed maglev Supertrains linking cities in the United States is beyond question.

GREEN LIGHT FOR FLOATING TRAINS

BREAKTHROUGH!

"The new trains will not require conductors,
but will use thousands of semi-conductors."
—*Former Pennsylvania Governor Dick Thornburgh*

AMERICA HAS SEEN DRAMATIC CHANGES IN TRANS-portation, changes dominated by the desire to travel faster. Less than 175 years ago, Americans still journeyed pretty much the way the Romans had—they took bone-jarring trips by horse-drawn carriages of one sort or another.

Change came incredibly fast. A frenzy of railroad building linked most of the country by the late 1800s, and travel became easier than ever before. Henry Ford introduced the Model T, and by 1918 more than six million autos were rattling over America's dirt roads. The Wright Brothers went aloft just after the turn of the century, sparking another transport revolution. By the mid-1950s, massive government programs to build new airports and interstate highways were underway.

The nation's infrastructure has been built in waves, and now, superseding the highways and jetliners, come the Super-trains.

John H. Riley, former Federal Railroad Administrator, said, "High-speed rail is coming to the United States and I'm convinced that it is going to revolutionize the national transportation system in our lifetimes. The only questions are when, where, and what role each one of us is going to play in bringing that process about."

Officials in some states have no doubt about their role. Leaders in Florida, California, Nevada, and Texas are doing serious planning. Ohio and Pennsylvania have the process under way, too.

During the 1980s, the public and private sectors together, including foreign governments, have invested about $70 million on studies and proposals of high-speed rail in almost every North American population corridor of consequence.

"High-speed rail is a project that hasn't started in Washington, D.C., and been pushed down our throats. It's a program that started in the grass roots, and believe me, the General Assemblies of this country are the grass roots," said Pennsylvania state legislator Richard Geist.

If any place needs a good train system, it's Florida. The latest census calculated that Florida is the nation's fourth most populated state after California, New York, and Texas, and some predict Florida will rank third by the year 2010. The number of residents in the state is expected to nearly double over the next 15 years, to 21 million.

"Figures from the 1990 census showed that the fastest growing metropolises were in Florida—nine of the top 12," wrote Barbara Vobejda of the *Washington Post*. "Among the most striking patterns revealed in the new figures was the extraordinary concentration of metropolitan growth in Florida." The fast-growing areas included Naples, Fort Pierce, Fort Myers, Ocala, West Palm Beach, Melbourne-Titusville, Daytona Beach, and Bradenton. The Miami area passed the three million mark, Tampa exceeded two million people, and Orlando's population surged past a million. Florida also has a booming population of domestic and international tourists.

To meet transport demand, plans are afoot to build both a maglev line in Orlando and possibly a rail system to link Miami

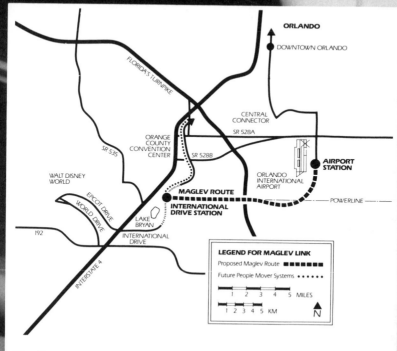

LEGEND FOR MAGLEV LINK

Proposed Maglev Route ■■■■■■■

Future People Mover Systems ●●●●●●

1 2 3 4 5 MILES

1 2 3 4 5 KM

N

The first super-speed link in Florida's magnetic levitation demonstration project will connect two stations — the Orlando International Airport with a tourist complex along International Drive.

(Maglev Transit Inc.)

with Orlando and Tampa. Estimates show that eventually as many as 14 million people annually are expected to buy tickets to ride the two advanced train services there.

"What a good idea for the state of Florida." With that understatement, the state's Supertrain began. Those words were uttered by Governor Bob Graham, now a Senator, while traveling on Japan's Bullet Train in 1981. He was allowed to "drive" the train on part of its run out of Toyko, and that turned him into a big booster. The program he started was continued by Governor Bob Martinez.

The first super-speed maglev line in America will be built in Florida by Maglev Transit Incorporated, a German-Japanese-American consortium, using the Transrapid technology, with the Bechtel Corporation serving as project manager. The train will link the Orlando International Airport with the tourist complex along International Drive, where developers will build a Grand Central Station complete with a resort hotel. In their proposal to Florida officials, Maglev Transit said the system could accommodate future extensions to other portions of the state, including the Space Coast and Port Canaveral.

The train will operate at 250 mph and cover the 13.3 miles in exactly 5½ minutes, making it the world's fastest scheduled train service. However, the train's neighbors will have few noise complaints. At that speed, the Transrapid's aerodynamic drag is expected to generate only 65 decibels, less than the 76 decibels created by an auto traveling at 65 mph.

This maglev train is privately funded, and the consortium paid the state a $500,000 fee for a franchise to build a line that will cost $596 million. "Our bankers say this is financially feasible without any public subsidy," said K. Sam Tabuchi, president of Maglev Transit.

In February 1991, after weeks of public hearings where 36 attorneys participated, Hearing Examiner Daniel Manry recommended that the Transrapid line be built. The project was approved by Governor Lawton Chiles, and Tabuchi said that "we expect to start operations in the fall of 1995."

Looking at Orlando, it isn't surprising that the city would attract a transportation breakthrough. "Central Florida is a place where technology has usually found warm welcome," said Tabuchi. "After all, John Glenn and Neil Armstrong began their epic space voyages from a launch site not 40 miles to the east of Orlando."

Nearly two decades ago when Disney World opened, less than a half million residents lived there, and the surrounding area was mostly orange groves. Orlando has developed many tourist lures over the years, and today it is home to Sea World, Universal-MCA Studios, and six major theme parks. In an area that sees more than 12 million visitors a year, mobility is a big issue. The Orlando Airport opened its third terminal in late 1990, part of a $700 million expansion.

Travelers will find the new line easy to use because it will, like European systems, offer hassle-free connections at the airport as well as with the proposed Supertrains to Miami and Tampa. Arrangements are being made to let people transfer to every conceivable local transit operation—the proposed "people-mover" and light-rail systems, hotel shuttle buses, Walt Disney World's transport systems, taxicabs and the downtown bus system.

Vacationers no longer will have to suffer the expense of renting a car. The Transrapid maglev line is expected to carry as many as 8½ million passengers annually, at fares as high as $12. Three types of travelers will ride—vacationers traveling from airport to hotels, employees commuting to work, and "at-

High Speed Trains

NORTHWEST
SEATTLE-MOSES LAKE
  Study underway of feasibility of new international airport at Moses Lake (a former military field), connected with Sea-Tac Airport by Maglev, eventually could be extended to Spokane.
  Renewed interest in High Speed Rail system to unite Vancouver, Seattle and Portland.

PACIFIC SOUTHWEST
CALIFORNIA-NEVADA SUPER SPEED
  California-Nevada Super Speed Train Commission has concept for HST connections between San Diego-Los Angeles-San Francisco-Sacramento-Reno-Las Vegas-Phoenix-Orange County. Same commission starting with Las Vegas-Southern California Route. Second commission studied Los Angeles-Sacramento/San Francisco route.

COLORADO
PUEBLO-COLORADO SPRINGS-DENVER BOULDER-FT. COLLINS
  Legislative effort to create High Speed Rail Commission.

NEW MEXICO
SANTA FE -ALBUQUERQUE
  New Mexico Department of Transportation completed a feasibility study, which had positive findings, for Santa Fe-Albuquerque.

ARIZONA
PHOENIX-TUCSON
  Arizona DOT official has rquested federal funding for study of a new airport midway between Tucson and Phoenix, to be connected by high-speed trains.

TEXAS
DALLAS-HOUSTON-SAN ANTONIO-AUSTIN- DALLAS
  High Speed Rail Authority approved franchise to Texas TGV for 5.7 billion high-speed train network that eventually will serve up to two-thirds of the state's population. The Dallas-Houston line will open in 1998; other segments later. Project is led by Morrison Knudsen Corp., a U.S. engineering and construction firm.

HIGH SPEED RAIL ASSOCIATION

206 Valley Court, Suite 800, Pittsburgh, PA 15237

July 10, 1991

Coming To North America

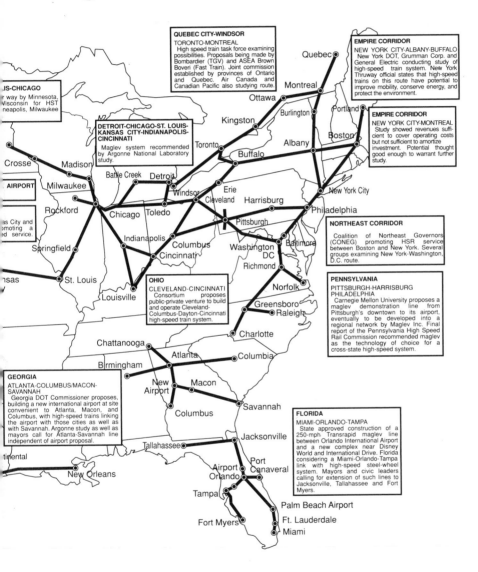

QUEBEC CITY-WINDSOR
TORONTO-MONTREAL
High speed train task force examining possibilities. Proposals being made by Bombardier (TGV) and ASEA Brown Boveri (Fast Train). Joint commission established by provinces of Ontario and Quebec. Air Canada and Canadian Pacific also studying route.

EMPIRE CORRIDOR
NEW YORK CITY-ALBANY-BUFFALO
New York DOT, Grumman Corp. and General Electric conducting study of high-speed train system. New York Thruway official states that high-speed trains on this route have potential to improve mobility, conserve energy, and protect the environment.

EMPIRE CORRIDOR
NEW YORK CITY-MONTREAL
Study showed revenues sufficient to cover operating costs but not sufficient to amortize investment. Potential thought good enough to warrant further study.

...IS-CHICAGO
r way by Minnesota, Wisconsin for HST neapolis, Milwaukee

DETROIT-CHICAGO-ST. LOUIS-KANSAS CITY-INDIANAPOLIS-CINCINNATI
Maglev system recommended by Argonne National Laboratory study.

AIRPORT

as City and omoting a ed service.

NORTHEAST CORRIDOR
Coalition of Northeast Governors (CONEG) promoting HSR service between Boston and New York. Several groups examining New York-Washington, D.C. route.

OHIO
CLEVELAND-CINCINNATI
Consortium proposes public-private venture to build and operate Cleveland-Columbus-Dayton-Cincinnati high-speed train system.

PENNSYLVANIA
PITTSBURGH-HARRISBURG
PHILADELPHIA
Carnegie Mellon University proposes a maglev demonstration line from Pittsburgh's downtown to its airport, eventually to be developed into a regional network by Maglev Inc. Final report of the Pennsylvania High Speed Rail Commission recommended maglev as the technology of choice for a cross-state high-speed system.

GEORGIA
ATLANTA-COLUMBUS/MACON-SAVANNAH
Georgia DOT Commissioner proposes, building a new international airport at site convenient to Atlanta, Macon, and Columbus, with high-speed trains linking the airport with those cities as well as with Savannah. Argonne study as well as mayors call for Atlanta-Savannah line independent of airport proposal.

FLORIDA
MIAMI-ORLANDO-TAMPA
State approved construction of a 250-mph Transrapid maglev line between Orlando International Airport and a new complex near Disney World and International Drive. Florida considering a Miami-Orlando-Tampa link with high-speed steel-wheel system. Mayors and civic leaders calling for extension of such lines to Jacksonville, Tallahassee and Fort Myers.

tinental

Pacific southwest regional Supertrain network could result from the success of the Anaheim–Las Vegas Transrapid line. Steady economic revival in Texas, combined with opposition to expanding the Dallas-Fort Worth Airport, means a set of Supertrain links would make a positive contribution to the state by carrying tens of millions of passengers by the turn of the century.

(High Speed Rail Association)

traction riders" who will climb aboard just for the novelty. In spite of the expected gradual decrease in joy-ridership, which is heaviest in the initial years of operation, the overall patronage will increase with time.

High ridership is only one reason for building a maglev in Orlando. Gilbert Carmichael, the Federal Railroad Administrator, said in Senate testimony, "That's one of the smartest sales places to put a technology, if you want to merchandise it, that you can imagine anywhere in the world. Millions of people will see that and go home. So what the Germans are doing down there is building a sales model for this technology."

Florida's other Supertrain, the Miami–Orlando–Tampa system, has been in planning longer. One group, the Florida High Speed Rail Corporation, has proposed building a 150-mph steel-wheel system, using the Swedish-Swiss Fastrain design.

"The fact that we had to go to Europe and Japan to see these advanced technologies tells us something about the state of the high-speed train technology in the United States—there is none," said David Rush, chairman of the Florida High Technology and Industry Council and longest-serving member of Florida's High Speed Rail Commission.

A ready statewide market exists for the trains because of the continuing tourist explosion. Charles H. Smith, executive director of the Florida High Speed Rail Commission, said, "An important aspect of Florida's transportation need is the 40 to 50 million visitors who come here each year to enjoy the sun, the sand, the tourist attractions, and all of the other amenities Florida has to offer. This tourist population is expected to grow to 70 to 90 million people per year by the year 2000.

"If we are to accommodate the future highway travel market

in south Florida, it has been estimated that 44 new lanes of freeway would be needed between Fort Lauderdale and Miami. There simply isn't enough room nor can these facilities accommodate the tremendous growth in travel markets in the future," Smith continued.

Considering the cost of I-595 completed in March 1991, the state cannot afford such a monolithic highway. "The construction of I-595 represents the largest public works project ever undertaken by the state of Florida," reported Smith's aide, Nazih K. Haddad. "This project includes the construction of a new 13.4-mile interstate highway . . . at a cost of \$1.2 billion. This translates to an average of \$89.6 million per mile."

Travel growth is everywhere. Miami expects to welcome twice the number of cruise passengers by the year 2000. Port of Miami Director Carmen J. Lunetta said, "The industry is enjoying annual growth of about 12 percent and demand for cruise vacations is increasing." Tourism is so big that Florida accounts for about 18 percent of the nation's total car rental revenue, generating some \$1 billion in 1988.

Florida's travel boom meant that, in 1989, three major airlines, American, Pan Am, and USAir, boosted the amount of service they offered. Foreign airlines expanded, too. Martinair Holland launched nonstop service from Amsterdam to Tampa and added flights to Miami. "The expansion is caused by the increasing demand of Europeans for travel to Florida," said Henk Guitjens, vice-president for the airline.

Capacity increases to handle long-term ridership gains cannot continue unabated. Aviation proponents say the state needs to build 18 new airports, including five in South Florida, through the year 2005. Such an expanded system would handle 56 million passengers compared to 32 million in 1989. However, environmental objections are sure to halt most of those plans.

The train trip from Orlando to Miami is expected to take a mere 1 hour and 45 minutes, and ridership will grow year after year. It is estimated that more than 2½ million passengers will use the high-speed line in its first year, growing to more than 3.7 million after the turn of the century.

The Florida High Speed Rail Corporation stated that "service will provide 16 round trips that will start from downtown Tampa and Miami at 6 A.M. Trains will leave hourly except during the mid-day period, 10 A.M.–2 P.M, and evening period, 8 P.M.–10 P.M., when service will be provided every two hours. The last trains will leave Miami and Tampa at 10 P.M. Service will be increased above these levels as demand warrants."

In the first phase, Supertrains will run from the Miami Airport to Hialeah, Fort Lauderdale, West Palm Beach, Orlando, Lakeland, and Tampa Union Station. Stops would be established in downtown Orlando and at the city's airport. That means both maglev and steel-wheel Supertrains would serve the air terminal.

"Service to the airport, ultimately, should be provided on a 24-hour basis," said Richard R. Bonner, the airport's deputy executive director. "As the project becomes increasingly important in Florida's intercity transportation system, it will become increasingly important for it to provide 24-hour connections to other 24-hour transportation modes."

Later expansion would establish Supertrain stops in downtown Miami and in Deerfield Beach-Boca Raton, Martin-Palm Beach County, and Fort Pierce. One stop planned for Osceola County, southwest of Orlando, will be next to a development proposed by the Walt Disney company. Traffic at that Supertrain station will benefit from Disney's 20-year plan to build a major shopping, business, and residential complex there.

The Supertrain line would follow an existing railroad right-of-way, Florida Power and Light transmission lines, and Florida's Turnpike. Locating the rail line with other facilities cuts construction costs, reduces disruption, and makes environmental sense.

Service would be phased in gradually, starting with a new, fully separated high-speed track would exist only between West Palm Beach and the outskirts of Orlando. For access to Miami and Tampa, the trains would use existing CSX Transportation freight tracks. In its second phase, separate tracks would open between Orlando and Tampa and between Miami's airport and downtown. The last phase would bring new high-speed tracks to the remaining gaps in Miami and Orlando. As each stage in the 300-mile system is completed, travel times would be reduced. Planning dates are uncertain.

The Fastrain consortium initially had proposed to bankroll the $3.6 billion project—about double that amount when interest and dividends are included—through tax-exempt bonds and complex real estate transactions. "The consortium . . . plans on receiving exclusive development rights along the tracks in exchange for building the line," reported Don Phillips of the *Washington Post* early in 1990. "The group envisions a $25 billion string of developments that together would be the largest in Florida history."

According to R. Redding Stevenson, Jr., president of the Florida High Speed Rail Corporation. "It is a long-term investment," he said. "It is not a project for the faint-hearted." Participating in the Boca Raton-based consortium of 30 companies are CRS Sirrine Incorporated, a Houston-based design and construction company; Asea Brown Boveri, a world leader in the development of high-speed trains; and AmeriFirst Development Corporation.

But the crumbling 1990 real estate market, combined with other recession-induced ills, and the savings and loan debacle,

made it impossible for any developer to finance the program totally with private funds. That's when complications set in.

Florida High Speed Rail Corporation officials said if the state wished to benefit from the many advantages of a Supertrain rail system, it was reasonable to expect support similar to the help government gives highways and airports.

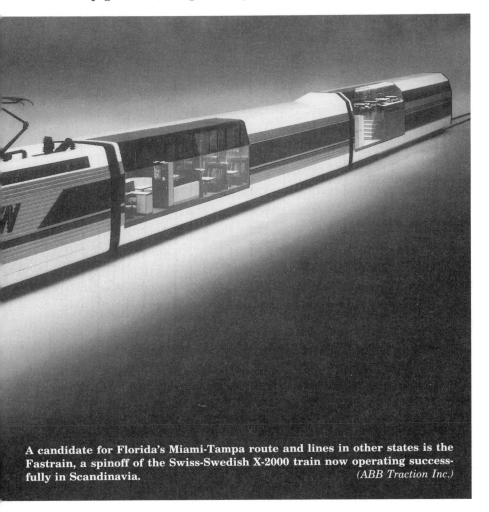

A candidate for Florida's Miami-Tampa route and lines in other states is the Fastrain, a spinoff of the Swiss-Swedish X-2000 train now operating successfully in Scandinavia. *(ABB Traction Inc.)*

BREAKTHROUGH!

As a consequence, the consortium in a revised proposal sought $2.5 billion in state help. It suggested a complex plan to establish local benefit assessment districts, tax increment financing, and impact fees. "Unfortunately that plan soon collapsed amidst a chorus of local government and media attacks," wrote Donald M. Itzkoff in *Railway Age*. A later financing plan "included a request for state bonding authority of $5.35 billion ($214 million annually for 25 years), together with imposition of a 10 percent tax on high-speed rail tickets; a two-dollar surcharge on automobile license tags; and a 2.5 cents per gallon increase in the motor fuel tax." That last idea was the riskiest of all, because federal and state gas taxes had just been increased while fuel prices were skyrocketing from the Middle East crisis.

Florida has been through three financing plans, and observers predict delays to the Supertrain program until the issue is resolved. That a Miami–Orlando–Tampa system will be built someday, however, is certain because of the state's booming population and opposition to more airports. Planners may start with a smaller route, a 70-mile stretch linking Orlando and Tampa.

Florida, with its drawn out and costly review procedures, has not made the process easy on companies that want to build Supertrain systems. The Florida High Speed Rail Corporation has been required to submit so much information that it filed a 14-volume application with the state commission in 1988, followed by another 10-volume set in 1990. Some in the private sector believe that the commission's procedures, established by law, have been unnecessarily litigious.

Yet, the state has a strong High Speed Rail Commission. Its executive director, Charles Smith, is respected throughout the nation for his abilities as a transportation planner. Among his credits is the modernized and successful Maryland commuter rail system that carries thousands of people daily in the Baltimore and Washington, D.C., areas.

The commission can help the eventual builders of Supertrain lines. According to the president of the state Senate, Harry Johnston, the Florida High Speed Rail Act granted the commission sufficient muscle to meet its goals. It has the power of eminent domain; the authority to negotiate with county, city, or private land owners; to acquire land for station development areas; to issue tax-free bonds; and the right to use all publicly owned land and interstate highway rights-of-way such as I-4, I-95 and I-75.

Right from the beginning, Supertrain organizers worked to build a consensus. They spent two years determining public need and benefit. Planners aligned themselves early with the Audubon Society, the Sierra Club, and other defenders of the environment. Officials spoke to the League of Women Voters, Kiwanis, Rotary, City Commission, and Chamber of Commerce in as many places as they could. To the visionaries, it was more important to determine the public interest in Florida's future through such technology than to begin working on an engineering study from day one. In effect, they helped form the grass roots movement.

Today, voices speak up for expanding the train system beyond its original plan. An extension from Tampa to West Shore Airport and across Tampa Bay to Pinellas County, where St. Petersburg is located, is part of the long-range thinking.

Also being discussed are additional high-speed segments in the next century. Growth in Jacksonville could justify links to the Supertrain system through Orlando. Jacksonville's mayor, Tommy Hazouri, in leading an economic development drive, said, "For a long time, we've said we want to be the next Atlanta. Now

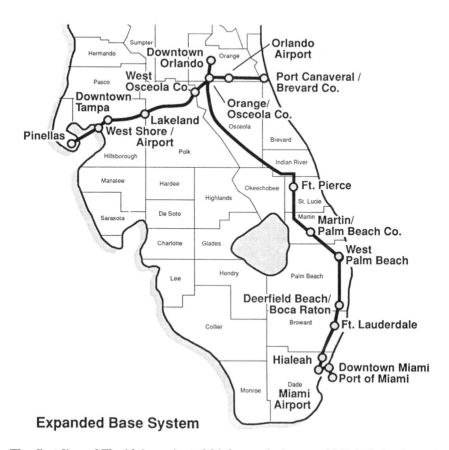

Expanded Base System

The first line of Florida's projected high-speed plan would link Orlando and Tampa. Extensions are possible to Miami, Pinellas County on the Gulf of Mexico, and Brevard County, home of the John F. Kennedy Space Center, on the Atlantic Coast. Visionaries want to add still other cities to future plans, namely Daytona Beach, Jacksonville, Gainesville, Tallahassee, Sarasota, and Fort Myers. *(Florida High Speed Rail Corporation)*

we want to be better than Atlanta." If such an extension is built, Daytona Beach attorney Pete Heebner is fighting for it to serve his city. Ocala realtor Chuck Pardee, on the other hand, wants the line to pass through his home town as well as Gainesville, home to the University of Florida. Others have declared that the

Supertrains, eventually, should serve Tallahassee, Sarasota, Fort Myers, and Naples.

Florida has been the site for historic moments in transportation. It's little known, but in 1565, the first road cleared by Europeans in North America connected two Spanish forts near St. Augustine. In 1912 railroad pioneer Henry M. Flagler completed the Florida East Coast Railroad over a chain of islands to Key West. The "railroad that went to sea" was an engineering feat noted worldwide. It's fitting that Florida, with its Supertrains, is setting the stage for engineering feats appropriate to the 1990s.

— — —

"Something B-I-G is beginning to happen!" said the ebullient William H. Briare in testimony to Congress when he was mayor of Las Vegas. That "something" is a fleet of super-fast Supertrains to southern California.

The California-Nevada Super Speed Train Commission wants to build a system where Transrapid maglev trains would cruise at 300 mph between Anaheim in southern California and Las Vegas. Estimated project cost is between $5 billion and $6 billion.

"The two states have identified specific purposes to be met by the system," said Paul Taylor, the commission's executive director. "It is to provide quick and convenient transportation; it should follow the route of Interstate 15 and reduce congestion on it so that scarce highway funding will not have to be spent to increase its capacity, and it should provide economic benefits to both southern California and Nevada." Taylor knows plenty about mobility problems. He is a planner who spent eight years developing a 150-mile public transportation system for southern

BREAKTHROUGH!

California, including the Los Angeles subway and the Long Beach light rail transit line.

"It's our intention to make this line as much a part of the transportation system in southern California as it is for travel between Las Vegas and Anaheim," said Taylor. Intermediate stations would be located in burgeoning San Bernardino and Riverside counties. California Congressman Ronald C. Packard is working to persuade the Federal Highway Administration to grant access to I-15 for a Supertrain line.

The Transrapid maglev may be built by a consortium led by Bechtel and could be in operation by 2001, connecting the two metropolitan areas in 75 minutes, compared to a five-hour auto trip. Twenty-two trains a day, sometimes running at 30-minute intervals, would run between 6 A.M. and 1 A.M.

Richard Katz is a key player in the Supertrain proposal. He is a California state legislator, chairman of the Assembly Transportation Committee, and possible candidate for governor. In 1989, while chairman of the California-Nevada commission, Katz laid out Supertrain benefits in testimony before the United States Senate:

"The super-speed train has the potential to serve over six million interstate travelers a year. . . . Included among them are as many as a million people who would otherwise be driving their own cars and adding to traffic congestion, contributing thousands of tons of pollutants from tailpipe emissions, and burning millions of gallons of fuel each year were the train not to be realized. The commission and legislature are particularly interested in the commuter potential for super-speed train service that could link growing bedroom communities in the inland empire of San Bernardino and Riverside counties with the job centers in Los Angeles and Orange counties."

Some of the freeways in the corridor are carrying over 250,000 vehicles a day, most of them in bumper-to-bumper traffic. Round-trip commutes in the area can take four hours, daily. Preliminary numbers indicate that the super-speed trains could carry a minimum of a half million commuters a year.

The Transrapid system is expected to operate at a profit. The Supertrains will be capable of earning enough revenue to pay operating costs, repay capital costs, provide for maintenance and future equipment replacement, and give a good long-term return to investors.

The ambitious plan has been pushed by Las Vegas for some time. Former mayor Briare said, "As with most great projects, the idea of a train between Las Vegas and southern California was born out of a crisis. The oil crises of the 1970s, the long lines waiting for gasoline, and the high prices threatened the very life-blood of our town. Discretionary travel was greatly reduced all over the country. And as we looked down the road, we didn't see any solutions to this situation."

Gridlock in southern California has caused communities to maneuver to be on the Supertrain line. The *Los Angeles Times* reported that "the cities of Anaheim, Los Angeles, and Palmdale have tried to persuade the commission to locate the terminal in their back yards." Taylor added, "At least nine communities want to be served by a super-speed train."

California's population continues to grow, with 1990 census figures showing the Los Angeles metropolitan area up 26 percent, to fourteen and a half million people, and Orange County up almost 17 percent from the prior decade. Rancho Cucamonga, located but a few miles from the proposed Supertrain, grew by nearly 84 percent to 101,409, making it the second fastest growing city in the nation. The state leads the nation in motor vehicle ownership with 19 million cars and trucks registered, prompting the League of Women Voters to ask the state to look at ways to reduce auto use.

A 1990 California Aviation System Plan warned that congestion at the state's airports will skyrocket from the 48.6 million passengers handled in 1985 to an estimated 114.7 million in the year 2005, a 136 percent increase. The major Los Angeles airports will experience the biggest share of that growth. The plan reported that "New technology in surface transportation, such as high-speed rail and magnetic levitation systems . . . could either supplement or supplant air travel for trips of 300 to 500 miles or could provide high-speed links between outlying airports and the urban centers."

Those comments were not lost on local planners. For 20 years, proposals have been made to turn a small airfield at Palmdale into a major facility that would relieve congestion at Los Angeles International and serve as an alternative to the Burbank, Long Beach, Ontario, and John Wayne airports. The Palmdale site comprises 23,750 acres of largely undeveloped land, seven times the size of the Los Angeles airport. The problem has been the lack of easy access to Palmdale, located in the Antelope Valley north of Los Angeles, over the San Gabriel Mountains. One recommended solution is for the Anaheim—Las Vegas Transrapid system to include a line linking the San Fernando Valley to the Palmdale Airport.

Another maglev line to Palmdale has been proposed by Los Angeles County Supervisor Michael D. Antonovich, a direct link from Los Angeles International using the HSST technology. Trains would run at perhaps 100 mph on the 69-mile line, on tracks elevated along the San Diego, Golden State, and Antelope

Valley freeways. Los Angeles Mayor Tom Bradley endorsed the proposal, as did Clifton A. Moore, general manager of the Department of Airports. The $1.3 billion project could be funded through a public-private partnership.

It's not the first time a link to the Palmdale airport has been proposed. "The need for a high-speed or super-speed train system was first articulated by Howard Hughes in response to a study [in the mid-1960s] conducted by the Los Angeles Airport Authority, which was concerned about the congestion, noise, and physical impact supersonic jet transports would have on the Los Angeles Basin," said Richard Welch, a spokesman for the City of Las Vegas.

Another airport proposal has been tied to the Supertrains. Community leaders in Victorville and Adelanto want George Air Force Base turned into an international airport, with Transrapid trains stopping there, too. "The remoteness and inconvenience of George Air Force Base for Orange County passengers is a big problem," editorialized the *Los Angeles Times*. "The only way the long trip to the airfield can be overcome is if the proposed high-speed rail service between Anaheim and Las Vegas becomes a reality."

The California-Nevada commission has been circulating an ambitious plan to forge Supertrain links between the major southwest cities of San Diego, San Francisco, Reno, and Phoenix, as well as Los Angeles and Las Vegas. "We envision an eventual network of trains operating up to 300 mph among the major centers of the Pacific southwest region," said Katz. A long-range Pacific southwest plan could take 50 years to complete.

Increasing environmental concerns have caused officials to consider Supertrains because of their ability to operate without emitting pollution along their routes. The California Air Re-

MAGLEV TRAIN ANAHEIM - LAS VEGAS

From one tourist mecca to another. Composite photo shows how a Transrapid train arriving from Las Vegas would fit in with the surroundings at Anaheim Stadium. Passengers would be able to transfer to Amtrak trains at a station not visible here.

(Dean D. Hesketh, Photomation Photo Lab, and Transrapid International)

sources Board noted that while automobile emissions have been cut 80 percent from their historic high, they need to be reduced another 75 percent to offset increases in travel. The board recommended increased transit use.

The United States Environmental Protection Agency has presented southern California with a grim view of its air pollution problem, including—horror of horrors in the land of freeways—the possibility of a ban on gasoline-fueled automobiles. EPA has proposed setting strict new parking restrictions to force greater use of transit.

The Natural Resources Defense Council, a feisty group staffed by lawyers, opened an office in Los Angeles in 1989 to specifically address these concerns. "Environmental activism is blossoming in Los Angeles and throughout southern California," the group reported. "Los Angeles's air quality, poorest in the nation, and other equally serious problems . . . present grave threats to public health and local resources."

Pollution isn't the only California public health issue faced by transportation planners. Earthquakes pose a real danger to any transportation system, but technology affords a measure of safety to Supertrain operations. Should the ground shudder, a Supertrain line would be protected the same way the Japanese safeguard their Bullet Train. There, seismometers are installed at substations every 12 miles along the line, and are also placed every 50 miles in other locations.

The Japanese detection system alerts a central control system, and trains are stopped automatically during earthquakes. The network is so sophisticated that it transmits information by satellite when land cables are damaged by large ground movements. In its 25 years, the Bullet Train has been completely unaffected by Japan's frequent earthquakes.

The Transrapid Supertrains, built to modern standards and protected by train-stopping devices, would be safer than southern California's freeway network. "In the event of a major earthquake either along the San Andreas Fault or the Newport-Inglewood Fault," the *Los Angeles Times* reported, "experts anticipate major damage to the highway network in Los Angeles County as a result of landslides, liquefaction, roadway ruptures,

and bridge failures." Highway officials say as many as 100 motorists or their passengers could die on the Long Beach, San Gabriel River, and San Diego freeways as a result of a major quake on the Newport-Inglewood Fault.

Californians, however, aren't the only ones who need Supertrains. Las Vegas continues to attract record numbers of vis-

Californians in Adelanto want the Transrapid line to serve the proposed site of a new airport. International flights would use the facility if it were linked to the Los Angeles basin by fast trains.
(Dean D. Hesketh, Photomation Photo Lab, and Transrapid International)

itors; hotel construction there has been spurred by the city's ranking as the nation's third largest convention city. In the

BREAKTHROUGH!

three-year period prior to 1992, more than 20,000 hotel rooms will be added to the 61,000 existing rooms. Soon, Las Vegas will be home to nine of the world's 10 largest hotels. Also, a $1 billion expansion of McCarran International Airport is under way.

Adequate transportation is vital to Las Vegas because so many tourists flock to the city's casinos and entertainment. In addition, the city's permanent population continues to grow— its 60 percent population gain put Las Vegas near the top of the 1990 census list of fastest-growing cities in the nation. These new residents also need another option to easily reach southern California.

Earthquake Detection along the Coast

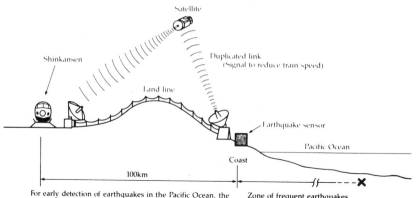

For early detection of earthquakes in the Pacific Ocean, the sensor system uses a telecommunications satellite.

California earthquakes need not be a danger to Supertrain riders protected by Japan Bullet Train countermeasures. Planners installed seismometers at regular intervals along the *Shinkansen* route and the Pacific Coast. Sensors immediately report earthquakes and control systems automatically slow trains until officials know lines are undamaged. So thorough is the network that it transmits information via satellite when land cables are damaged. In more than a quarter century, Bullet Trains have been unaffected by Japan's frequent earthquakes. Experts say that, during a California earthquake, people on Supertrains will be safer than those on freeways.

(Shinkansen *Holding Corporation*)

Anaheim, home of Disneyland, hosts about 35 million tourists annually, according to Don Roth, a member of the Super Speed Train Commission and an Orange County supervisor. He has worked to make sure the city is the California terminus of the line. Thinking ahead, he wants the terminal to be integrated with the Amtrak station, providing easy travel connections to Los Angeles, San Diego, and other California points.

Some have dubbed the project a "gambler's special" that would benefit Nevada at California's expense. While there are long-term benefits to Las Vegas, about 85 percent of the immediate benefits would go to southern California. The project will create about 11,000 jobs and generate $4.6 billion in construction benefits in California.

The case for this train was made by Nevada Attorney General Brian McKay, who said, "The Las Vegas to southern California corridor is a natural. Both areas are growing rapidly, and the need is there. If you've never been on Interstate 15 heading from Los Angeles to Las Vegas on a Friday afternoon, or going the opposite way on a Sunday afternoon, the old saying, 'You ain't seen nothing yet' absolutely applies in terms of traffic.

"It would seem to me that some method of super-speed mass transit is inevitable. The interstate is loaded now. What's it going to be like in 10, 15, or 20 years? The airways are crowded today! Could commercial aviation handle a 25 percent increase in the Los Angeles center? What about 40 years from now—with a 50 or 100 percent increase?"

McKay addressed criticism head-on: "Much has been made of the so-called 'Gambler's Train' and the perception in some quarters is that its benefits will mostly favor Las Vegas. Look at the nine million non-Californian visitors who visit Las Vegas each year. How many will opt to try out an exciting new mode

BREAKTHROUGH!

of transportation, and take in Disneyland, or a Dodgers game, or watch the Rams or Raiders play, or visit the beaches, or California's most famous location—Hollywood? Travel agents would have unlimited possibilities."

Tourist travel to all of southern California will continue to grow, aided by work to increase by about 2½ times the capacity of the Los Angeles convention center by 1992, making it the biggest convention facility on the West Coast. Orange County, not to be outdone, is expanding the Anaheim Convention Center for the third time in a quarter-century.

The first California-Nevada commission meeting was held on September 14, 1988, in Anaheim. There, Las Vegas City Councilman Arnie Adamsen, later to become commission chairman, said, "I think it's quite appropriate that we hold the first meeting at the Disneyland Hotel, in that Walt Disney was famous for saying, 'If you can dream it, you can do it.'" His optimism was shared by Commissioner Roth who said, "This is a mark in history for all of California and Nevada. It may be the catalyst for high-speed trains, maybe throughout the United States."

— — —

The spark is back in the economy of Texas as the state attracts new business in a big way. Late in 1989, Exxon Corporation, the world's largest energy company, announced it would move its headquarters from New York City to a Dallas suburb. Writing in the *Washington Post*, Elizabeth Hudson catalogued other shifts to Dallas: "J.C. Penney Company moved its corporate headquarters from New York to Dallas; Kimberly-Clark Corporation moved to Dallas from Wisconsin; and Diamond Shamrock moved to Dallas from Cleveland. GTE Telephone will break ground . . . for its new headquarters in suburban Irving, near the Dallas-Fort Worth airport, which also will be the location of the new Exxon headquarters." These continue a trend started in 1979 when American Airlines moved there from New York.

Fortune magazine ranked the Dallas-Fort Worth metropolis its top-ranking city in 1989 for a pro-business climate. The area's population is near four million, and growing. Houston has begun to revive from the oil bust and in the 1990 census displaced Philadelphia as the nation's fourth largest city. San Antonio has an area population that has grown to about 1.4 million. The city, home to the Alamo and the tourist-dependent Riverwalk complex, is at the forefront of the convention industry with more than 10 million visitors annually.

Greater prosperity, however, brings traffic problems. The Texas Department of Highways and Public Transportation in 1988 conducted hearings and surveys to gather public opinion. Highway officials learned that 77 percent of those responding believe traffic is tied up too frequently now "and a whopping 90 percent anticipate traffic congestion to be a serious problem by the year 2000." Investing in passenger trains was frequently suggested by those surveyed.

Allan Rutter, a budget and transportation adviser to former Texas Governor Bill Clements, said the amount of air and highway traffic between Dallas and Houston made it a prime market for Supertrain service. There may be wide open spaces between Texas cities, but gridlock strangles urban areas.

Interstate 610 in west Houston, for example, has a volume of 231,000 vehicles per day on one stretch, making it the busiest highway in the state and one of the most congested in the nation. "The Texas Turnpike Authority conducted a survey that showed there was more than enough traffic between the two cities to justify a high-speed train," Rutter said, "and that's been verified by the interest from the French and Germans."

Congestion has hit the Texas aviation system—more than 12,000 people a day travel by air between Dallas and Houston —and environmentalists are objecting to more runways. Dallas-Fort Worth Airport officials are facing resistance from nearby towns to plans to build two new runways. The $200 million project would double capacity to 1.2 million takeoffs and landings annually by the year 2010, causing noise and pollution the communities say they don't want.

In mid-1989, Governor Clements signed legislation creating the Texas High Speed Rail Authority. The action followed a feasibility study by the Turnpike Authority, which concluded that super-speed trains could meet future travel demands on routes linking Dallas, Fort Worth, Houston, San Antonio, Austin, and Waco. About half the state's population call these cities home, but planners say the service area of the trains will accommodate nearly two-thirds of the state's residents.

The study recommended using the French TGV or German ICE trains to serve between 5 million and 9.7 million riders in 1998. A later estimate showed nearly 15 million riders by the year 2015.

Travelers using the Supertrains, which one wag suggested be called the *Longhorn Limiteds*, can expect to get from Dallas to Houston, about 250 road miles, in approximately 90 minutes. "Texas could become the first entity in North America to compensate for the limits of air and highway travel with a safe and economical alternative," the study observed.

Train stations would be located in central business districts

200 MPH.

TEXAS · HIGH · SPEED · RAIL

Bumper sticker showing the barometer of public opinion in Texas.
(Texas FasTrac Inc.)

in each city, at the Dallas-Fort Worth Airport, and at a suburban site in Houston.

A German team has been at work in Texas since 1985. Texas FasTrac Incorporated, a consortium of three prominent Texas companies and a similar number of German multinational firms, said its ICE trains could operate every 10 minutes, as passenger demand increases. One marketing idea: attract business travelers by crediting Supertrain trips to a major airline frequent-flyer program.

Herman Eisele, marketing manager for Siemens AG, said that "the Houston–Dallas corridor is probably one of the best high-speed rail corridors in the United States" in terms of travel volume. He said his ICE train project "will leave a greater economic impact on Texas than the supercollider," a 53-mile long atom smasher to be built south of Dallas, in Waxahachie.

"I've made well over 250 speeches about high-speed rail in the last five years," said Pike Powers, a former state legislator and now an attorney with the Texas law firm Fulbright and Jaworski, working with the German team. "Nobody has ever told me it was a bad idea."

Late in 1989, William M. Agee, chairman of Morrison Knud-

BREAKTHROUGH!

sen Corporation, announced the formation of the Texas TGV consortium. Based in Austin, it includes major domestic and French interests competed against the German ICE team. Agee made the rounds of Texas cities to describe the TGV *Atlantique*. He was joined by Jean Francois Maechel, a vice-president for GEC Alsthom, the French manufacturer of the TGV, and former Texas Lieutenant Governor Ben Barnes. "This efficient form of public transportation is profitable in France and it can be profitable in Texas," Agee said.

Each team, showing its serious intent, filed a non-refundable $500,000 franchise application fee with the Texas High Speed Rail Authority on January 16, 1991.

In forming the authority, Governor Clements appointed to its board a mixture of prominent public- and private-sector figures. Named chairman was Charles J. Wyly, Jr., of Dallas. Wyly, vice-chairman of Sterling Software Incorporated, was a founder of Bonanza restaurants, and has been a chairman or director of several other major companies.

Also appointed to the authority was former Texas Governor John Connally. He said the Supertrain system "could rebuild the economic base of Texas as no other project could." Connally has served in Washington in two cabinet-level posts, Secretary of the Navy and Secretary of the Treasury, and is a consultant to the First City Bank-Texas. He gained railroad experience as a board member of the New York Central Railroad.

Bob Neely, executive director of the Texas High Speed Rail Authority, said the ICE and TGV groups competing in the state had extensive experience in engineering and building complex facilities, transit lines, and advanced passenger trains. It's only fitting that the project turned into a Texas-sized competition.

It was a contest with a clear winner. On May 28, 1991, the nine authority board members unanimously granted a 50-year franchise to the TGV team. The decision was based on lengthy public hearings and the recommendation of Larry Montgomery, a hearing examiner, who wrote in a 700-page report that "it is for the public convenience and necessity" to select Texas TGV. The $5.7 billion project sets the Dallas-Houston leg for completion in 1998; San Antonio and Austin in 1999. As much as $4 billion may have to be raised through tax-exempt bonds, the largest such bond funding in United States history. Agee said the project is an "acceptable business risk" and the "cornerstone of a new age of transportation."

— — —

"Faster than a speeding bullet, more powerful than an ordinary locomotive, able to sweep across tall hills without a single sound. Look! Down in the Ohio fields! It's a blur! It's a train! It's Supertrain!" So wrote Bryce Nelson of the *Los Angeles Times* about an early Ohio plan for super-speed trains.

A snowbelt state that has seen better days, Ohio is fighting to return to prosperity. Cleveland has suffered greatly in the last two decades but is on the rebound. Many of the city's old factories have closed, but entrepreneurs are developing new technology-oriented companies. Columbus is gaining in population and jobs.

Ohio is considering an advanced train service on the heavily traveled Cleveland–Columbus–Cincinnati route. Riders leaving Cleveland could reach Columbus in about 45 minutes and Cincinnati in less than 1½ hours.

Early in 1989, Ohio released a study indicating that as many as 4.6 million passengers would ride the line each year. Between 24 and 36 trains a day traveling at 170 mph would cruise over tracks that, for the most part, would be totally dedicated to passenger service. A private group would work with the state to jointly finance the project to put French, German, or Swedish Supertrains in service. It should be an attractive investment. An investment-grade ridership study states that revenues from Cleveland–Columbus–Cincinnati high-speed trains will exceed operating costs by more than $100 million annually.

The project is viewed by Robert J. Boggs, Minority Leader of the Ohio Senate, as one more step in a long line of transportation improvements. Said Boggs, who has served as the chairman of the Ohio High Speed Rail Authority: "Before Ohio was known as the Buckeye State, it was known as the Gateway State. That is, we served as a gateway for thousands, well, millions of people, really, in the early days of our nation traveling from the East Coast to the prairie, to the Midwest, later on to the West Coast."

Former Lieutenant Governor Paul Leonard said, "We've learned some lessons the hard way. We now know that transport issues are economic development issues. And that's why we are committed to the high-speed rail project. Because it complements the direction of our economy. You can't have a 21st century economy in Ohio without a 21st century transportation system."

Ohio has talked about fast trains for years. In 1972, Senator Robert Taft, Jr., called for a network of high-speed trains to be built and operated apart from the federal government. His plan resulted in a study by the Ohio General Assembly's staff.

In 1975, Arthur Wilkowski, a determined state legislator from Toledo, armed with the study, began taking action. Inspired by the Japanese and European trains, energized by the Organization of Petroleum Exporting Countries (OPEC) oil embargo, and disenchanted with Amtrak, he began the movement to establish a state-based high-speed train system.

By the early 1980s, Wilkowski's grand plan envisioned high-speed lines in four travel corridors: Cleveland–Columbus–Cincinnati, Cleveland–Toledo, Columbus–Toledo, and Cleveland–Youngstown. The proposal gained public support from Wilkowski's thunderous proselytizing.

He conceived Ohio's first high-speed concept during the nation's first energy crisis. He declared that Amtrak would never provide the short-distance corridor services needed in states like Ohio, and was bitter in his denunciation: "The Amtrak system would not work in Ohio. We will build this system on the ashes of Amtrak."

A more constructive approach was taken by Thomas R. Pulsifer, a chairman of the Ohio Rail Transportation Authority, and Robert J. Casey, the agency's executive director. They helped bring the proposal to the forefront of public attention without heaping criticism upon Amtrak. The high-speed plans were crippled, however, when voters refused to approve a dedicated sales tax to build the system—a one-cent tax that would be in effect for 17 years.

"The greatest successes follow a period of failure, and I believe that to be true of Ohio," said Jolene Molitoris, who has held several state government posts involving the Supertrain proposal. "In 1982, Ohio had a failure at the ballot. An issue was defeated by the electorate, a one-cent sales tax to be used for the development of a complex system of high-speed rail, at a cost of over $8 billion. That sent Ohio back to the drawing board."

Discouraged but not defeated, state planners started over and have developed a new supertrain plan. In answer to the

HIGH SPEED ROUTE ━━━━━

PROPOSED ROUTE OF OHIO'S HIGH SPEED RAIL PASSENGER SYSTEM

The Buckeye State has considered a number of routings between Cleveland, Columbus, and Cincinnati, its largest cities. *(Ohio High Speed Rail Authority)*

question, "But haven't Ohioans already rejected high-speed rail?" a new state report said:

"In 1982 a one-cent increase in the state sales tax to fund a high-speed rail system was defeated by Ohio voters.... The vote was an expression by the voters that they did not want a second large increase in the state sales tax within a few months' time. The state was in a severe recession, and to balance the budget the General Assembly had been forced to increase the state sales tax by a full cent just prior to the vote on the high-speed rail tax. . . . We think the electorate was rejecting the method of financing such a program, and not the concept itself."

Public support today is evident. *Youngstown Vindicator* reporter Ron Cole wrote, "An AAA Ohio Auto Club survey in 1990 said 65 percent of those surveyed support a high-speed rail system and 82 percent would use it."

Ohio's planners are optimistic that proposed private financing has been a big boost. The *Columbus Dispatch*, usually skeptical, said in an editorial that "creditable private companies may provide the necessary fuel to propel a high-speed passenger train off the drawing board and onto Ohio tracks. . . . The new group of positive thinkers, the Ohio Railway Organization, [relies] on the backing of Credit Lyonnais, a French bank with assets of almost $200 billion."

Public funding will be considered, too, with perhaps use of bonds backed by taxes already paid by railroads, or loans or grants from the Ohio Department of Transportation.

The Ohio Railway Organization is a consortium of firms with worldwide credentials, including Parsons Brinckerhoff Incorporated, an engineering company that has worked on the New York, San Francisco, and Hong Kong subways and completed high-speed rail studies in other parts of the United States. The firm has assigned rail expert Robert K. Pattison, a former Long Island Rail Road president, to nurture Supertrain projects.

In an evangelistic speech to a High Speed Rail Association convention held in Cleveland, Lieutenant Governor Paul Leonard said:

BREAKTHROUGH!

"I hope the Wright Brothers are looking down on me tonight. They would be proud that this convention is being held in the state of Ohio. For they were individuals who had the kind of vision that we need to have if we are going to plan for the 21st century. To those of you who are skeptics about Ohio, let me remind you that John Glenn was born in this state, and he was the first man to orbit the Earth. The Wright Brothers were born in my home town, Dayton, and Neil Armstrong was born in Ohio and he was the first individual to step on the moon.

"We will move this country once and for all out of the 1980s and into the 21st century."

— — —

The Keystone State, Pennsylvania, is considering a high-speed line across the rugged Allegheny Mountains, roughly paralleling the busy turnpike. Transrapid has offered to participate in a public-private funding arrangement to build a cross-state maglev line in Pennsylvania. Despite what could be a blessing to the state's moribund economy, the governor gave the proposal a cold shoulder. The situation has pitted two men, both named Robert Casey, against each other.

It is an understatement to say that the two Caseys, who are not related, do not see eye-to-eye on plans to build a Supertrain link between Philadelphia, Harrisburg, and Pittsburgh. Robert J. Casey of Pittsburgh says that Robert P. Casey of Scranton "killed" the state's Supertrain effort on the eve of completion of a $4 million study. Robert P. Casey denies that he is against the Supertrains. It's a case of high intrigue.

Robert J. Casey is the former executive director of the state's High Speed Rail Passenger Commission. Robert P. Casey is the governor, and he won't respond to questions about why he put the state's Supertrain commission out of business on just 24 hours' notice.

Pro-train Robert J. Casey knows high-tech trains from the viewpoints of a vendor, consumer advocate, public carrier, and state bureaucrat—all of which made him an ideal choice for directing the independent, bipartisan commission.

He had been director of Ohio's high-speed agency and learned how a Supertrain plan could get into trouble. He had served in Amtrak's public relations department, a witness to government funding that was too feeble to allow Amtrak to capture new riders by the tens of millions. This Casey had Washington experience, having served with the National Association of Railroad Passengers, a consumer group. And he had become familiar with the technical side of railroads in a stint with the Pittsburgh-based Westinghouse Air Brake Company.

Under his direction and that of the chairman, Richard A. Geist, the Pennsylvania high-speed commission flourished. Planners studied route options between Philadelphia and Pittsburgh, undertook the most sophisticated ridership studies ever done in America, and reviewed available technologies.

A Republican state legislator from Altoona, Geist was a freshman when he interested Joe Kolter, a Democrat and chairman of the Transportation Committee, in jointly sponsoring legislation to create the commission. In an astonishing victory, the bill passed both houses unanimously.

Over the next few years the legislature voted unanimously on behalf of the commission in 12 out of the 13 votes taken. That kind of legislative support is rare in a state that is as highly partisan as Pennsylvania.

Said Geist: "Public support was evident in a series of community meetings held throughout the state concerning station

BREAKTHROUGH!

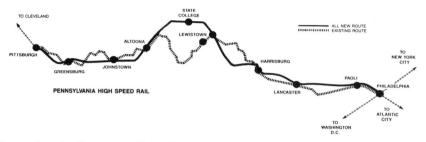

Pennsylvania Governor Dick Thornburgh liked the idea of Supertrains connecting Philadelphia with Harrisburg and Pittsburgh. His successor, Robert P. Casey, on only 24 hours' notice, killed the state's High Speed Intercity Rail Passenger Commission. Governor Casey went on to build more highways.
(Pennsylvania High Speed Intercity Rail Passenger Commission)

sites and everything that goes into development. In western Pennsylvania, the people gave us the attitude of, 'You guys have done enough studying. Let's build the darn thing.' In eastern Pennsylvania, we had people saying, 'Look, this thing's gonna work. Let's just go with it. Build it.' So, we've gotten fantastic support."

Governor Casey's administration boldly killed the commission despite the fact that it was popular and was doing its job in a noncontroversial way. In the words of Director Robert J. Casey: "On August 6, 1987, a day that will live in infamy, the governor's budget chief, Michael Hershock, sent word to me by a messenger that the entire commission staff was off the payroll as of five o'clock the next day. There was no reason given except they claimed there wasn't enough money. Not enough money when the state had a surplus of more than $300 million?

"We had only four months to go to complete the study. It was a scandalous affair and the editorials around the state were critical of the governor. Some of them said they may have not have been for or against the high-speed trains, but they were in favor of finishing the study because $4 million in tax funds were invested in it. They thought it was a crime not to have a product to give to the people after that kind of an effort," Casey said.

Complain the media did, as illustrated by an editorial in the *Harrisburg Patriot*, calling the abrupt funding cutoff "a shocking and ignoble end to a worthy and admirable project that deserved a better fate. . . . It seems to us that if the governor is genuinely serious about economic development, if he really believes in open and clean government, he has a lot of explaining to do about the how, the what and the why of the crude and premature end to the commonwealth's venture into high-speed rail."

Two years after the commission was killed, pro-train Robert J. Casey said: "The governor caused Pennsylvania to lose its lead in high-speed rail in America. We were ahead because in 1987 the study was almost completed. Had it been issued then, and the legislature acted in 1988 on its recommendations, then there would be an authority in place that would be making plans and a ground breaking could have been held by 1991 or 1992. We would be ahead of any other rail system in this country."

He continued: "The long-term effects are many. We have been deprived of setting the pace for a world-class system. Industry that might have located here will go elsewhere instead, and that prevents thousands of people from obtaining high-tech jobs. We have been sentenced to untold hours of highway and airport gridlock. What the governor did was an economic, transportation, and ecological disaster."

About a month after he uttered those words, the Environmental Protection Agency told Governor Casey that the state must tighten its air quality requirements and bring certain areas into compliance with federal clean air standards for ozone. The primary contributor to ozone formation is auto exhaust, and affected communities should look to ways to reduce driving. The cities on the EPA list included Altoona, Harrisburg, Johnstown, and Lancaster—all of which are stops on the proposed Supertrain system, a system that could lure people out of their autos for many intercity trips.

This Democratic governor's style was diametrically opposed to the progressive efforts of his predecessor, Dick Thornburgh, a Republican, who vigorously supported the high-speed rail program. Governor Thornburgh later became President Bush's Attorney General, but before going to Washington he said that high-speed rail systems would benefit the environment, create jobs, and help revitalize city centers.

Governor Robert P. Casey and his supporters underestimated Director Robert J. Casey, Chairman Geist, and their wrath. For quite some time, several commissioners and enraged staff members worked without pay to prepare the final study for publication. They turned a finished product over to the governor. The administration intensified its stonewalling when Commerce Secretary Ray Christman said he would refuse a federal grant to print the study. He delayed printing it for 18 months, but public and editorial pressure later changed his position.

It was worth the wait. The report urged that a magnetic levitation Supertrain be the technology of choice for a cross-state system, citing travel time on a 250-mph Philadelphia–Pittsburgh Transrapid maglev at a mere 1 hour 54 minutes. The study also said an advanced steel-wheel technology like the French TGV or German ICE should be considered an alternative, allowing a cross-state trip of about 2 hours 45 minutes.

Ridership forecasts estimated that by the year 2000, almost nine million passengers would ride annually on a maglev system and nearly eight million on a steel-wheel type. Ten years later,

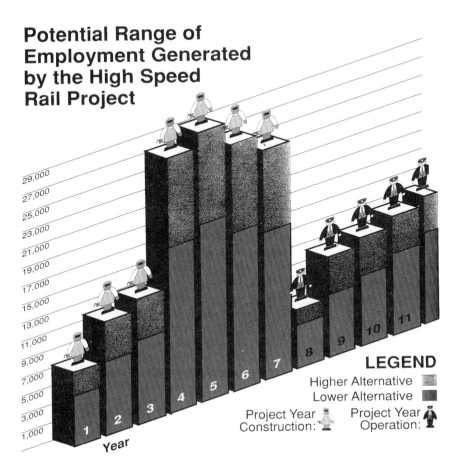

Potential Range of Employment Generated by the High Speed Rail Project

29,000
27,000
25,000
23,000
21,000
19,000
17,000
15,000
13,000
11,000
9,000
7,000
5,000
3,000
1,000

Year

LEGEND
Higher Alternative
Lower Alternative
Project Year Construction:
Project Year Operation:

Advocate **Robert J. Casey,** not to be confused with Governor Casey, wants Pennsylvania to build Supertrains to create employment as well as aid mobility. Shown here are the number of jobs that could be created over more than a decade of building and operating a Pittsburgh–Philadelphia line. Only a range of employment can be shown until the state selects the technology and final route. *(Pennsylvania High Speed Intercity Rail Passenger Commission)*

after the system will have gained broader use, the estimates rise as high as 14 million riders a year.

Planners did not want to be saddled with criticism that their projections were overly optimistic. That allegation had helped

BREAKTHROUGH!

kill an earlier Los Angeles–San Diego high-speed train proposal. Thus, the year-long ridership study was conducted according to stringent new guidelines. Result: no criticism of the estimates. *Planning Magazine* called the study "the most rigorous and accurate ridership projection so far."

Pennsylvania is an ideal candidate for Supertrain service because it has two large cities about 300 miles apart, the larger of which, Philadelphia, is anchored in the heavily traveled northeast corridor. In between is Harrisburg, the capital, as well as other smaller cities. In the words of pro-train Robert J. Casey —always said with a smile: "God made Pennsylvania for high-speed rail."

The eastern terminus for the Supertrains would be Philadelphia's 30th Street Station, offering connections to Amtrak's Boston–New York–Washington and Atlantic City services, and also to an extensive local suburban network including trains to Philadelphia International Airport. The western terminus would be a new station costing nearly $58 million next to Pittsburgh's Station Square, connecting with the light-rail and bus system.

The cost estimates run from $10 billion to build an all-maglev system from Pittsburgh to Philadelphia to $7 billion for an all-new steel-wheel system. Transrapid International and TGV experts protested the consultant's figures, saying the estimates were too high.

Transrapid has proposed a new option, building a magnetic levitation line between Pittsburgh and Harrisburg first at a cost of $3 billion. A major upgrading of the existing Amtrak-owned Harrisburg–Philadelphia line would allow service there at speeds as high as 150 mph.

"Few transportation improvements in history have been built all at once, and both the commission's consultants and

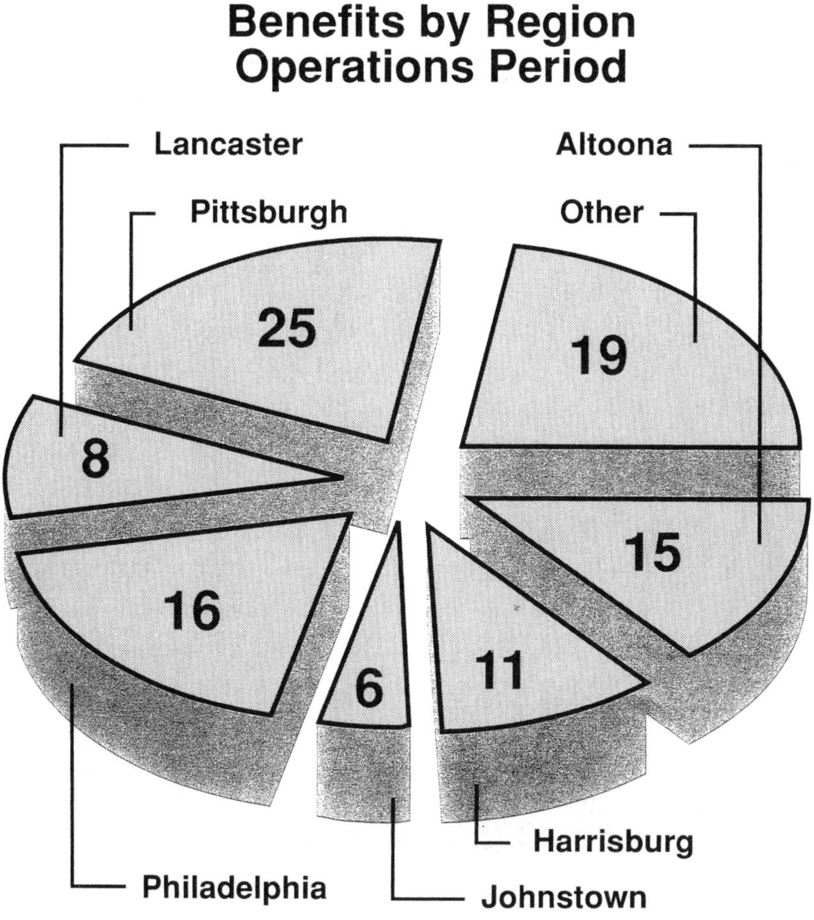

Benefits by Region
Operations Period

Lancaster

Altoona

Pittsburgh

Other

25

19

8

15

16

6

11

Harrisburg

Philadelphia

Johnstown

Employment will grow along the Pittsburgh–Philadelphia Supertrain line. Cities named above are expected to receive a percentage of the primary economic gains, with Pittsburgh being the biggest single beneficiary. In reality, the trains would stimulate economic benefits to even more of the state.
(Pennsylvania High Speed Intercity Rail Passenger Commission)

engineers representing maglev and high-speed steel-wheel systems have urged consideration of a staged approach," noted the commission's report. Such a deal would be a replay of October

BREAKTHROUGH!

1, 1940, when the Pennsylvania Turnpike opened its four-lane divided highway on the 160-mile portion between Harrisburg and Pittsburgh. The sections to the Ohio border and to Philadelphia, not part of the original plan, were built later.

Admittedly, a drawback to phasing in Transrapid maglev service is that it would require passengers to make a cross-platform transfer between maglev and steel-wheel trains at Harrisburg for an unknown period of time. Even with that change, however, millions of people would ride the Supertrains.

When the report was issued, Rick Geist reiterated his plans to keep the Supertrain issue alive: "The thing that's really on our side is the power of the idea. There's nothing stronger in politics than an idea." After the commission was abolished, the project was turned over temporarily to the Milrite Council, standing for "Make Industry and Labor Right In Today's Economy." The real goal of Geist and his fellow Assemblyman Joseph Petrarca, a Democrat, is to have the Pennsylvania Turnpike Commission arrange financing and oversee construction of the Supertrain line.

"Either way—with a steel-wheel system or a maglev—we can revitalize some of our oldest industries while building an entirely new one," Geist said. "Our state is home to a large number of railroad-supply industries, and has a history of railroad innovation."

Pennsylvania indeed has a rich railroad heritage. Its first major railroad was the Philadelphia and Columbia Railroad, and that was a product of the General Assembly. The first person to head that railroad was Thaddeus Stevens, who later became governor.

A host of railroads operated famous trains: the Pennsylvania Railroad with its *Broadway Limited* and the Baltimore & Ohio's

Capitol Limited are but two examples of the hundreds of trains that used to ply through the state. The mountainous terrain has also served as a test site for new technology. One venture in 1956 was operation of the General Motors diesel-powered Aerotrain between New York and Pittsburgh. Its low center of gravity allowed it to traverse the twisting Pennsylvania Railroad main line at higher than normal speeds.

Pennsylvania was the first state where proponents of high-speed rail passenger service began to speak up. In 1965, Governor William Scranton, a Republican, proposed building such a line between Philadelphia and Pittsburgh. Two years later, the Westinghouse Air Brake Company provided the state with a study that recommended a 150-mph system between those cities, a route it dubbed the "Keystone Corridor."

More activity followed. In 1969, the Washington-based National Association of Railroad Passengers issued a report calling for high-speed trains between Pittsburgh and Cleveland. Later, Democratic Governor Milton J. Shapp, who had campaigned on a platform of opposing the doomed Penn Central merger, said, "We should be rebuilding our railroads. Every other nation in the world is doing it. We are just assuming that railroads are a thing of the past, when actually they are the transportation of the future."

Governor Casey's policies have added little to Pennsylvania's railroad heritage. Meanwhile, his administration early in 1989 said it had more than $2 billion in highway construction under way and boasted of the governor's intent to finish the interstate system. The final new interstate corridor in the state, the 21.5-mile Blue Route, Interstate 476, in southeastern Pennsylvania, was placed under construction in 1988 at a total cost of more than $460 million. It's expected to be completed by 1991.

BREAKTHROUGH!

In other words, billions were available to fund new highways, but pennies were taken away from Supertrain planners. As a comparison, the $460 million for the 21.5 miles of I-476 would build 60 miles of the maglev line west of Harrisburg as well as some of the trains. Another costly highway can be found in Pittsburgh where a new 13.5-mile portion of I-79, opened in 1989, was built for more than $416 million.

It could be argued that the state is building an antiquated transportation infrastructure. Supertrains allow people to travel almost *six times faster* than the top speed allowed on the new highways being built. A transportation revolution is becoming apparent when Supertrains can be built at less cost than highways, yet offer superior, speedier service.

Nevertheless, highways continue to be Governor Casey's centerpiece. In mid-1989, the state adopted a plan to spend $13.9 billion on them through the year 2000. That sum could build a maglev line 1,790 miles long—just a few miles shy of the distance between Philadelphia and Denver, Colorado.

Pennsylvania's political environment will have to improve for the Supertrain program to advance. Scott Casper, when a member of the Pennsylvania legislative staff, said:

"High-speed rail operations had been supported by both the right and the left in Europe and Japan. A conservative French President gave the go-ahead to plan and build the TGV high-speed line, but it was a socialist president that cut the ribbon to make it operational. There was a lot more to that scenario than just irony. There was the consensus to make a commitment and place rail transportation high on the national agenda."

After the doors to the Pennsylvania commission were locked, pro-train Robert J. Casey went on to become executive director of the High Speed Rail Association. He remains puzzled by the turn of events. "The trains offer a rich promise, so what did the governor fear?"

Events have caused a bit of a turn-around in the state. Pittsburgh's Maglev Incorporated has proposed a Supertrain link between the city's Station Square area and its airport. In an apparent change of heart—and while up for reelection in 1990—Governor Robert P. Casey said he backed state aid to study the Pittsburgh idea.

"The potential short-term and long-term benefits of this project are enormous, and it is time now to see whether they can be realized," said Governor Casey.

Pro-train Robert J. Casey said it's about time that the other Casey came aboard. "We're choking on our east-west traffic, and the studies indicate that in a few years, the year 2000, there's going to be so much traffic that they just won't be able to cope on the Pennsylvania Turnpike. The same exists for air traffic. The 21st century is only a few years away. It's time for us to become visionaries."

Something big happened in Pennsylvania back in 1819. Then, 11 years before America's first railroad would be built, the state's forefathers had completed a surfaced highway from Philadelphia to Pittsburgh. One can only wonder—was it this much trouble back then, too?

—— —— ——

These projects are progressing at different rates, but they share a common foundation: key leaders in each state are hard at work to solve serious mobility problems. Florida, California, Nevada, Texas, Ohio, and Pennsylvania, far ahead of the rest of the country, will give birth to the first American Supertrains of the 21st century.

BREAKTHROUGH!

WAITING AT
THE STATION

"We can do as the Swiss did at the Zurich Airport which handles more trains per day than Chicago Union Station. Their airport is a bigger railroad station than our railroad station."
—F. K. Plous Jr., Chicago writer

IN PARTS OF AMERICA TODAY, SUPERTRAINS SEEM to be an idea that is all dressed up with nowhere to go. While they promise to help solve many social, environmental, and economic problems, proposals for Supertrain systems are struggling to gain acceptance in some sections of the United States.

One of the biggest reasons is that there is no TGV, no mag-lev, no Bullet Train—in short, no world-class, super-speed train—in the country to illustrate the possibilities, let alone suggest such tangible benefits as ease of mobility and time and money saved in travel. Another reason is that there's no established national constituency, or cheering section, for Supertrains with anywhere near the power wielded by aviation and highway interests.

It's not hard to see what kinds of obstacles, and what kinds of special-interest groups, stand in the way. Just look at the states and the regions in which Supertrains generate lots of talk, and nothing else. In some instances, powerful opponents have

crippled the idea. The states that are Supertrain leaders got to be that way by careful planning, hard work, and dedication. What's happened elsewhere provides case studies in how to side-track a great idea.

The Midwest is a good example of an area crying out for Supertrains, but which may get them last. Chicago, St. Louis, and Kansas City have been railroad hubs for nearly a century and a half. The gentle topography of the Midwest made railroad-building easy in the 19th century. That, coupled with the 250- to 500-mile distances between major cities *should* make the Midwest fertile ground for high-speed trains.

In the 1930s, many of the same conditions gave the Midwest proud passenger trains that were among the nation's fastest. The Milwaukee Road's *Hiawatha* unofficially hit speeds as fast as 120 mph on its daily dash between Chicago and Minneapolis —with a steam engine. The Chicago & North Western's *"400"* train sprinted the approximately 400 miles between those same cities in about 400 minutes.

But prospects for midwest Supertrains of today are clouded by uncommitted leadership, and private investors have been uncertain of an adequate return on investment. Unless and until the federal government steps in to provide a guiding hand, as it did with the interstate highway system, the initiation of super-speed trains in the Midwest will be complicated by the fact that most travel patterns cross state borders. It seems that European countries can more easily build high-speed lines across their borders than Americans can across state lines.

"We need to connect our city by high-speed rail to St. Louis, Detroit, Indianapolis, and Milwaukee, and probably to Cincinnati, Cleveland, and Minneapolis as well," said F. K. Plous Jr., an ebullient Chicago writer, known as Fritz to his friends.

The fastest regularly scheduled train in the world could be running in the United States and Canada. Starting Supertrain service in North America is a political problem; the technological problems have been solved.

(French National Railways)

This makes state planning for Supertrains more difficult, because for each line, at least two sets of legislatures and gov-

ernors must simultaneously agree before a single TGV-type rail is laid or the first maglev guideway support beam is bolted into place.

None of these difficulties changes the fact that Chicago needs Supertrains. It is the nation's third most populous metropolitan area. It has both congestion and renewed growth. In

WAITING AT THE STATION

the 1980s, the city saw an unprecedented building boom in down-town construction. The future will see three huge new devel-opments, including a 15-year project to build a "new city" on a site formerly occupied by the Illinois Central Railroad. Chicago Union Station, used by Amtrak and commuter trains, is one of the busiest in the country. Chicago's O'Hare Airport is legendary as being among the nation's busiest centers, and highway travel is increasingly congested.

"We could relieve the stress on our airports," said Fritz Plous, "by diverting from air to rail most of the passenger trips of less than 300 miles and a substantial number of trips in the 400-mile range." Such short-distance travel represents more than 25 percent of the trips handled to and from O'Hare, ac-cording to Plous.

The Argonne Report on magnetic levitation vehicles con-tained a map showing large midwestern cities served by a web of Supertrains radiating out of Chicago to points Plous men-tioned. But Argonne's proposals were even more ambitious, add-ing lines to Pittsburgh, Louisville, Kansas City, Topeka, and points as far away as New York, Boston, and Montreal.

Traffic on the Midwest's highways is worse than ever. Truck traffic jumped 44 percent between 1980 and 1988 nationwide, much of it in the Midwest. Roads leading to Chicago, the "cross-roads of the nation," often present oppressive snarls. Traffic tie-ups in the Illinois-Indiana area where interstates 80 and 94 meet have been so bad that Congress has appropriated $500,000 just to study potential solutions at that junction, yet rail-based so-lutions have been in the works for years.

Back in January 1967, a Midwest High-Speed Rail Transit Conference was held in Chicago where arguments were made that the Midwest was perfectly suited for high-speed trains. In

1970, Anthony Haswell, founder of the National Association of Railroad Passengers, told the Illinois Commission for Economic Development that the state of Illinois should establish a regional program for high-speed rail service.

Anticipating the day when planning gives way to building, officials in six states—Illinois, Indiana, Michigan, Ohio, and Pennsylvania, with New York a late joiner—formed an interstate compact to share data in an effort to bring about Supertrain service. Ohio State Senator Robert J. Boggs said, "If the states represented by the compact were a single nation, we would be among the handful of the most powerful nations of the world, whether you would view that by gross national product or by any other economic or political or social statistic."

The compact was conceived in 1979 by Ohio State Legislator Art Wilkowski, and the other states signed on after lobbying by Ohio's Jolene Molitoris. Federal approval was needed and two Pennsylvanians—Senator John Heinz, a Republican, and Representative Joe Kolter, a Democrat—sponsored the necessary legislation, which was signed by President Ronald Reagan on July 18, 1984. The compact has been unsuccessful in bringing about a Philadelphia–Chicago Supertrain line, its original objective. It has however, established communication among the states.

Despite the lack of visible progress, the Midwest has been subjected to more studies than any other part of the country. One example is the Chicago–Detroit line, scrutinized separately by Amtrak, Michigan State University, the Council of Upper Great Lakes Governors, the Federal Reserve Bank of Chicago, a group called the Advanced Rail Consortium, and the Argonne National Laboratory.

Although different options were studied, and the findings

on finances conflicted, all reports agreed that a significant travel market exists along the corridor. The French TGV and Japanese Bullet Train officials have also examined the route, but the results of their studies were not publicly released.

Proposed is a tri-state high-speed rail commission to nurture Chicago–Detroit proposals. "Illinois and Michigan have passed legislation, signed by the governors, to form a 15-person commission," said Robert L. Kuehne of the Michigan Transportation Department. "Similar action by Indiana is necessary for the commission to be formed." Al Ronan, chairman of the Illinois State House Transportation Committee, said he would like to see trains operating as fast as 180 mph between Chicago and Detroit.

Indiana, according to state Senator John Bushemi, was the first state in the country to dedicate its interstate highway rights-of-way for possible future high-speed rail use. Although it took that farsighted action in 1982, little has happened in the state since.

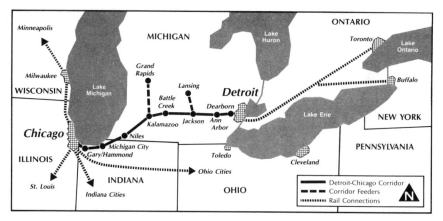

Chicago–Detroit high-speed rail has been subjected to a half dozen studies. Most of the ridership findings have been positive. Getting financing help from aviation- and highway-dominated governments has been the primary obstacle to service on this route. *(Advanced Rail Consortium)*

Other travel corridors have been considered as well, including high-speed trains between Chicago and the Twin Cities. Leonard W. Levine, when serving as Minnesota Transportation Commissioner in 1990, said Supertrains on that route could ease traffic on I-94 and I-90, and reduce airport noise by cutting some of the 135 flights a day between Minneapolis, Milwaukee, Madison, and Chicago. "Nothing has captured the public's attention in the Twin Cities like high-speed trains," said Levine. Ronald R. Fiedler, Wisconsin's transportation secretary, said the Supertrains could operate via Milwaukee and Madison.

The states agreed to conduct a preliminary study, which was issued early in 1991. The report indicated that a corridor via Milwaukee and Madison as well as LaCrosse and Rochester would produce better results than a northern route via Green Bay and Eau Claire.

This effort was a repeat performance, in a way, for Wisconsin. In the early 1980s, the Wisconsin Electric Power Company studied a Chicago–Milwaukee maglev system, prompted by Congressman Henry S. Reuss, Milwaukee County Executive William F. O'Donnell, and Wisconsin Governor Lee S. Dreyfus. Had the idea been implemented, 24 daily round trips would be operating on a 32-minute schedule, an hour faster than today's trains.

Looking at another route, Transportation Secretary Sam Skinner late in 1989 told the Chicago Association of Commerce and Industry that Rockford and Chicago should work toward developing a high-speed rail link between their airports.

One Missouri visionary, Rich Pisani, is speaking up in favor of high-speed trains on a St. Louis–Kansas City route. He leads a volunteer group dedicated to luring both the World's Fair and the Olympics to St. Louis and Kansas City in 2004, with events connected by TGV or ICE trains. Larry Malone of Kansas City, a backer of the 2004 scheme, is talking up magnetic levitation trains through his group, Maglev For The Heartland. St. Louis Mayor Vincent C. Schoemehl, Jr. and former Kansas City Mayor Charles Wheeler have endorsed the idea of connecting the cities with super-speed trains.

No matter what kind of futuristic trains people envision for the Midwest, or what route draws the most study and attention, Chicago will always be at the center of things. City leaders there operate one of the finest commuter rail systems in the nation, but must find the political will to bring alongside it a new kind of city-to-city travel—the Supertrains.

———   ———   ———

Another region with even more promise is the Boston–New York–Washington corridor, an area where people use trains in great numbers. Amtrak carries more passengers there than anywhere else in the nation. It's also a region that, after suffering declines in the 1970s, has experienced some renewal. While not achieving the double-digit population growth of the sunbelt states, the Northeast in the 1980s registered gains from southern New Hampshire all the way to northern Virginia.

New York City, for all the bad press it gets, continues in its role as the nation's center of commerce. *Fortune* magazine noted: "Any company hoping to maintain a significant national or global presence in finance, business services, communications, or the arts will remain in New York. No fewer than 110 Fortune 500 and Fortune Service 500 companies are headquartered in the five boroughs alone. That's more than 2½ times as many as anywhere else. Manhattan is where the big deals still get done."

The Census Bureau reported that New York City grew in the 1980s, in part because Manhattan enjoyed its first big jump in residents since before World War I. The city's immediate neighbors, Connecticut and New Jersey, also added residents.

Senator Claiborne Pell of Rhode Island, known as the father of the *Metroliner*, has recognized the unique nature of the corridor. In 1966 he observed that New York was only the core of a massive population belt stretching along the whole northeast coast in an unbroken procession of urbanized counties, a "Megalopolis" stretching from Virginia to New England.

The region suffers from gridlock on the ground and in the air, and miles-long traffic snarls are legendary. In Boston, it takes longer to drive to Logan International Airport than it takes to fly from Logan to New York.

Carol Blair, transportation manager for Boston's Metropol-

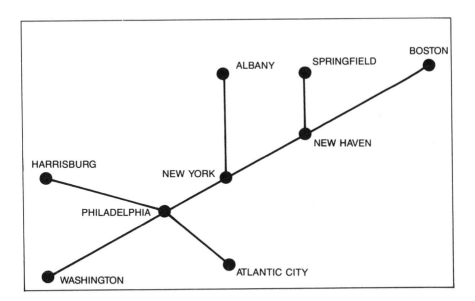

The congested northeast corridor sees a significant amount of intercity train ridership. As growth occurs in other parts of the nation, and as mobility problems begin to resemble the Northeast's, demand will increase for Supertrains.

WAITING AT THE STATION

itan Area Planning Council, said estimates show area auto traffic will double by the year 2000. A $4.5 billion project to dismantle a key portion of the city's highway system and put it in underground tunnels will only compound the area's congestion.

Connecticut planners estimate that as many as 10 additional lanes would be needed on Route 15, the Wilbur Cross-Merritt Parkway, and Interstate 95 between New Haven and the New York state border just to handle traffic to the year 2010. The cost would be prohibitive, and the project would be an "unacceptable infringement on private and public lands," stated the Connecticut Department of Transportation, adding that it has "no intention of building 10 additional lanes in this area."

Further south, mammoth highway work is planned in New Jersey. Although the last transport plan issued by former Governor Thomas H. Kean stated, "The era of building new roads in New Jersey has come to an end," it discussed spending $2.7 billion to widen the New Jersey Turnpike for just 27.1 miles south of Newark. That is $300 million more than the federal government spent to upgrade Amtrak's entire 457-mile Boston–Washington line. Farther south, suggestions have been made for another major new highway between Baltimore and Washington, D.C.

Aviation in the Northeast took the spotlight in 1989 when New York financier Donald J. Trump bought the Boston–New York–Washington air shuttles from Eastern Airlines. The service was spruced up and, to no one's surprise, the new airline was named the Trump Shuttle. Competitor Pan Am countered with hard-hitting advertising and new airport lounges to pamper travelers. Despite all of this one-upmanship, Amtrak still carries more passengers between New York and Washington than either airline.

Yet schedules for both airlines in the future can only get worse, not better. The Northeast's airfields are at the top of the Federal Aviation Administration's list of facilities suffering delays. New York's La Guardia and John F. Kennedy airports are operating at twice their designed capacity and are among the 10 busiest airports in the nation. Boston's Logan and Washington's National Airport have both reached their limits. Philadelphia International Airport has seen a passenger increase of nearly 100 percent over the last decade, cause for an expansion program that will not be finished until 1995.

All of this airway and highway congestion translates into a latent market, which better trains could tap. Gerry Spencer, a transportation expert with the Bechtel Corporation, said, "Let's get the Amtrak corridor up to 150 or 160 mph where it should be, cut the travel time New York to Washington to 2 hours and 15 minutes, and clear up a lot of airspace congestion both in New York and Washington."

It isn't the first time 150-mph trains have been proposed. In 1963, Professor Richard Rice of Princeton University urged construction of a high-speed "bypass" line in the Northeast. The pioneering plan would have created a route parallel to existing rail lines, but farther inland. Also in that year, New Jersey Highway Commissioner Dwight Palmer said, "This would seem to be the one area in this country where an installation similar to the New [Japanese Bullet Train] Line could not only be justified but make a substantial contribution to economic advancement of this seaboard corridor."

Groups today have similar thoughts. The SuperMag Coalition, chaired by Arthur B. Shenefelt, wants to see federal backing for a Northeast Corridor Magnetic Levitation Commission. It has proposed a government-private sector partnership, with a

WAITING AT THE STATION

federal commission offering a franchise in the manner of the Florida and California-Nevada commissions.

A maglev bandwagon has hit the nation's capital area. A Baltimore–Washington maglev study was undertaken by Charles River Associates of Boston, under sponsorship of the Baltimore-based Abell Foundation. Still another plan has been suggested by the Washington-Baltimore Regional Association for a 300-mph maglev link between the two cities and New York. Their report estimated travel time between Washington and New York City, including current stops, at 45 minutes. A third organization, Maglev USA, headed by lobbyist William J. Boardman, urges that the Baltimore-Washington International Airport be linked to its namesake cities with a maglev demonstration line, a proposal endorsed by Maryland Senator Barbara Mikulski.

As in the Midwest, the jumble of states and cities with conflicting priorities clouds true prospects for Supertrains. These trains will come more easily to the northeast corridor, an area of eight states and the District of Columbia, when the federal government shows more leadership.

Not all of the interest in north-south trains has been along the Boston-Washington axis. In a 1985 study, Supertrains were considered for use between New York, Vermont, and Montreal. With French TGV trains operating at 186 mph, it was estimated that the trip would take about three hours, attracting an estimated 3.1 million passengers. The report on this system, estimated to cost $2.3 billion to build, was a joint effort by New York and Vermont, the Provence of Quebec, and the City of Montreal. Trains would leave Montreal's Central Station, cruise along the east side of Lake Champlain through Burlington, Vermont, and head south through Albany to New York's Penn Station.

"The population is greater than 23 million just including the end points," said John K. Lussi, former director of rail planning for New York's Transportation Department. "There's additional population in the Albany metropolitan area and through Burlington."

Running as many as 14 New York–Montreal trips a day would bring in a net annual profit of $26 million, the study showed. This was, in Lussi's words, "not a generous contribution toward capitalization. On the other hand, it would appear adequate to finance equipment replacement." The findings showed that high-speed rail for the New York–Montreal route is at least in "a gray area," according to Lussi. "We can't rule it out."

In mid-1990, Assemblyman William B. Hoyt, chairman of the energy committee, proposed a bigger plan, perhaps using maglev. "I'm talking about a system that would start in Long Island, through New York City, up the Hudson Valley to Albany, westward to Utica, Syracuse, Rochester and Buffalo, splitting with a spur line to Niagara Falls while the main line traveled the lake shore route to Cleveland and eventually Chicago."

Hoyt has received support from the chairman of the Assembly Transportation Committee, Michael J. Bragman, who has asked the New York State Thruway Advisory Council to consider using thruway tolls—about $100 million annually—after bond retirement in 1996 to help finance a maglev system. Remarkably, New York Thruway Executive Director John Shafer said that he does not see maglev as competition and is open to the idea.

A pro-Supertrain attitude is evident right at the top. Governor Mario Cuomo, in his 1991 State of the State, said, "Magnetic levitation and very high speed rail offer the potential to be the major transportation modes of the next century." A task force under Lieutenant Governor Stan Lundine is studying Supertrain alternatives.

At the southern end of the northeast corridor lies another, highly unusual, Supertrain possibility. Washington, D.C., to Pittsburgh is not usually thought of as a candidate because of the sparse intermediate population. Paradoxically, however, it does have Supertrain potential. According to *Fortune* magazine, Pittsburgh, often called the Renaissance City because of its sparkling downtown redevelopment, ranks fourth as a headquarters city for Fortune 500 companies. That business base results in a strong travel affinity with the nation's center of government.

Also, according to David Houston of the University of Pittsburgh, the city has had one of the highest out-migration rates in the country. During the 1960s and 1970s when Pittsburgh's economy plunged, much of that mass migration ended up in Washington where jobs have been plentiful.

These transplanted Pittsburghers would use Supertrains to visit families and friends back home, providing a large untapped leisure train market. Such travelers would avoid driving the Pennsylvania Turnpike and I-70, part of the Turnpike in western Pennsylvania and a lengthy stretch of the heaviest traffic congestion on the toll road, if they could. Also, highway travel over the Allegheny Mountains, while scenic, is plagued with numerous curves, and is dangerous during bad weather.

Richard A. Uher of Carnegie Mellon University's High Speed Ground Transportation Center sees Supertrains as an option on the route. "If I think of my own trip from Pittsburgh to Washington, it takes me 4½ hours by air, counting time to and from the airports, five hours by automobile, and by maglev . . . it would take me only two hours."

The Argonne study showed the Pittsburgh–Washington route as a connecting link between high-speed lines along the East Coast and the Midwest. Maryland and the District of Columbia ought to join the interstate compact to officially explore the potential.

— — —

Supertrain fever is spreading in the West, particularly in California where ballooning growth is forcing planners to come up with better solutions to transportation problems. The state's population is expected to grow by 11 million people by the year 2020, giving California a total of 40 million residents.

The effect on its airports could be crippling: "Between 1985 and 2005, the number of passengers at California's 43 air-carrier airports will rise by 136 percent with the major airports continuing to carry the greatest share of traffic" noted a state government report. By the year 2000, gridlock on the runways may force commercial flights to be redistributed from San Francisco International to Metropolitan Oakland, San Jose International, and a new airport.

Parts of the Bay Area are growing rapidly enough to pose a threat of stopping traffic on Interstate 80, commonly called "Northern California's Main Street." Planners are considering a rail passenger link between San Jose and Sacramento via the Great America amusement park, Oakland Airport, and Berkeley, dubbing it the Pacific Sierra Corridor. The population in the area continues to expand—San Jose, for example, has grown into America's 11th largest city, ranking ahead of Indianapolis and Milwaukee.

Futuristic thinking was demonstrated by Wilfred Ussery, a

board member of the Bay Area Rapid Transit (BART) system, who has ideas about maglev trains zipping to Sacramento, Reno, Salt Lake City, and the San Joaquin Valley. Planning for a new BART line to Livermore, he said, should allow for a maglev line.

"The Livermore corridor is the most likely to be used for a high-speed train and BART combo," Ussery commented. "I don't want us to lay our track in such a way as to preclude someone else from operating there."

In a separate move in southern California, three counties formed the Rail Corridor Agency to upgrade Amtrak service between Los Angeles and San Diego. While not talking Supertrains, the group's formation represents a shift in priorities for the nation's most auto-dominated state. It also reflects an increased awareness in San Diego of the limitations of Lindbergh Field, an airport located only two miles northwest of downtown that has but one runway for commercial jetliners.

Looking at a wider geographical area is the California-Nevada Super Speed Train Commission, which has proposed Supertrain links from San Francisco to Los Angeles and San Diego, as well as from the Bay Area to Sacramento and on to Reno. Another line would extend that network to Phoenix.

The state formed a second commission whose name is a mouthful: the Los Angeles-Fresno-Bay Area/Sacramento High Speed Rail Corridor Study Group. Created through the efforts of Assemblyman Jim Costa of Fresno, the group concluded that an advanced north-south rail link is needed. "High-speed rail is not pie in the sky; it's happening all over the world," said Paul Bartlett, chairman of the working committee.

The study showed that Supertrains could take travelers from the Bay Area to Los Angeles in as little as 2 hours and 13 minutes. It also pointed to a direct correlation between train speeds and number of prospective customers: a 125-mph network would carry as many as 3.8 million riders annually; trains at 185 mph would serve up to 7.3 million; and a 300-mph maglev system could attract 8.1 million.

The group recommended incremental improvements to existing railroad lines—first to 110 mph, then 125 mph, and finally to 185 mph—because an "integrated already constructed statewide rail system" allows great compatibility. It also found justification to build high-speed routes on new alignments between Bakersfield and Los Angeles, and from the San Francisco area to the Central Valley via new lines over Altamont Pass and Panoche Pass.

Amtrak President Graham Claytor said he thought the Los Angeles–Fresno–San Francisco line was a possible candidate for maglev, suggesting it would be easier to build than a rail line across the mountains from Los Angeles to Bakersfield.

Talk like that pleases Fresno's Sarah Adams, who thinks maglev trains are a good idea along State Route 41 to Yosemite National Park. "I think we need to get cars out of the park, and electrified trains are the way to go," said Adams. "Trains make sense—I want them." She admits that she is not a maglev expert, but she has been pleased with her trips aboard Amtrak's *Metroliners* and trains in Germany. In addition, as Yosemite photographer Ansel Adams' granddaughter, she is sensitive to the ecology of the park.

The right-of-way of the abandoned Yosemite Valley Railroad remains intact as far as El Portal, about 15 miles west of the Ahwahnee Hotel in Yosemite Valley. "It's a gradual climb to El Portal, and after that the grades are steep," said Adams. "Maglev can climb steep grades. It's fast and quiet. It's clean—I think we can use something like that."

WAITING AT THE STATION

Presumably, these efforts can be financed through an existing state agency, the California High Speed Rail Financing Commission. But even in western states without California's population, Supertrains are receiving serious consideration.

When Toney Anaya was New Mexico's governor in 1985, he commissioned the Rio Grande Corridor Rapid Rail Feasibility Study that found conditions favorable to connect the state's capital at Santa Fe with the downtown and airport of its largest city, Albuquerque. Ronald C. Sheck of the state's Transportation Department said the proposal has been scaled back to where trains would run only at 90 mph, but it illustrates how discussions of high-technology trains have spread to unlikely areas. Real estate interests are involved. Catellus Development Corporation, the nation's largest publicly traded land development company, has helped to fund a new 1991 study. Bryan Marsh III, project manager for Catellus in Dallas, said the company owns a large piece of undeveloped land near Santa Fe's downtown.

Colorado also joined the fold. State Representative Charles Duke plans to create a commission that would wrestle with the concept of steel-wheel or maglev Supertrains on a Fort Collins–Denver–Colorado Springs–Pueblo routing. He called the route "nearly perfect" for high-speed trains because "80 percent of our population lives along I-25," the main north-south traffic artery. "If I had a high-speed train from the new Denver Airport to Aspen, I'd probably put New Hampshire out of business as far as skiing is concerned," Duke said.

Arizona has recognized that Supertrains may fly across the desert. Citing congestion, Gary Adams, administrator of the state's Aeronautics Division, is looking at a plan to link a proposed new airport to Tucson and Phoenix with Supertrains rather than widen I-10 further. The state's population has more than doubled in recent years, and pressure for the trains will build.

In Washington state, gridlock is spreading and highway costs are out of control. Between 1980 and 1988, the number of daily vehicle-miles in King County, where Seattle is located, and neighboring Pierce and Snohomish counties, grew by a whopping 77 percent. A 1990 state forecast said that as much as $34 billion would be needed by the year 2000 to meet roadway needs.

The state conducted a study in 1984 of train service between Vancouver, British Columbia, and Portland, Oregon, on a routing that would include Seattle and perhaps suburban Bellevue. The report examined several options, finding a trip time from Vancouver to Portland, about 320 miles, of only a little more than two hours with France's TGV steel-wheel train and under two hours with Germany's Transrapid maglev.

Interest fizzled when the study estimated construction costs as much as $12.7 billion—a miscalculation since the price tag could be less. The report was silent on the enormous capital costs of building facilities for other modes. That means the public had no Supertrain-versus-highway cost comparisons to review, or Supertrain-versus-airport considerations to evaluate.

Furthermore, the findings of that study have been outdated by advances in maglev and rail technologies. In 1989 the Argonne Report listed the Vancouver–Seattle–Portland route as a candidate for maglev service, and that again thrust the issue into the spotlight.

The idea was revived early in 1991 by Representative Ruth Fisher, who chairs the state House Transportation Committee,

Pat Patterson, chairman of the equivalent committee in the Senate, and House Speaker Joe King. In turn, Seattle Mayor Norm Rice and Portland Mayor Bud Clark were enthusiastic, with Clark suggesting the federal government divert highway funds into transit projects like Supertrains. Such trains could replace many of the frequent flights operating from Seattle-Tacoma International Airport to Portland and Vancouver.

Washington state legislators have been looking at another option, building a maglev line to a proposed new super-airport. In 1989, Sea-Tac Airport's traffic reached levels not expected for another decade, and officials began looking at ways to build a new airport elsewhere because expanding Sea-Tac will be costly and unpopular with neighboring communities.

Some planners want to locate a new international jetport twice as big as Sea-Tac at Grant County Airport in Moses Lake, east of the Cascade Mountains, with Supertrains linking it to Seattle. A maglev train could make the 178-mile trip over the mountains along I-90 in less than one hour. State legislators Mike Patrick, Phil Talmadge, Roy Ferguson, and Glyn Chandler pushed the idea, optimistic that support for the plan would spread. "By connecting an airport in eastern Washington with Puget Sound, high-speed rail would drop the 'Cascade Curtain' and spread residential population and prosperity across the state," said Patrick.

"Our officials are greatly concerned with relieving the congestion and indigestion caused by too many automobiles on the roads today," said Legislative Staff Aide Susan Casey Summer. "As the current Sea-Tac Airport is saturated, and expansion of the facility is out of the question, the Moses Lake airport and super-speed train proposal is a logical solution."

Pointing to the Transrapid maglev line scheduled for Florida, Sumner asked, "Shouldn't we, in the opposite but equal corner of America, take a look at such systems? If it works to Moses Lake, shouldn't we consider expanding it to Spokane, Vancouver, and Portland?" State Transportation Secretary Duane Berentson said the idea "is farsighted and is going to happen, not now, but it will happen." Support has spread to neighboring Oregon, where William McCoy, a State Senator from Portland, has called for a task force to examine Supertrains. "There will be high-speed rail in the Willamette Valley at some point in time," said Robert Bothman, director of the Oregon Transportation Department. "I don't think that's in question."

A maglev study was unanimously approved by both houses of the Washington legislature in a vote shortly before the death of Representative Chandler. One of Chandler's last acts was to pass a note to an aide concerning the maglev proposal.

Seattle has been waiting a long time for a realistic discussion of trains—any kind of trains—to take place. The city is peculiar in that environmentally clean rail transit and commuter train services have had difficulty winning voter approval there, which is odd, considering the number of people in the area who profess to be environmentalists.

— — —

Someday, states in yet another expanding area of America, the South, may catch the Supertrain. A broader economy and a growing population presents a rich potential market. The Argonne study envisioned Supertrains running from the nation's capital to Richmond and Norfolk in Virginia, as well as to Raleigh, Greensboro, and Charlotte in North Carolina.

WAITING AT THE STATION

In a 1984 study, William Zuk, an architect and civil engineer on the University of Virginia faculty, anticipated proposals to use the interstate highways for high-speed trains. The report pointed to Washington's Metrorail transit line built in the median of I-66 in northern Virginia as a way to integrate a new rail line with highways.

"If there is an interstate route in Virginia that would be a candidate for the incorporation of a high-speed rail system in the future, it is I-95 between Richmond and Washington," Zuk wrote. "Even now, the traffic volume is extremely large on this route. High-speed rail service in this location could reduce the growing vehicular pressure on this heavily traveled highway."

Some Supertrain construction would pose difficult challenges. Zuk writes: "At a massive interchange, as on I-95 near the Pentagon in Arlington County, options are limited to either a dug tunnel or a high elevated structure with long spans, both of which are expensive." Although the report didn't say it, Supertrain structures there would be less costly than trying to squeeze more highway lanes through "condo canyon"—the neighborhoods in Alexandria that bracket I-95.

Zuk's report concluded that Supertrains are viable. Perhaps the positive view stemmed from Zuk's futurist outlook—he is a research scientist and has written extensively on emerging technologies, robotics, and structures planned for the 21st century.

Northern Virginians are awakening to the prospects of maglev trains. McLean lawyer James "Ed" Ablard has formed the non-profit Maglev Mid-Atlantic Working Group to look at ways to link the area's three airports, Baltimore-Washington International, Dulles, and National. They meet regularly with airline personnel, with former state Transportation Secretary Vivian

Watts, and others. Perhaps in response to such activity, in March 1991, Virginia Governor L. Douglas Wilder asked Congress to consider building a maglev line between Norfolk, Richmond, and Washington, D.C.

Another state where Supertrains could shine is North Carolina. Its cities, too, are beginning to choke on traffic. A state report noted that the number of urban vehicle-miles grew by 132 percent between 1970 and 1985, "and the pace of growth is accelerating." Gridlock bothers officials because the travel and tourism industry supports more than 200,000 jobs.

The state continues to grow in population as well as activity. In the 1980s, Charlotte obtained a National Basketball Association expansion team, the Hornets, and plans a downtown stadium for a prospective National Football League team. In the 10 years leading up to 1989, personal income in the state rose 136 percent, higher than any other southeastern state except Florida.

Governor James G. Martin has established a Rail Passenger Task Force. While limited to looking at Amtrak, this group has focused on public opinion. In a scientific "1988 Carolina Poll," residents said they believe, by a two-to-one margin, that the state should "provide money for railroad passenger service" and should buy rail rights-of-way for future use.

"We're looking at high-speed rail for between Raleigh and Charlotte, maybe via Greensboro," said Robert Grabarek of the state DOT's mass transit division. It's only a matter of time before Supertrains are taken more seriously here.

Perhaps no state illustrates so vividly the gap between hope and reality as Georgia. The state considers itself to be the symbol of the "New South," a symbol reinforced by the International

Olympic Committee's selection of Atlanta and Savannah as sites for the 1996 Summer Olympics. In transportation, however, old politics are still calling the shots.

The first effort to promote high-speed trains there came in 1985, when the legislature created an authority to study a link between Atlanta, Macon, and Savannah. French experts touting the TGV traveled to Georgia to meet with officials, pointing out that TGVs could link Atlanta with Savannah in 2 hours and 23 minutes.

Excitement spread quickly. The Atlanta Chamber of Commerce sponsored a trip to France for a ride on the TGV for 100 of its members. Atlanta Mayor Andrew Young rode the TGV and met with French President François Mitterrand about possible help in establishing a Supertrain. "I think the TGV is wonderful," Young said. "It helped bring France together." The effort also was endorsed by Mayor John Rousakis of Savannah.

However, nothing happened. Plans went into limbo when Governor Joe Frank Harris refused to appoint anyone to the authority board. His press secretary said, "It's a proposal that's not feasible at this time." However, the governor killed an agency whose very purpose was to investigate that feasibility. Since Governor Harris did not know if Supertrains are feasible or not, it was preposterous to pour cold water on the proposal.

The governor would not comment on the Argonne Report's finding that showed potential for Supertrain routes out of Atlanta to Savannah, Jacksonville, Columbia, Birmingham, and Chattanooga. Substituting Supertrains for short-haul air service that is a major cause of congestion at Atlanta's airport was the main thrust of the Argonne recommendations. Federal aviation officials rank Atlanta's Hartsfield Airport as the nation's second worst, after Chicago's O'Hare, for delays due to thick air traffic.

Many Georgians were disappointed. Pressure from powerful aviation interests may have caused the governor to table the plan. Atlanta's Hartsfield airport boasts Georgia's largest work force in one spot—37,200 employees with an annual payroll of $1.7 billion.

As in most areas, auto traffic is escalating. From 1980 through 1988, the volume on Georgia's highways rose 38 percent. The state Transportation Department says it might have to spend as much as $32.8 billion on highways through the year 2005 to meet the needs of growing numbers of travelers.

The potential for Supertrains is there. Atlanta continues to grow as a regional headquarters for hundreds of major firms and has been selected as the United States home for a growing number of foreign corporations. It would be logical indeed for Atlanta's first Supertrain to travel to Savannah since the city's rich history and restored downtown draws many tourists. Savannah also is a gateway to coastal resorts and is the largest port in the Southeast.

Although development of Georgia's Supertrains has been stalled, that may be changing. Hal Rives, commissioner of the state Transportation Department, has proposed building a new airfield on the Fayette-Coweta county boarder, in the middle of a triangle made up of Atlanta, Macon, and Columbus. Rives said he would connect the new Georgia International Airport—bigger than Hartsfield International—with those cities and with Savannah by building a maglev system.

Louisiana has stirred. New Orleans, home to the Superdome, could be home to a Supertrain. State Representative Quentin Dastague envisions a new regional airport north of Lake

Pontchartrain, in St. Tammany Parish, with maglev train connections to New Orleans, Baton Rouge, Biloxi, Jackson, Pensacola, and perhaps Houston.

———   ———   ———

No matter what part of the country Supertrains try to break into first, the obstacles will be difficult until the federal government starts to take a more enlightened viewpoint.

Federal Railroad Administrator Gilbert Carmichael has publicly supported Supertrains, asking Congress: "Just stop a second and imagine the impact on airport and highway congestion if a maglev system connected Los Angeles and San Francisco."

Congressmen have trouble imagining that, because so few of them know anything about Supertrains. Bijan Yarjani of the Southern California Association of Governments said that if he had $3 million to spend, he would send all 535 members of Congress to Europe to ride high-speed trains.

It would be money well spent because most of the blame for inaction on Supertrains lies with the federal government. Would the states have constructed interstate highways without federal initiatives? In 1940, for example, there were 3 million miles of highway in the United States, all but 11,000 miles of which were two-lane.

History shows the states would not build the four-lane interstates, at least not until President Dwight D. Eisenhower agreed to raise the money to pay for the overwhelming majority of the costs. Would the air traffic control system be what it is today if the states had to agree and cooperate on its design, function, and maintenance, and pay for it?

After years of ignorance, Washington has discovered Supertrains. In 1990, Congress held hearings, issued reports, and funded more studies.

"These systems, I can predict, will be built in the United States in this next decade," said Carmichael. "It's my belief that high-speed rail and maglev projects should be developed by the private sector where they are subjected to the scrutiny of the marketplace. Preliminary evidence from prior studies suggests that there is a United States market for these projects and that they will meet the financial standards of the investors."

Anyone who says high-speed rail can't be profitable "is just plain dumb," Carmichael said. "I'll tell you this in simple terms. If you can take 250 passengers on an airplane and make money, you can take 250 passengers on a high-speed train, at 160–250 miles an hour, and make money. The international bankers already know it makes money; they've already put two and two together."

Government expenditures for transportation infrastructure and services came to $83 billion in 1986, an increase of almost 60 percent from 1980. Most of the funds went into highways, streets, and the aviation system. About two percent of that went to transit and Amtrak. As big as the overall numbers are, public works outlays as a percentage of the Gross National Product have steadily declined since the 1960s.

States with little movement toward Supertrains have almost no understanding of how to pay for the systems. There are three ways Supertrain systems can be funded: totally by government, as are highways; through a public-private partnership, the mechanism with the broadest appeal; or totally by private enterprise, which is unrealistic in light of subsidized competition.

Construction financed totally by the federal and state governments may not seem like a good idea, especially with demands on public agencies rising while the national debt remains a problem. However, some people think otherwise.

James Nelson of the United Electrical, Radio and Machine Workers, representing General Electric workers in Erie, Pennsylvania, said, "Since working people in this country pay the majority of the taxes, high-speed rail service should be a social priority, not simply something that's referred to as being a matter for the private sector to discuss and develop."

Others point to potential savings if Supertrains were built in place of more costly air and road networks. The Argonne Report showed that chronic airport delays have raised costs for airlines, which pass the added expense along to consumers in higher ticket prices.

The FAA estimated the total annual cost of aviation delays, to airlines and to passengers, at $5 billion, and that is growing because new airports are not being built. Within 20 years, $100 billion worth of congestion costs will have to be paid by somebody.

Compared to airports or highways, Supertrain systems would be less of a drain on taxpayers. The Argonne Report noted that for a typical intercity corridor, a double-track maglev system would cost about $15 million per mile. By comparison, interstate highways on a per-mile basis often cost more than $30 million in urban areas, between $15 and $25 million in suburban areas, and in the $5–$10 million range in rural areas. New airports, if they can be built, will cost as much as $5 billion each.

The most readily apparent method for bringing Supertrains to a region is a public-private partnership. According to an estimate by William G. Reinhardt in *Public Works Financing*, almost $100 billion in privately financed infrastructure projects are proposed for the United States and many are transportation projects. Some of those funds are available to Supertrains, thanks to legislation that put high-speed trains on somewhat the same tax basis as other transport modes.

The bill was sponsored by Florida's Lawton Chiles in 1987, then a senator. He was supported by Senator Lloyd Bentsen of Texas even while Bentsen was busy running for the vice-presidency on the Democratic ticket with Michael Dukakis. For the first time, it allowed tax-exempt industrial revenue bonds to be used to finance Supertrains just as such bonds have funded airports, highways, and port facilities.

Abelardo L. Valdez, an attorney engaged in trade and investment law, and former United States Ambassador and White House Chief of Protocol, explained that "the train must be reasonably expected to operate at speeds in excess of 150 miles per hour" in order to qualify for the tax exemption. He said that the high-speed rail facility bonds differ from other bonds in that the facilities financed need not be government owned, and "the public and private sector enter into a financing partnership which promotes overall cost effectiveness."

Bonds are ideal for these projects because they are a form of long-term borrowing that makes it possible to build public facilities with capacities based on future population estimates. In addition, bonds allow the cost to be spread over the life of the facilities.

Senator Harry Reid of Nevada has called for a $10 billion investment in the development of maglev routes. He would do this through federal guarantees to reduce state fears of assisting with tax-free industrial revenue bonds, similar to what the French did to build their TGV lines.

The proposal echoes past policy, in a way. The government has guaranteed loans to bail out Chrysler, Penn Central, and Lockheed. Perhaps it's time for federal officials to use guarantees

for new infrastructure instead of relying on them only as a life preserver to save giant transportation-related corporations from going under.

United Electrical Workers, United Steel Workers, and other labor organizations want domestic manufacturers to be licensed to build foreign-designed trains in the United States. Companies in Vermont, New York, and Pennsylvania are willing to tackle such work. Shown above is the TGV nearing final assembly in France; at the left is an Italian ETR-500. European rail suppliers have big backlogs, and some foreign builders welcome North American partnerships.
(TVG: GEC Alsthom; ETR-500: Breda Transportation Inc.)

American institutions could be persuaded to invest in carefully planned Supertrain projects. After all, banks in the United States have invested in the TGV Paris–Lyon line and in the Channel Tunnel between England and France. Investors here have put almost a quarter of a billion dollars into the French system, with Morgan Stanley of New York being a large part of the syndicate.

"They glommed onto many an American dollar to do part of that. Far from objecting, I think that is fine. The world is better off," said former Congressman Henry Reuss of Wisconsin. "The

WAITING AT THE STATION

American investors are clipping a nice coupon as a result of it. It simply shows if we could get Morgan Stanley to look homeward, angel, we could do it here."

The cornerstone of raising funds in the private markets is believable ridership estimates. Jean Bouley, president of Europe's International Union of Railroads, said, "In France, the TGV estimates for the first line were so reasonable that the reality was 30 percent more than what was projected. That's like a check in the pocket for the bankers."

"I have been concerned from the start that ridership forecasts be of investment quality," said Robert W. Blanchette, former head of the Federal Railroad Administration. "You can't go in there [to bankers] with a Ouija board."

No Supertrain project will be a purely private-sector effort because of numerous public issues involved, including access to highway rights-of-way or publicly built and maintained airports.

Precedents have been set in transportation projects through public-private partnerships. For example, by 1995, the Times Square subway station will be transformed from a "dingy labyrinth of tunnels, corridors and stairwells" to a less congested, architecturally pleasing environment, according to Karen DeWitt of the *New York Times*. "The Times Square Subway Improvement Corporation will oversee the $140 million project. The corporation is a subsidiary of the 42nd Street Development Corporation, which is run by the city and state and financed by developers who are receiving tax breaks and zoning variances." The station work is part of a $2.5 billion Times Square redevelopment project.

Special assessment districts work, as shown by a 50-block New York area surrounding Grand Central Terminal. "The largest special assessment district in the United States, Grand Central Partnership incorporates more commercial space—51 million square feet—than do the downtowns of all but three other United States cities," wrote Barbara M. Walker in *Urban Land*. The district has financed major improvements to the train station, cleaner streets, crime prevention, and improved retail stores. New business has moved to the area and Chemical Bank said it would remain in Manhattan rather than move to New Jersey because of the district's success.

According to John Riley, the Federal Railroad Administrator during most of Ronald Reagan's time in office, this approach is nothing new: "It is, in effect, the modern-day land grant. It's not anything that hasn't been tried before. . . . The trolleys in California in the early part of this century used exactly the same approach. If you go to Japan, you can see how effectively they have done something very similar to this in the development of their stations."

Paul Taylor of the California-Nevada Super Speed Train Commission said of the line to Las Vegas: "It will be financed over the long run from passenger revenues. The construction financing will probably be done through bonds that are issued by the franchisee, perhaps with some assistance by the commission." He cautioned that the bonds "would not be backed by any collateral or full faith and credit of the commission but would be obligations solely of the private company."

The Transrapid maglev line in Orlando is being financed privately through an international deal that includes Germany's Transrapid International and the Japanese consortium, Maglev Transit, Incorporated. That program also includes some real estate development.

Experts like Frank Schmidt of Smith Barney, and Harriet Stanley of Investors Service Corporation, both vice-presidents with years of financial experience, point out that potential investors face many risks. What happens if construction is delayed? Are cost estimates realistic? Will a system carry the numbers of riders the studies said it would? What are the real life-cycle costs? What are the real interest rate figures?

"Some people are expecting high-speed rail to break the mold and be self-supporting when very few transportation systems are," Schmidt told *Washington Post* reporter Don Phillips. "If these things were as self-supporting as many people try to make them, then they would already be built."

These experts say that to sell bonds, the planners had better have good answers. If not, there are so many other sound tax-exempt revenue bonds on the market that buyers will look elsewhere.

The United States has not made it easy to finance Supertrain systems. As a consequence, there will not be one single way to finance high-speed rail. Nothing like the open spigots of highway or aviation trust funds is available for Supertrains.

However Supertrain systems are financed, they will generate billions of dollars' worth of construction throughout the country. The increased mobility and commerce, and the jobs created later to run the systems, will add up to a positive economic force.

High-speed rail construction costing as much as $60 billion might be undertaken in the next 15 years in the United States, and could reach $300 billion worldwide. Such large capital projects generate other economic benefits by a factor of two or three times the original spending, when secondary and spinoff spending is counted.

Jobs would be created in the manufacturing sector if domestic firms were licensed to assemble foreign trains, and through the government-industry effort to design new Supertrains. Benefits would cascade through many American companies—railway suppliers, aerospace, steel, electrical, concrete, and so forth.

"It could mean the revitalization of many ailing industries," said John H. Reck of the United Steel Workers of America. "We view it as a program that will not only enhance transportation, commerce, and communications products, but also steel-making for tracks, wire, bridges, and the fabrication of steel and other metals for various related products."

Economic benefits will come in the construction process. Richard Welch, a management analyst with the City of Las Vegas, pointed out that for the Las Vegas–Southern California line, the guideway, stations, parking lots, and signals represent 80 percent of the total capital cost of the system. Studies show that as many as 10,800 jobs will be created in California during the peak year of the line's construction. Even if the train sets are built elsewhere, they represent only 15–20 percent of the system's cost.

Robert E. Chizmar, executive director of the Ohio High Speed Rail Authority, estimates that his state's system would produce as much as 75,000 "person-years of employment" over the eight-year construction period, and that 80 percent of the expenditures could be captured by firms located in his state. In economically battered Pennsylvania, as many as 25,000 jobs would be created in peak construction years for a maglev line, and a somewhat smaller amount for a steel-rail system.

"Construction and operation of high-speed systems will spark a major upturn in employment in many of the same industries that built the interstate highways, that is, the earthmovers, the pavers, bridge builders, fence makers, and related

WAITING AT THE STATION

fields," said former Pennsylvania Governor Dick Thornburgh.

Rail labor supports Supertrains, particularly after taking such a beating over the years. The unions have seen railroad mergers, line abandonments, and automation eliminating thousands of jobs. At one time, railroads employed more people than any other American industry. In 1955, the railroads could claim more than a million workers, but by 1990, the number had dropped to less than a quarter of that. It's no surprise that the Railway Labor Executives' Association has supported Supertrain concepts in Washington.

"There are two things that high-speed rail might provide for our craft that would satisfy me," said Larry D. McFather, former president of the Brotherhood of Locomotive Engineers. "One, safer jobs. Two, more of them."

The freight railroads also have a stake in the development of Supertrain routes stemming from selling rights-of-way. The CSX Corporation has sold a lengthy stretch of track in Florida to the state, and according to John Snow, the company's president is willing to part with more. That means that CSX property in 17 states could be available for locating Supertrain lines.

What contractors would run the Supertrains once they are built? "It could be American Airlines, Amtrak, or the German Federal Railroad," says Pennsylvania's Richard Geist. "I look at Lufthansa as being able to do it—if they can run trains in Germany, they can run them here."

Such internationalization is increasingly common. In the telephone business, for example, Bell Atlantic, the company that provides service to six eastern states, will operate phone systems in Argentina and New Zealand as well as join in a venture to build cellular telephones in Czechoslovakia.

The travel business is a sure-fire growth industry poised to both support and gain from creation of new Supertrain lines. The National Tour Association said that by the year 2000, tourism will be the nation's largest retail industry. Population growth is one factor; increased leisure time is another.

Don Wynegar of the United States Travel and Tourism Administration said the number of international visitors reached a record of 38.5 million visitors for 1989, and was estimated to increase to more than 41 million in 1990. Tourism is highly dependent upon infrastructure and quality transportation. In states that have actively pursued Supertrains, this industry will boom even more.

The Bureau of Census reports America's population will increase by 44 million by the year 2020. How are all of these people going to move between the nation's largest cities?

"It is clear to me that every industrialized nation has either developed a high-speed rail system, or is moving toward the implementation of high-speed passenger rail," said John Riley. "It is inconceivable to me that the United States is going to be the one nation in the industrialized world left behind."

Most states flirted with super-speed trains by taking a quick peep into the future, then did little. The situation suggests that planners in some states have a lot to learn. However, the task of persuading skeptical officials will be easier when the first Supertrains begin carrying passengers in the United States. Then, residents of inactive states will demand to know why they've been left waiting at the station.

WAITING AT THE STATION

BULLET TRAINS FOR AMTRAK?

*"The Europeans and Japanese ride in speedy comfort,
but after years of dithering, Washington can't even
decide what to do with Amtrak."*
—John Chancellor, NBC-TV Nightly News

AMERICANS, AFTER HAVING SAMPLED JAPANESE
Bullet Trains and other fast trains overseas, are starting to ask
why Amtrak doesn't run them here. Word is getting around that
the federal government has a pathetic "can't do" attitude when
it comes to trains. Amtrak, which has endured a titanic struggle
just to stay alive, is not about to bring super-speed trains from
drawing boards to reality. Most Supertrains in America's immediate future will be brought to life courtesy of state governments and public-private ventures.

At one time, the passenger train occupied the premier spot
in the United States travel picture as crowded expresses and
locals crisscrossed the country. Right after World War II, railroads accounted for three-quarters of the common-carrier share
of intercity traffic. Airplanes and buses shared the other one-
quarter. The railroads introduced new multi-million dollar
streamliner fleets with great fanfare—trains such as New York
Central's *20th Century Limited* between New York and Chicago,
or Santa Fe's *Super Chief* between Chicago and Los Angeles.

But even as these gleaming new trains were being showered with champagne, America's rail passenger service began a long, sorry decline. Railroads failed to tap the growing demand for short-distance trips, a classic case of failing to adapt to changing market conditions. By 1950, more than half the nation's trains had disappeared, not so much a victim of technological obsolescence as they were the subject of management neglect, stubborn union attitudes, and overwhelming government favoritism to other modes.

"Much of the blame rests with the railroad industry, which missed untold opportunities for growth after the war, then gave up and began to discourage patronage," wrote Donald M. Itzkoff in his book *Off The Track: The Decline of the Intercity Passenger Train in the United States*. "The federal government also deserves responsibility, for Congress, the executive branch, and the judiciary watched impassively and even exacerbated the decline while a major component of the national transportation system disintegrated."

Also, Itzkoff wrote, economic special interest groups—particularly the automobile and aviation industries cloaking themselves in "progress"—diverted national attention away from trains, reaching into the public till for superhighways and airports. By the late 1960s, the passenger train network was a shrunken image of its former self.

Enter Anthony Haswell of Chicago, a modest attorney and a train travel enthusiast. While with the Illinois Central Railroad, Haswell witnessed firsthand attempts by management to discourage riders. Then, with reduced traffic, the railroad would receive permission from regulatory agencies to discontinue the trains. Determined to fight such actions, Haswell founded the National Association of Railroad Passengers in 1967, where he waged a decade-long campaign to save, then to improve, America's passenger rail system.

In one of his first acts, he issued a scorching document that included solid evidence of the Southern Pacific Railroad's ruthless attempts to drive the passenger business away. The report —reinforcing the thesis that railroads deserted the passengers, and not vice-versa—caused an uproar in the railroad industry, emboldened passenger train advocates, and got the government's attention.

Some passenger trains, notably those of the Santa Fe, Union Pacific, Seaboard Coast Line, Southern Railway and Baltimore & Ohio, still operated with style and pride.

Many others did not. In a petition to the Interstate Commerce Commission, Haswell crisply described just how bad some had become: "There are many instances where train service has been downgraded by lengthening schedules, discontinuing dining and lounge facilities, and otherwise. Service in many places has become undependable; equipment, roadbed, and station facilities have been inadequately maintained; and employees too often seem indifferent. . . . First class fares in the East have been raised to prohibitive levels. A few roads have sharply curtailed operation of special trains for groups and excursions. The decline bears no relation to the potential passenger market; the most marked decline in service has been in the East, the most densely populated part of the country."

Haswell's view of government aid to other modes was that the public was not voting the passenger train out of existence: "We believe that public support for highway and airport spending merely indicated a desire to have these services *along* with railroads, rather than *instead* of them. The economic bind in

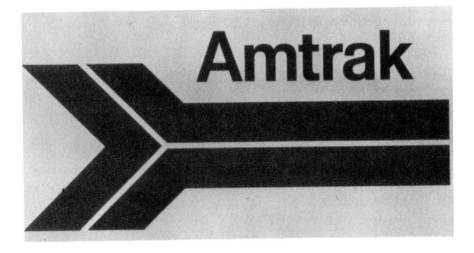

which such policies have put passenger trains was not an intended consequence."

While the passenger train declined, Haswell played a leading role in the creation of Amtrak and, later, in urging improvements to its system. At the same time, planners in Europe and Japan were designing new high-tech, high-speed trains—the ones that are running today.

Americans were reluctant to let rail passenger service become extinct, and Congress acted. In October 1970, Congress passed and President Richard M. Nixon signed the Rail Passenger Service Act, creating Amtrak. A novel quasi-public corporation, Amtrak was charged with reversing the decline in railroad passenger service.

On May 1, 1971, Amtrak took over almost all intercity passenger trains, immediately discontinuing at least half of them. "Tracks are Back!" was its first slogan. When Amtrak trains

BULLET TRAINS FOR AMTRAK?

began to roll, survival, not starting Supertrains, was on its collective corporate mind. The initial funding amounted to a pitiful $40 million grant and $100 million in loans, prompting the *Philadelphia Inquirer* to observe: "When compared to the multiple billions of dollars placed in the Interstate highway system . . . the puniness of this effort is all the more apparent."

Within a fairly short time, many people worried that Amtrak was doomed. "As Amtrak nears its first anniversary," wrote Haswell in the *Chicago Sun-Times*, "there is imposing and accumulating evidence that it is in reality a passenger train euthanasia program, with next year's funeral ceremony already being planned."

He pointed out that no permanent improvements were being made, concluding, "In short, the baby is being strangled in its crib. By whom, why and what can we do about it?" Later it was learned that John Ehrlichman and Bob Haldeman, advisors to President Nixon, were researching ways to kill Amtrak.

Haswell asserted that the freight railroads, with influence in the White House and a presence on the Amtrak board of directors, were in a strong position to achieve Amtrak's demise. That would clear their tracks of passenger trains that interfered with their freight train movements.

In an open act of hostility, Southern Pacific President Ben Biaggini sharply attacked Amtrak during an interview with *U.S. News & World Report*, saying, "I think Amtrak's function should be to preside over an orderly shrinkage of rail passenger service." Rail activists denounced Biaggini's comments, finding them to be fresh evidence of the resilience of the American railroads' anti-passenger mentality.

Amtrak ought to be recorded as one of the worst business ventures in history. At first, it did not own any tracks, any stations, any rail yards or repair shops, any locomotives, or any passenger cars. Trains were outfitted with a pathetic collection of hand-me-down leased cars, most built two decades earlier and poorly maintained, with inoperative air-conditioning, broken steam-heating systems, shattered windows, burst pipes, and loose seats. Many of the stations looked as if they had been owned by slumlords, and some in fact were.

"Who in this room would volunteer to begin a business with resources like that?" Edwin E. Edel, Amtrak's first public relations vice-president, regularly asked his audiences. "It boggles the mind. It would be roughly parallel to all of our airlines trying to handle their customers with only DC-3s that had little upkeep since World War II."

Edel held one of the toughest posts in Washington, a job that would test his levelheadedness. The *Saturday Evening Post* described Edel as a "man who speaks quietly and kindly," a considerable feat in that Edel's work days were filled with responding to attacks from media as nationally influential as CBS's "60 Minutes" or from parochial local papers.

Amtrak and its first president, Roger Lewis, inherited disgruntled employees from railroads such as the bankrupt Penn Central, the Burlington Northern, and the notorious Southern Pacific. The "reservation system," consisting of an uncomputerized set of paper diagrams, was so inefficient that the average telephone call requesting schedule and fare information took 18 minutes. This meant that one operator could handle less than 25 calls in a day.

"Imagine the bedlam and public anger this created when thousands of prospective passengers attempted to reach Amtrak before a busy weekend or during the energy crisis, and could not get anyone to answer the phone," Edel said.

BULLET TRAINS FOR AMTRAK?

An Amtrak *Metroliner* running at 120 mph links New York's Penn Station with Washington Union Terminal in 2 hours 40 minutes. With that downtown-to-downtown performance, the *Metroliners* carry about two million passengers a year, more than either the Trump Shuttle or Pan Am Shuttle. This train was photographed about a mile north of Bowie, Maryland.   *(Alex Mayes)*

For the first two years, Amtrak was totally dependent on the private railroads over which its trains ran. A customer could make a reservation, buy a ticket, and complete a round-trip journey, including eating in the dining car, without ever coming into contact with any Amtrak staff.

The railroads did a poor job in handling Amtrak's day-to-day contact with passengers. The tidal wave of complaints overwhelmed Amtrak's small consumer relations department: lines at the ticket windows were too long; conductors were grumpy; credit cards weren't accepted; trains were late, and dirty; coaches were too hot or too cold; dining cars ran out of food; and on it went.

Hostility to Amtrak by private railroads was only part of the company's problems. Congress gave Amtrak just a two-year

BULLET TRAINS FOR AMTRAK?

experimental period of life, with no fixed route structure beyond that time. The politicians had made it excruciatingly difficult, indeed impossible, for Amtrak to plan improvements. Amtrak supporters have disagreed about what Amtrak should become. Some wanted 150-mph "trains of the future" running in populated corridors while others called for restoration of great "name trains" of the past on long-distance lines.

"The company had faced this massive dilemma since its creation," said Edel. "There were those who said Amtrak should cut back all long-distance routes right away and concentrate on high-volume, high-density corridors where there was better hope of making a profit. Then there were those who would not permit the reduction of one single mile of the national system."

America could have had better passenger trains years earlier, had the federal government instituted a "Railroad Trust Fund" for trains as it had for highways and aviation. Although virtually unknown today, there was a time when the nation's train travelers paid hundreds of millions of dollars in user fees to Washington in the form of taxes.

Federal taxation of railroad travel started in World War II, when unprecedented demand strained the nation's rail lines. Once travelers reached stations, they had to push through thick crowds to reach the trains. Passenger cars operated by the railroads and the Pullman Company, then numbering more than 50,000 coaches and sleeping cars, were stretched to their limits carrying people in crush conditions.

The War Department was worried that congested tracks would slow troop movements and shipments of critical supplies. Congress wanted to discourage frivolous travel on trains and slapped a 10 percent excise tax on the hapless public.

When the war was over, the government refused to rescind the tax because it was generating big revenues. Thus, Washington taxed train riders, and most likely some of that money helped finance new airports and highways. Not until 1962—a long 17 years after the war's end—was the excise tax on railroad travel repealed. By then, the trains' ability to give the public adequate service had been crippled.

At one point, Congress discussed proposals to allow railroads to keep revenue from the 10 percent tax, but rejected the notion because it would mean a public subsidy to the private individuals who were railroad stockholders. In other years, Congress voted for subsidies to airlines, with no apparent concern about aviation's "private individuals" who were shareholders.

"Railroad passengers have paid a double penalty," said Ross Capon, executive director of the railroad passengers' association. "No rail trust fund was ever established, yet substantial rail user charges were collected for many years." Between 1942 and 1962, railroad passengers paid $2 billion in federal ticket taxes, and rail freight shippers sent $3.1 billion to Washington in freight taxes.

"Imagine what United States transport would look like now if we had given equal treatment to passenger trains by earmarking ticket tax revenues for rail passenger service improvements, starting when trains were dominant," said Capon. "Actually, the $2 billion in federal ticket taxes paid by railroad passengers simply went into the Treasury while the government built more highway, air, and waterway facilities." It's hindsight now, but an Amtrak created between the end of World War II and the early 1960s would have stood a far better chance of early success.

BULLET TRAINS FOR AMTRAK?

Amtrak still does not enjoy the benefit of support from a trust fund, and may have had a tenuous start, but it has improved the service. Some good planning in the 1970s under the leadership of its second president, Paul Reistrup, has helped. Then, Amtrak ordered the Amfleet and double-decker Superliner cars used on most of its trains in the 1990s. However, Reistrup's goals of developing 125-mph services in parts of the country outside the Northeast never received government funding.

One of the darkest moments for Amtrak was in 1979 when, during a nationwide gasoline shortage, President Jimmy Carter's Administration sought to reduce Amtrak's system. Because of the Arab oil embargo, America was literally running low on gasoline. Prices at the pump skyrocketed, lengthy lines formed at filling stations, and police at times had to control violence among motorists frustrated by long waits for fuel.

In that crisis environment, when record numbers of travelers were clamoring to get aboard Amtrak trains, the shortsighted Carter administration, through Transportation Secretary Brock Adams, axed six long-distance trains that were experiencing double-digit ridership increases. Angry protests, heated editorials, and distressed governors targeted the Carter policy of cutting trains during an energy crisis. Amtrak trains represent the most efficient transport system available, according to Oak Ridge scientists and others, and ought to be kept running, said the critics.

The firestorm of opposition saved some trains, but when the clamor died down Amtrak proponents felt like second-class citizens. If the federal government won't fully support Amtrak when its trains are full, they wondered, will it ever do so?

However, Amtrak survived, and in some corridors it has flourished. Thanks mostly to state aid, Amtrak has improved service between New York and Buffalo, Milwaukee and Chicago, Los Angeles and San Diego, and between San Francisco and Bakersfield, and has started serving Atlantic City. On its own, Amtrak also increased the number of New York–Washington *Metroliners*.

By 1990, Amtrak's cash registers took in more than $1.3 billion, an all-time record, and it came closer to paying its way than ever before. "We're pleased that revenue is covering 72 percent of our costs," said Amtrak spokesman Clifford Black. "As recently as 1981, Amtrak covered only 48 percent of its costs."

Also in 1990, Amtrak carried 22.2 million riders and racked up an all-time record of more than six billion passenger-miles. It was the eighth record year in a row. Amtrak carried another 18 million riders on commuter trains it operates separate from its intercity system, with such traffic increasing everywhere.

A survey conducted for *Travel Weekly* showed that 1989 travel agency sales for rail bookings totaled more than $3.2 billion, up from $1.9 billion two years earlier. The good news reflected increased purchases of Amtrak tickets at agencies as well as a big jump in Eurailpass sales as more Americans planned to hop aboard the Supertrains and express trains of Europe.

The biggest cost of providing passenger service has traditionally been labor. For decades, obsolete work rules contributed to poor financial results. For example, since 1919 locomotive engineers have been paid on a mileage basis, earning a day's pay for a 100-mile trip that by the 1940s took just two or three hours to complete. Conductors and brakemen earned eight hours pay for traveling 150 miles. Labor organizations fought to keep the "featherbedding" practices despite the harsh fact that artificially high labor costs were contributing to the death of passenger trains.

BULLET TRAINS FOR AMTRAK?

Starting in the late 1980s Amtrak began to reduce expenses through new agreements, an effort that is succeeding because of unprecedented cooperation from unions. Amtrak began paying engineers hourly wages, which means that eight hours of work, finally, equals eight hours of pay. America today would have more trains running to more places if labor's attitudes had changed earlier. Nevertheless, the turnaround in labor relations is the single most important factor in reducing Amtrak's costs.

Although Amtrak is more successful than ever, the Reagan and Bush administrations tried to abolish Amtrak for six years in a row, from fiscal years 1986 to 1991. One group said of President Bush's budget: "Our members are incensed at the priorities reflected in the administration's proposal to continue to do nothing for Amtrak . . . while spending 73 percent more on aviation the next five years," said Ross Capon of the National Association of Railroad Passengers.

Amtrak inherited the first *Metroliners*, which were improperly maintained, from the bankrupt Penn Central Railroad. The flat ends lack any aerodynamic styling and at least three paint schemes have adorned the units. *(Amtrak)*

BULLET TRAINS FOR AMTRAK?

The justification for Reagan and Bush's treatment of Amtrak is difficult to understand. In 1985, Amtrak President W. Graham Claytor, Jr., said airline travelers were subsidized at $42 per passenger, substantially more than the then $30 per passenger subsidy to Amtrak. In other words, Washington expects train riders to give up service to help balance the federal budget, but powerful airline interests can keep playing with their bigger grants of free money.

Bush budget documents admit that the trust funds pay for only part of the cost of providing facilities for the other modes. In 1990, the government expected to collect only about $3.9 billion in aviation taxes. Total funding for aviation was $7.1 billion, far exceeding the taxes collected, according to DOT's assistant secretary for the budget, Kate L. Moore.

Most Americans do not realize how Washington *really* spends their money. Based on how much of each cost dollar is subsidized by the general taxpayers, aviation gets 50 cents, not counting the money from the trust fund or the massive indirect subsidies to aircraft builders; highways, 39 cents, again, not counting trust fund money; and Amtrak, 28 cents, with no trust fund for added help. Amtrak is doing better, on a dollar-per-dollar basis, in covering costs than its competition does.

Rarely is it reported to the public that way. The most visible difference between aid for Amtrak and subsidies for its competitors is that Amtrak's funding comes in the form of direct appropriations primarily from one source—the federal government. Highway and aviation interests get money from many sources—subsidies kept on the ledgers of federal agencies, 50 states, and thousands of cities and counties. It is quite easy to determine how much aid Amtrak receives; it's very difficult to determine how much aid aviation and highways receive.

Amtrak has a hard time overcoming its stigma as a loser, particularly when federal partisans repeatedly moan about Amtrak's "subsidy" while referring to federal aid to aviation and highways as an "investment." Such prejudiced treatment often causes uninformed people to call for an end to Amtrak, but these same people would never think of calling for an "end to highways" or an "end to aviation."

W. Graham Claytor, Jr., Amtrak's chairman and president since 1982 and a respected Washington figure, is struggling with this problem. A Harvard lawyer, he has served as former chief executive officer of Southern Railway and as the Secretary of the Navy. He is optimistic about Amtrak's future.

"This country cannot get along with a passenger system that's limited to the highway and the air—no other industrialized country in the world has been able to do that," said Claytor, who believes Amtrak someday will operate without a government subsidy. "We require 40 percent less federal operating assistance today than we needed just eight years ago," Claytor said. "Indeed, if other recipients of federal support could have been as successful as Amtrak in reducing their needs, this country would not now face a federal deficit."

He's right. It's difficult to find another government-subsidized program where federal aid as a portion of costs has declined so much over the years. Claytor told Congress that the federal government's fiscal problems cannot be solved on Amtrak's shoulders alone: "Federal appropriations to Amtrak constitute 5/100ths of 1 percent of the total federal budget."

His arguments mattered little to some. Congressman Robert S. Walker, a Republican from Pennsylvania and a partisan of subsidized aerospace interests, initiated an amendment in 1989 that would have killed all federal aid to Amtrak. During the

BULLET TRAINS FOR AMTRAK?

debate, Congressman Richard J. Durbin of Illinois, a Democrat, argued that Walker "would spend billions of dollars for a space station to the stars, but deny railroad service for people traveling to work. He would spend millions to go to the moon, but deny railroad service to America's families. This is not a visionary amendment, it's a reactionary amendment." Fortunately for travelers, Durbin and his colleagues defeated the ill-advised Walker move.

Claytor has set a goal that Amtrak will cover 100 percent of its day-to-day costs through ticket sales and other revenues by the year 2000. To do so will require capital spending for new passenger cars, and Claytor says Amtrak has established itself with the investment community and can borrow money to match federal funds for that purpose.

"We are becoming the victims of our own success—the growing demand for Amtrak service nationwide is outstripping our capacity to provide it," Claytor said. "Unless serious steps are taken to provide Amtrak with the means to acquire new cars and locomotives, millions of passengers who depend on our service will be forced to stand on trains or be denied service altogether."

It's true that Amtrak's performance could be better if it owned more cars to carry passengers. "In my hometown of Meridian, Mississippi, they're turning away as many as 1,300 passengers in a peak month," said Federal Railroad Administrator Gilbert Carmichael. "When my wife wanted to come to Washington for my swearing-in ceremony, Amtrak didn't have room."

By and large, Washington has ignored strong public support for Amtrak. Around the nation, people have been trying to tell public officials they want more and better train service through voting on referenda, answering opinion polls, and riding trains in great numbers on those occasions when more trains have been added on selected routes. Again and again across the country, the people speak: In 1990, California voters approved bond issues that will finance $2.9 billion in improvements to intercity and local rail systems there. In the prior year, voters in 17 counties with about 78 percent of the Golden State's population approved use of state gasoline taxes for rail purposes.

A *Frequent Flyer* magazine survey two years before that said, "A surprisingly high 57 percent of respondents said that they had traveled by rail, either in the United States or abroad, during the past year." The *Chicago Sun-Times* stated that three of four people questioned would prefer using improved Amtrak midwest corridor trains to flying.

More sophisticated national surveys have shown decisive mandates to upgrade intercity trains. Americans by a margin of 64 percent to 22 percent favored continuing Amtrak service "even if it means federal subsidies," a Harris survey found in 1972, when Amtrak was still in its infancy. Two subsequent coast-to-coast polls, with timely results for the Reagan and Bush administrations, showed similar results. The federal government cannot claim ignorance of America's pro-train support, expressed for at least two decades.

Washington's procrastination is partly due to the fact that too few organized groups speak up for Amtrak. The National Association of Railroad Passengers and a few rail labor unions have nowhere near the clout that the dozens of aviation and highway groups wield in favor of their government-supported programs.

Washington regularly overlooks the fact that more than two million passengers ride Amtrak's best short-distance trains, the *Metroliners*, annually. From 1983 to 1989 these New York–

Washington express trains saw ridership increase by 90 percent despite big fare increases, making the service a vital part of life in the region.

Amtrak saw another jump in *Metroliner* use beginning in April 1991, when the new Westside Connection was put into service in New York City. The new track allowed Amtrak trains from Buffalo and other upstate points to use Penn Station, which is on the line to Washington, rather than Grand Central Terminal. For the first time, passengers transferring between these two routes will not have to change stations in traffic-choked Manhattan. Look for Westchester County business travelers headed for Philadelphia, Albany tourists headed for Atlantic City, and upstate New York groups to Washington, to switch to Amtrak in increasing numbers. New York Governor Mario Cuomo played a key role in bringing about the new connection.

When the Reagan administration tried to abolish Amtrak entirely, including the *Metroliners*, Claytor described the possible result:

"If Amtrak northeast corridor service were eliminated, these riders would be forced to fly between Washington and New York. To carry just the 4,200 passengers who daily travel between New York and Washington—over a million and a half annual ridership—an additional 60–70 airline flights would be required each day, mostly during peak travel times. It would be physically impossible for the already overcrowded Washington and New York airports to handle all of the passengers now traveling by Amtrak, and new airport facilities are unlikely."

Claytor is right. In a February 1990 calculation, the northeast corridor saw a total of 1,041 *daily* commercial flights between the five major cities of Boston, New York, Philadelphia, Baltimore, and Washington. Uncounted were hundreds more private executive flights that added to airway crowding. Trains are indisputably essential in the congested Northeast: despite population shifts to the west and south, the area is still home to more than 33 million people.

Metroliners are a part of America. Before being inherited by Amtrak, they originated as a result of the efforts of Senator Claiborne Pell of Rhode Island, who spearheaded the High-Speed Ground Transportation Act in 1965 that authorized a demonstration project in the Boston–Washington corridor.

When the senator proposed the acquisition, upgrading, and operation of railroad passenger facilities from Boston to Washington, the news made page one of the *New York Times*. On the inside pages, it reprinted the full text of Pell's statement, a *Times* honor usually reserved for messages from heads of state. In 1966 he wrote his book *Megalopolis Unbound* promoting high-speed trains, before there was an Amtrak or even a Department of Transportation.

Widespread popular support for faster trains as well as persistence by Senator Pell paid off. President Lyndon B. Johnson, in his 1965 State of the Union address, said, "I will ask for funds to study high-speed rail transportation between urban centers. We will begin with test projects between Boston and Washington." The first *Metroliner* departed New York's Penn Station at 8:30 A.M., January 16, 1969, a year that saw 604,000 passengers ride the trains. By 1990, that figure would grow to two million travelers.

The ridership gains were possible in part because the federal government improved the corridor under a $2.4 billion program. Even that potential bonanza for Amtrak, however, turned into a headache when President Gerald R. Ford's Transportation Secretary, William T. Coleman, Jr., insisted on keeping control of the project. Coleman had called Amtrak "outmoded outhouses" and had urged airlines to oppose Amtrak subsidies. When later given charge of the Northeast rail improvement program, Coleman assigned federal bureaucrats to the work instead of Amtrak's more professional engineering staff, resulting in the delay of urgently needed work, while costs needlessly rose. When money ran out sooner than expected, plans to electrify the line between Boston and New Haven were abandoned. Meanwhile, Secretary Coleman, like his predecessors and followers, accelerated plans to build better highways and airports.

Between New York and Boston, Amtrak schedules suffer because trains must be pulled by diesel locomotives north of New Haven, Connecticut. Electrification of the line is necessary for faster running times. This train is crossing the Mystic Bridge in Connecticut. *(Amtrak)*

Despite all that, Amtrak improved speed and service. Amtrak added trains to the schedules, outfitted the service with new equipment, and vastly improved the stations. In fact, rents for retailers in busy Washington Union Station are among the highest in the nation. Amtrak also began offering amenities such as free meals in first class and credit card activated on-board telephones. Late in 1990, Amtrak began running a conference car on selected *Metroliners*, accommodating those who want to have formal business meetings while traveling.

Metroliners run at a top speed of 125 mph, connecting New York with the nation's capital in as little as 2 hours and 40 minutes. In 1985, Amtrak for the first time became the largest single carrier between New York and Washington, carrying more passengers than either the Trump Shuttle or Pan Am shuttle. It is Amtrak's goal to increase the speed between Washington and New York to as high as 150 mph, reducing travel time to approximately two hours between the cities.

Amtrak in the Northeast is surviving, but it pales in comparison to the Supertrains overseas. Amtrak's work between Boston and Washington brought parts of the line up to modern standards, but many portions of the infrastructure are obsolete: one-quarter of the 776 bridges on the line were built before 1895; signals are a mixture of modern and outdated systems; and in New England, Amtrak and motorists continue to be plagued with highway-rail grade crossings. Putting it mildly, this is not a Japanese Bullet Train.

In the 231 miles between Boston and New York, where the top speed is only 90 mph, the route weaves and twists. If all those pretzel-like track curves were put together end to end, they would make 10 full circles. Clearly, this is not a French TGV system, either.

Prodded by Massachusetts Governor Michael S. Dukakis, the Coalition of Northeast Governors formed a high-speed rail task force with members from New Hampshire, Vermont, Rhode Island, New York, New Jersey, and Pennsylvania. Dukakis said rail upgrading is necessary between Boston and New York "to avert an airborne gridlock in the skies that threatens to cripple travel for millions and strangle our regional economy." Dukakis called for higher train speeds of 125 mph.

Federal Aviation Administration figures show that Boston–New York is the busiest air travel route in the country, with more than 3.3 million passengers a year flying between the two cities and 40 percent of all domestic flights from Logan International Airport bound for New York. "The market strength of Boston–New York is more than twice the size of the Paris–Lyon market and actually larger than London–Paris traffic," said Matthew A. Coogan of the Massachusetts Office of Transportation and Construction. He says of the government's northeast corridor improvement project: "That project was only half done."

The task force would like to see a trip time of three hours between Boston and New York instead of the current 4½ hours. Several options have been studied, such as straightening the curving trackage, installing electrification from New Haven to Boston, and running tilt-body trains to allow higher speeds around curves.

"If I can get under three hours New York–Boston, I'll take a third of the business away from the airplanes right there," said Claytor. "If that were successful, it might spark spending even more money to maybe relocate some track and do other things that are more expensive, like running trains at 150 mph."

Amtrak reported that the best way to speed trains north of New York was through a $1 billion program to electrify the line

Amtrak could cut Boston–New York travel time by running the Fastrain, a derivative of the Swedish X-2000 shown here. The hydraulic tilting mechanism (inset) allows the train to take curves at speeds as high as 150 mph while at the same time giving passengers a comfortable ride. *(ABB Traction Inc.)*

BULLET TRAINS FOR AMTRAK?

into Boston (the 300-mile Washington–New Haven leg already is electrified), eliminating a 10-minute locomotive change at New Haven and allowing higher speeds. Amtrak predicts, after purchasing new trains and boosting service to 22 round-trips daily, tripling ridership between Boston and New York, and generating an annual profit of as much as $40 million.

During the autumn of 1988, Amtrak ran a series of tests, using foreign-designed trains on the Boston–New York line. The Federal Railroad Administration gauged passenger comfort with computerized measuring devices. Researchers also noted other factors, for instance, the number of drinks spilled when the trains went around curves. Results showed that almost one out of every five drinks spilled on cars now used on the line, but only about one out of every 10 on the foreign tilt-car trains.

Finally a move is underway to electrify Amtrak's New Haven–Boston line, thanks to New Jersey Senator Frank Lautenberg. As chairman of the Senate Transportation Appropriations Subcommittee, he provided $125 million in fiscal year 1991 legislation to start the job.

Some state-inspired programs are more ambitious. Look at California, the land of congested freeways. California may actually pump more money into capital investments for Amtrak than Uncle Sam does for Amtrak's *entire* national system. Washington ought to be embarrassed.

Amtrak runs eight round-trip trains daily at a top speed of 90 mph in the San Diego–Los Angeles corridor, now Amtrak's best-used route outside of Washington–Boston. From carrying slightly more than 300,000 passengers in 1973, ridership on the California route grew to about 1.7 million by 1989. Amtrak released figures that showed its gain in another way—since 1975, Los Angeles–San Diego ridership jumped 376 percent, proving that even at modest speeds, clean, dependable rail service will lure Californians to trains.

Several studies show that more than 50 percent of the riders on the San Diego route would have driven the freeways if rail service had not been available. Gridlock in Los Angeles and Orange County is well known, but it has spread to San Diego, now the nation's sixth largest city. Interstate 5, the San Diego Freeway, has become so busy during rush hours that local governments are starting commuter trains from *en route* communities into Los Angeles and San Diego.

Counties along the line have formed the Rail Corridor Agency to start a $250 million program to improve track, signaling, grade crossings, and stations, and to purchase more train equipment for Amtrak. Goals include increasing train frequency to 12 round-trip trains, while reducing Los Angeles–San Diego travel time from nearly 3 hours to 2¼ hours by 1995. If all work is completed, the line could be carrying as many as 3.9 million intercity passengers by the year 2000.

The agency is chaired by James Mills, former President Pro-Tempore of the state Senate and a former Amtrak director. A native of San Diego, Mills is widely regarded as the father of the city's popular trolley system.

The effort to initiate Supertrain service to Las Vegas will again boost passenger use of Amtrak's San Diego line. Plans call for the Supertrains to share Amtrak's Anaheim station, and that will mean plenty of additional passengers transferring to and from Amtrak at that point.

Despite pockets of real progress, it's unlikely that Amtrak will build Supertrains. Such visionary thinking, with a few exceptions, has been nonexistent in the federal establishment that decides policies for Amtrak, and only occasionally evident in

Amtrak itself. Amtrak is obligated by law, as well as by politics, to run a national system. It cannot as a practical matter turn one of its routes into a true showcase system—if it does, charges of favoritism will fly from regions that feel neglected.

Former Amtrak president Reistrup explains: "I hope Amtrak continues to improve the northeast corridor, but they can't build new high-speed lines elsewhere because Amtrak has to serve too many publics. They've got a board of directors of 535 people in Congress—how can they bring about high speeds between point A and point B? It won't work. Amtrak has to be too many things to too many people." Sad, but true. Congress resists appropriating a substantial amount of cash to improve any one single line, no matter how worthy the project.

Amtrak's Claytor confirmed that Amtrak has to scatter its improvements around the nation: "Oklahoma and Maine, currently without Amtrak service, have requested studies to assess the possibility of getting it. The suspension of our Washington–Montreal train created a steady cry for its return. North Carolina is requesting new intrastate trains."

Reistrup, as Amtrak's president, argued for faster trains. In the 1977 five-year capital plan, Amtrak proposed starting a network of such trains, with recommendations for different regions of the nation. Chicago–Detroit and Los Angeles–San Diego were shown as top routes deserving improvements.

Congress reacted like a spoiled child. It was unhappy with Amtrak's plan, which suggested trading off poor routes for promising ones that would attract many more riders and greater profits. No Congressman wanted to let Amtrak discontinue a train in his district, even a poorly performing one, so that people elsewhere would benefit. As a result, virtually nothing was done to speed up Amtrak's short-distance trains anywhere in the nation. Where a program was undertaken, between Boston and Washington, it was inadequate.

Amtrak tried again, completing what it called the *Emerging Corridor Studies* in 1981. However, its modest, indeed timid, recommendations were crippled by the transportation secretary at the time, Drew Lewis. In a cover letter to the report, Lewis wrote: "The department is opposed to expanding rail corridor services. . . . There is no justification in the report to support additional funding for corridors in addition to Amtrak's existing system."

Lewis's heavy-handed criticism of the Amtrak studies alleged that "none of the markets could be served by rail corridor trains without an increase in public subsidy." However, his letter did not volunteer that he, like others before him, was increasing subsidies to the competing air and highway networks.

Amtrak's president at the time, Alan S. Boyd, himself a former transportation secretary, disagreed with Lewis. Calmly and painstakingly, Boyd proved that the government had relied on misleading and meaningless figures to reach inappropriate conclusions. Also, Boyd said, the government was totally ignoring the massive outpouring of pro-train testimony gathered at 30 community briefings.

When Lewis succeeded in carrying Reagan's anti-Amtrak banner to victory in Washington, he let ideological concerns interfere with the task of improving transportation. In sum, nothing had been accomplished. By defeating attempts to strengthen Amtrak, Reagan's supporters thought they were the winners, and, as air and highway congestion worsened, America's travelers were the losers.

The federal government has hampered Amtrak in the worst way by letting it starve for capital, which restrains its ability to lure more customers. Washington time and again has exhaustively debated what "size" Amtrak should be, but the bigger question of how "good" Amtrak should be has been left virtually unexamined. In countries with Supertrain systems, the debate is often the reverse. That's why Amtrak trains run faster than 100 mph on only two routes in the entire nation. That's why Amtrak's capital plan to the year 2000 calls for buying only 270 locomotives and 477 cars, none of which can top 125 mph.

Whenever Americans ask, "Why don't we have trains like they have in Europe and Japan?" The simple answer is that Europeans and Japanese are committed to effective capital investment in their rail networks. Washington simply never considers giving Amtrak $40 billion to upgrade America's trains, yet Washington regularly gives the Pentagon between $40 billion and $60 billion *and more* for single weapons systems. Similar amounts go to NASA, aviation, and highways.

"The 12-nation European Community has embarked on an ambitious project to provide high-speed rail service between the major cities on the continent," said Amtrak's Claytor. Europe's program, which would make trains the first choice for trips of 350 miles or less, could cost more than $100 billion by the year 2000. In contrast, Washington's total capital investment in Amtrak's Boston–Washington improvement program has amounted to a mere $2.4 billion.

Another problem hampering Amtrak is that in most of the nation it still operates over tracks owned by the freight railroads. Those private companies, some of which are more concerned with reducing their physical plant than improving railroad services, have little incentive to help boost Amtrak train speeds on their tracks, and the government certainly isn't interested in improving private railroad property. Fortunately, steel-wheel Supertrains will use separate tracks for the most part, having little need

Three Amtrak trains are ready to depart Atlantic City's new train station.
Feeder routes like this to Amtrak's Boston–Washington line help sell train
service overall.   *(Amtrak)*

to operate over the tracks belonging to private railroads, and maglev Supertrains won't intermingle at all with the freight railroads.

Not only is Amtrak, as it is presently organized and funded,
unlikely to develop true Supertrain services, but its governing
law makes some Supertrain planners wary. Amtrak's original
legislation contains a provision that says no one may, without
Amtrak's consent, operate rail passenger service over any route
served by Amtrak.

"No one at the time this provision was passed thought about
the effects requiring Amtrak consent would have on private initiative in high-speed rail—there was no such thing," said attorney Mari M. Gursky, a partner in the Philadelphia firm of
Dechert, Price & Rhoads. "The question then is how to ensure
that Amtrak cannot demand a percent of the profits when the
system is funded privately. For nothing will take the shine off
those high-speed tracks in the eyes of private investors like having to share an increasing percentage of any profits they realize
with Amtrak."

BULLET TRAINS FOR AMTRAK?

She concluded that states and private firms would not need approval from Amtrak to operate high-speed rail systems when new lines are built, lines that did not exist when Amtrak was formed. The law could have been much worse. One of the early fears of pioneers in the current high-speed train movement was that Amtrak would grab control of all Supertrain proposals. Robert J. Casey of the High Speed Rail Association explained:

"We formed the Association on August 4, 1983. Within a few weeks—we had not even gotten organized yet—I got a call from Tom Wagner who at that time was at the Texas Railroad Transportation Company in Austin. He asked if we knew that Congressman Jim Florio of New Jersey wanted to give Amtrak

The *Empire State Express* from Niagara Falls heads south along the Hudson River. Effective April 7, 1991, for the first time in history, intercity trains linking New York City with upstate points began serving Penn Station instead of Grand Central Terminal. Amtrak will benefit financially by operating out of one New York City facility instead of two, and passengers find it much easier to connect between different Amtrak lines. *(Amtrak)*

exclusive jurisdiction over rail passenger service anywhere in the United States.

"A group of us walked into the Congressman's office, unannounced, and were able to get Florio to see us," Casey said.

"We explained our position and several weeks later he dropped that provision. I'm a fan of Amtrak. We need Amtrak. But if Amtrak had exclusive authority to bring about high-speed trains, we'd never have any in America."

Fortunately, Amtrak management seems to realize that Supertrains can only help Amtrak. Claytor said in a speech late in 1988 that Amtrak could help as a contractor to build the new steel-wheel Supertrain rail lines because it already had the machinery to do so.

Once they are built, whether steel-wheel or maglev, Amtrak would compete for a contract to operate them as it does commuter trains in the Northeast. Amtrak is teamed with Bechtel on the Los Angeles–Las Vegas maglev Supertrain proposal: Bechtel would build it and Amtrak would run it. Claytor said Amtrak could provide reservation and other services to all Supertrain systems. Amtrak's reservations system is tied to most major airline systems and is accessible to some 25,000 travel agents around the country.

Amtrak will profit in a big way if Supertrains use its stations. For example, a Supertrain line across Pennsylvania would pour an additional five million passengers a year into Amtrak's 30th Street Station in Philadelphia, travelers who could be induced to continue on Amtrak to other destinations such as New York. Amtrak will profit by charging fees to the Supertrains for using its stations, and real estate development opportunities will expand within and around each Amtrak station that serves Supertrains.

"Graham Claytor has pledged support for high-speed rail efforts," said Casey. "You can see why—systems in Pennsylvania, Florida, Texas and California all propose to share facilities with Amtrak. The financial rewards at just one station can be worth millions of dollars to Amtrak. Amtrak will not gain one

BULLET TRAINS FOR AMTRAK?

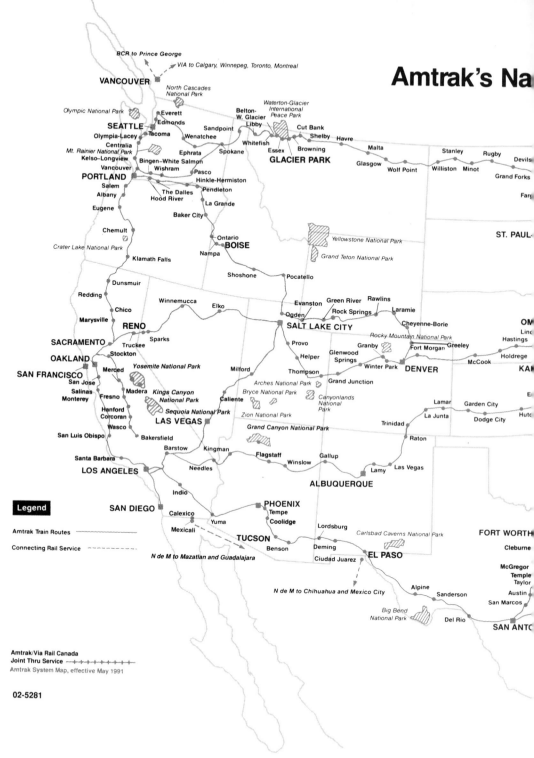

Amtrak's Na

BCR to Prince George

VIA to Calgary, Winnipeg, Toronto, Montreal

VANCOUVER

North Cascades
National Park

Olympic National Park
Everett
Edmonds
SEATTLE
Olympia-Lacey Tacoma
Centralia
Mt. Rainier National Park
Kelso-Longview
Bingen–White Salmon
Vancouver Wishram
PORTLAND
Salem
Albany
Eugene
Chemult
Crater Lake National Park
Klamath Falls

Belton-
W. Glacier
Libby
Sandpoint
Wenatchee
Whitefish
Ephrata Spokane
Essex Browning
GLACIER PARK

Waterton-Glacier
International
Peace Park
Cut Bank
Shelby Havre
Malta
Glasgow Wolf Point

Stanley Rugby
Williston Minot

Devils
Grand Forks
Farg

ST. PAUL-

Pasco
Hinkle-Hermiston
The Dalles Pendleton
Hood River
La Grande
Baker City
Ontario
BOISE
Nampa
Shoshone Pocatello

Yellowstone National Park

Grand Teton National Park

Dunsmuir
Redding
Chico
Marysville
RENO
SACRAMENTO Truckee
Sparks
OAKLAND Stockton
SAN FRANCISCO
San Jose
Salinas
Monterey Fresno
Hanford
Corcoran
Wasco
San Luis Obispo
Santa Barbara
LOS ANGELES

Winnemucca Elko
Merced
Madera
Yosemite National Park
Kings Canyon
National Park
Sequoia National Park
LAS VEGAS
Bakersfield
Barstow Kingman
Needles
Indio

Evanston Green River Rawlins
Ogden Rock Springs Laramie
SALT LAKE CITY
Cheyenne-Borie
Provo
Helper Granby
Glenwood Fort Morgan Greeley
Springs
Winter Park DENVER
Thompson
Grand Junction
Arches National Park
Bryce National Park Canyonlands
Caliente National
Zion National Park Park
Grand Canyon National Park
Flagstaff
Winslow Gallup
Lamy Las Vegas
ALBUQUERQUE
Raton

Milford

OM
Linc
Hastings
Holdrege
McCook KA

Lamar Garden City
La Junta Dodge City
Trinidad

Hutc

SAN DIEGO
Calexico
Mexicali
Yuma

PHOENIX
Tempe
Coolidge
Lordsburg
TUCSON
Benson Deming
Ciudad Juarez
N de M to Mazatlan and Guadalajara

Carlsbad Caverns National Park
FORT WORTH
Cleburne
McGregor
Temple
EL PASO Taylor
Austin
Alpine San Marcos
Sanderson
SAN ANTO

N de M to Chihuahua and Mexico City

Big Bend
National Park Del Rio

Legend

Amtrak Train Routes ─────────

Connecting Rail Service ─ ─ ─ ─ ─

Amtrak/Via Rail Canada
Joint Thru Service ┼┼┼┼┼┼┼┼┼
Amtrak System Map, effective May 1991

02-5281

SUPERTRAINS
260

al Rail Passenger System

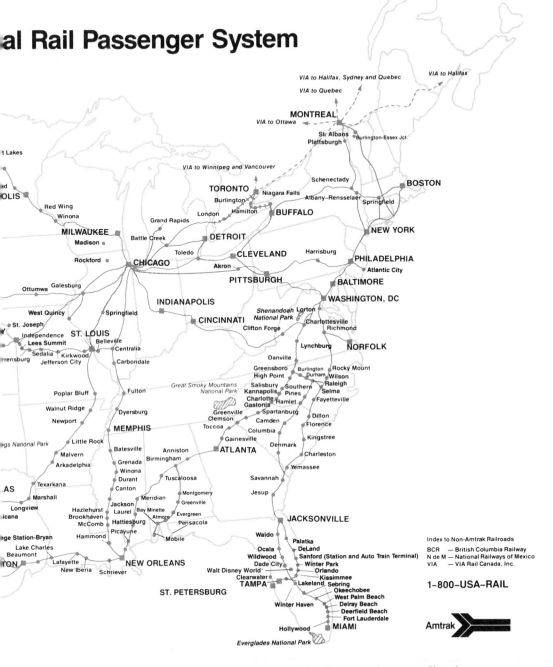

VIA to Halifax, Sydney and Quebec
VIA to Quebec
VIA to Halifax

VIA to Ottawa

MONTREAL

St. Albans
Plattsburgh
Burlington-Essex Jct.

VIA to Winnipeg and Vancouver

Schenectady
BOSTON

TORONTO
Niagara Falls
Albany-Rensselaer
Springfield

Burlington
Hamilton
BUFFALO

London
Grand Rapids

Red Wing
Winona

MILWAUKEE
Battle Creek
DETROIT
NEW YORK

Madison

Rockford
CHICAGO
Toledo
CLEVELAND
Harrisburg
PHILADELPHIA

Akron
Atlantic City

Galesburg
PITTSBURGH
BALTIMORE

Ottumwa

INDIANAPOLIS
WASHINGTON, DC

West Quincy
Springfield
Shenandoah
National Park
Lorton

St. Joseph
CINCINNATI
Clifton Forge
Charlottesville
Richmond

Independence
ST. LOUIS
Belleville

Lees Summit
Kirkwood
Centralia
Lynchburg
NORFOLK

Sedalia
Jefferson City
Carbondale
Danville

Poplar Bluff
Fulton
Greensboro
Burlington
Rocky Mount

High Point
Durham
Wilson

Salisbury
Southern
Raleigh

Walnut Ridge
Dyersburg
Kannapolis
Pines
Selma

Newport
Charlotte
Hamlet
Fayetteville

Gastonia

MEMPHIS
Greenville
Spartanburg
Dillon

Clemson
Camden
Florence

Toccoa
Columbia

Little Rock
Gainesville
Denmark
Kingstree

Batesville
Anniston
ATLANTA
Charleston

Malvern
Birmingham

Arkadelphia
Grenada
Winona
Yemassee

Texarkana
Durant
Tuscaloosa
Savannah

Marshall
Canton

Longview
Meridian
Greenville
Jesup

Hazlehurst
Jackson
Bay Minette

Brookhaven
Laurel
Evergreen
JACKSONVILLE

McComb
Hattiesburg
Atmore

Hammond
Picayune
Pensacola

Waldo

Lake Charles
Mobile
Palatka

Beaumont
Ocala
DeLand

Lafayette
Wildwood
Sanford (Station and Auto Train Terminal)

New Iberia
Schriever
NEW ORLEANS
Dade City
Winter Park

Walt Disney World
Orlando

Clearwater
Kissimmee

ST. PETERSBURG
TAMPA
Lakeland
Sebring

Okeechobee

West Palm Beach

Winter Haven
Delray Beach

Deerfield Beach

Fort Lauderdale

Hollywood
MIAMI

Everglades National Park

Great Smoky Mountains
National Park

Great Lakes

Index to Non-Amtrak Railroads

BCR — British Columbia Railway
N de M — National Railways of Mexico
VIA — VIA Rail Canada, Inc.

1-800-USA-RAIL

Amtrak

Amtrak's national system means it must satisfy Congress by spreading improvements here and there. The rail carrier also has been capital-starved for two decades, able to make only modest improvements. Result: it is impossible, thus far, for Amtrak to invest in any single line to bring about a true Supertrain service.
(Amtrak)

iota if more highways or airports are built, so these new trains should be considered the best type of friend Amtrak will have in the future."

Amtrak, lucky to be alive, can use the added business. For a company that many did not expect to survive, Amtrak has established itself in some markets and now enjoys a public mandate to stay in business. One great Amtrak challenge is finding the means to buy new equipment just to replace 1,000 passenger cars built between 1948 and 1964 that have reached retirement age. An even bigger challenge in the 1990s is expanding its capacity to meet growing demand.

Where will the capital funding come from to improve Amtrak? How about earmarking a one cent per gallon tax on gasoline to upgrade Amtrak? Samuel E. Stokes, Jr., of Alstead, New Hampshire, has been advocating just that: "The United States is the richest country in the world with the cheapest gasoline in the world. We can afford it."

"A balanced national transportation system requires a balanced approach to funding," said Claytor. "A penny a gallon from gasoline tax revenues, used to fund Amtrak, would enable Amtrak to engage in meaningful long-term planning, not now feasible. It also would de-politicize the funding of rail passenger service. . . . A dedicated funding source would give non-federal financial institutions more confidence in the long-term future of Amtrak and encourage them to finance capital and rolling stock programs."

A one-cent gas tax for Amtrak would meet all its capital costs for its system nationwide, Claytor told Congress, including Boston–New York schedules of 2 hours 59 minutes and New York–Washington times of 2 hours 15 minutes. Vigorously supporting the idea of the "Amtrak penny" is John R. Martin, president of the National Association of Railroad Passengers.

Amtrak is willing to contract to build lines for Supertrains that will run in-
dependently of Amtrak's system. The company has built 125-mph tracks and
can adapt its methods to bring about tracks good for still higher speeds. This
gargantuan track-laying machine is upgrading the northeast corridor. The
machine removes old rail and ties, plows away the ballast, lays new ties, and
places new welded rail on top, all in one operation. Amtrak completes these
tasks at a rate of 1,200 feet per hour with laser-alignment precision.

(Amtrak)

So what's the verdict on Amtrak? It all depends on expectations. Those who wanted Amtrak to make conventional train
travel a decent experience, instead of the horror it once was on
certain railroads, consider Amtrak an effective program. Amtrak
is experiencing its greatest success, providing improved service
at less cost to the taxpayers. Those who hoped Amtrak would
develop super-speed trains on densely populated corridor routes
have been disappointed. However, Amtrak may win contracts to
operate Supertrains built by others. And it appears that independent Supertrains and Amtrak trains will coexist nicely in
the 21st century.

As Bill Poling, a Washington reporter for *Travel Weekly*, and
a keen observer of Amtrak's ups and downs, noted, "For Amtrak,
it could be a whole new era. But, as always, a lot depends on
the politicians."

BULLET TRAINS FOR AMTRAK?

WINGLOCK!

*"We can build more airplanes, and we can
even build more airports. But try as we might,
we cannot build more airspace."*
—*Senator Daniel Patrick Moynihan*

JOSEPH ZUCKER LOVES
trains. He has gladly
taken rail trips in
frigid

Canada, sweltering India, and parched Australia. He's ridden on slow trains in Brazil and fast ones in Germany, quaint trains in Panama and noisy ones in Kenya. Now, Zucker is in his glory: he's a Los Angeles public relations man paid to boost interest in trains run by his overseas employer.

He eagerly touts his firm's rail passenger service in talks with the news media and travel agents. His office is stocked with brochures that show trains cruising through a scenic region dotted with small villages and vineyard-covered hills.

United States airlines could learn from the way Lufthansa operates passenger trains out of its Frankfurt air terminal to Cologne, Bonn, and other cities. The trains connect to and from European and international flights, with ticketing and baggage transfer the same as if they were jetliners. Lufthansa thereby eliminates short-distance flights, opening up scarce takeoff and landing slots for aircraft that serve long-distance routes. The airline does not argue to build more airports—it wants to expand its intercity train network.

(Lufthansa German Airlines)

Americans who never think of traveling by train have found that the services his company runs are comfortable and fast, and the trains arrive on schedule 98 percent of the time. Travelers could fly between the same cities served by Zucker's trains, but many pass up jetliners after riding the rails but one time. Nearly two million passengers have boarded his company's trains on one route in just a few years of operation.

So, what is the overseas railroad Zucker works for? The German Federal Railway? The French? Maybe the Japanese? The answer is: none. He works for an airline, and an internationally respected airline at that—Lufthansa.

"We offer an intercity rail service as part of our 'flight' network," said Zucker. "The trains are listed as *flights* in any travel agent's computer anywhere in the world, and we're so successful we have a crowding problem." Called the *Lufthansa Airport Express*, these "planes without wings" connect Frankfurt's airport, the major hub for the airline, to Bonn, Cologne, and Dusseldorf. The airline shifted passengers to rail as an alternative to flying more aircraft in the busiest airspace in Germany.

The Lufthansa trains make the trip from Frankfurt's Rhein-Main Airport to the city of Cologne in two hours and to Dusseldorf in 2½ hours, about twice as long as flight times, on days when there are no air traffic delays. Painted in Lufthansa's yellow and blue, the trains transport 127 passengers in cars with interiors that look like the interior of a jetliner. One big difference is that the trains have large windows, which allow easy viewing of the beautiful Rhine River valley, including the ancient castles that hang on cliffsides high above the rails.

The streamlined Lufthansa express trains, leased from the German Federal Railway for an undisclosed fee, operate four times daily in each direction. The railroad provides the engineers, while Lufthansa flight attendants pamper the passengers.

"This intercity rail service is a true part of our network—our cabin attendants serve passengers drinks and meals at their seats just as if they were aboard an aircraft," said Zucker. "Booking, ticketing, everything, including baggage transfer for the *Airport Express* is the same as for any connecting Lufthansa flight. The crew will accept a ticket from any airline. You can arrive from Moscow on Aeroflot and get aboard."

Lufthansa officials are unhappy that the company's image as a punctual airline is being jeopardized by airport congestion. In a meeting with Larry Johnson and Donald Rote of the Argonne National Laboratory, officials said they would like to replace all Lufthansa flights on the Frankfurt–Bonn–Cologne–Dusseldorf route with *Airport Express* trains. They would, Lufthansa said, shift use of limited airport takeoff and landing slots from short hops to higher value long-distance flights and save the airline money.

"If Lufthansa had faster trains (maximum speed is 125 mph), then they believe that most of their passengers would use the train," wrote the Argonne researchers. "What Lufthansa is especially interested in is a Transrapid maglev link between the Dusseldorf and Cologne airports (about 40 miles), thereby enabling Cologne to become a major European hub."

Widespread European air traffic delays cost Lufthansa about $50 million in 1989, and that figure did not count the loss of revenue from travelers who avoided flying altogether. So it is not surprising that the airline looked for other routes where it could use trains, and in 1990 started another *Lufthansa Airport Express*, this one between Frankfurt and Stuttgart. The operator of the Frankfurt airport said demand for trains at that "station" was so great he felt he needed three additional tracks.

WINGLOCK!

Lufthansa Airlines is interested in leasing new ICE trains and replacing the older equipment in its train network. Jetliners often suffer excessive delays during bad weather, but the trains are unaffected and keep punctual schedules.
(German Rail)

The railroad has bolder plans to meet future demand, approving plans for a second airport station at Frankfurt due to be completed in 1997. The airline is so serious about using trains that it has set up a joint subsidiary with the German Federal Railway called Airport-Express. Lufthansa Chairman Heinz Ruhnau explained why: "By the end of this decade airports will not require feeder services by aircraft—all will be operated by rail. New runways are not the only answer. The railways are an answer to the airport capacity problem."

Regardless of the air carrier, at other European airports, such as Geneva, Zurich, and Amsterdam, arriving air travelers can transfer easily to intercity trains. Sabena World Airlines offers its full-fare passengers free rail travel on local trains to and from Brussels' Zaventem International Airport. More joint terminals are coming—at Paris' Charles de Gaulle Airport and Rome's Leonardo da Vinci Airport, both intended for high-speed trains.

Overseas airlines also have supported technological advances in Supertrains. Lufthansa has participated in developing Germany's Transrapid maglev. Japan Air Lines backed the HSST maglev program until 1985, when it sold the project to a company made up of its former employees.

Some aviation leaders in the United States are warming to the idea of developing a high-speed train network. In comments before several hundred people in Washington, USAir Chairman Edwin I. Colodny asked whether America in the 1990s should move more people in densely populated short-haul markets by train.

"What will be the role of high-speed rail? You may find it odd to hear an airline CEO raising the prospect of high-speed rail, but it is something that needs to be explored," said Colodny. "Using all of the airspace capability we have in the northeast corridor—Boston–New York–Washington—for duplicate shuttle services, one should question whether that's the most efficient way to run the system when you can't add runways in the New York area."

Experience is on Colodny's side. When the TGV began operating between Paris and Lyon, so many passengers diverted to the trains that airline traffic on that route plummeted by 50 percent. In the 1960s, the launching of Japan's Bullet Train caused many travelers to switch to rail service between Tokyo and Osaka.

Colodny sees no incompatibility between aviation and surface transportation, saying, "Perhaps United States carriers will also someday get into the ground transportation business."

The airlines know that trains are easy to sell. In 1990, no less than three airlines based in the United States promoted travel on trains overseas. Pan American World Airways ran advertisements in major American newspapers promoting a tour package in France headlined "Ooh La La! *C'est magnifique!*" Shown in the photo was the French TGV, saying the offer included "a trip on one of the world's fastest and most sophisticated trains." That promotion was followed by American Airlines, whose ads also touted French train travel. Said Dagobert Scher of French National Railway's New York office: "That is good. We want all the airlines to advertise our trains." Northwest Airlines took a different approach, touting use of the British Rail System by offering a BritRail Flexipass under certain conditions. Singapore Airlines and Avianca also offer Air-Train travel packages.

"Amtrak and United Airlines offer a special package that allows travelers to combine air and train travel at a price competitive with existing round-trip airline excursion fares," reported Timothy P. Gardner, Amtrak's vice-president of passenger marketing. "We know we can attract thousands of new passengers with this program."

Air freight experts are speaking up. Said James E. Tyler, Jr., of Federal Express: "There is a serious need for alternate means of transportation, such as high-speed rail. Properly operated, it can offer real advantages that aircraft, by their very nature, may never be able to match. Not the least of these are all-weather reliability and *en route* sorting [of packages]."

Harried airport directors are also warming to Supertrains. Officials at Massport, which runs Boston's Logan International Airport, say traffic will double by the year 2010 and suggest building a high-speed Amtrak line to New York. The first regularly scheduled commercial flights in the United States, established in 1927, started between Boston and New York.

Massport is not the only organization to see trains as a tool for managing airport growth. The Los Angeles Department of Airports, long worried about congestion, has studied new airport sites for 25 years. The agency has urged construction of a Supertrain line to remote Palmdale where it wants to build a giant new airport. There, the City of Los Angeles owns 36 square miles of empty Mojave Desert, purchased in 1968 for a super-airport five times the size of Los Angeles International.

Clifton Moore, executive director of the Los Angeles Department of Airports, has urged that the Supertrains to Las Vegas do double duty by carrying passengers to the Palmdale airport. Palmdale Mayor Pete Knight, lobbying for his town, said officials will provide land and help build a Supertrain terminal at the new airport.

A 1989 California Republican Party resolution said the state was in "virtual *winglock* at all major airports with long delays in take-off and in landing clearances" and endorsed privately financed Supertrains. The author, Angie Papadakis, chairs the party's transportation committee and is a commissioner of the California-Nevada Super Speed Train Commission. "We have to face reality out here," said Papadakis. "It's not likely that the number of people driving or flying will diminish, so we have to provide alternatives." She coined the term "winglock" for the resolution.

Even unlikely federal officials have spoken up. In a speech to aviation experts, J. Lynn Helms, the former head of the Federal Aviation Administration, said, "Our business is moving people. We must not let our personal desires overshadow our responsibility to the traveling public. We must include high-speed rail transportation in our planning." He wasn't the only FAA administrator to speak favorably about trains. Donald D. Engen, Helms' successor, while addressing safety issues in 1987, said, "The way to achieve safety—true safety—is to put the planes in the hangar, lock the doors, and everybody take the train."

Aviation is starting to see Supertrains as a solution to its congestion just in time because few new airports are on the horizon.

"With a near unanimity rare in the travel industry, airlines and aviation organizations predict that overcrowding in the air and at airports is sure to get worse," wrote Barbara Sturken in *Travel Weekly*. "More people are flying now than the system was built to accommodate, and still more will want to fly in the future."

Moreover, some say that the sheer discomfort of air travel is worse than ever. A California legislator, David Roberti of Los Angeles, wants to establish a special state office simply to field calls from angry airline passengers and publish the findings. The number one complaint to the FAA by passengers focuses on cancelled and delayed flights, which often result from air system congestion. Four months after Roberti's call for action, a Washington agency issued a report that said the nation's airlines cancel thousands of flights a month because of weather and because they don't have enough passengers or sufficient crew members.

"The General Accounting Office said that about 4,700 flights a month are canceled for these reasons but are reported as late flights and counted with flights that are more than 15 minutes behind schedule," reported David Field in a *Washington Times* story headlined, "Airlines Cover Up Canceled Flights."

When Japan's Bullet Trains began running, airline patrons on the Tokyo–Osaka route switched to the trains in big numbers.
(Japan National Tourist Organization)

WINGLOCK!

Congestion affects air safety, too. For example, the 28 busiest airports in the Los Angeles Basin handle about six million takeoffs and landings annually, and that number is growing. Near mid-air collisions happen so often that the region has "the dubious distinction of being Number 1 in the nation for near misses four years running," according to Kathleen Burton, a small-plane pilot writing in the *Los Angeles Times Magazine*. Los Angeles International Airport had 57 near collisions between 1986 and 1988, but not all such incidents are counted that way. In March 1991, a Pan Am jetliner and a United Express commuter jet narrowly missed one another in cloudy skies. Air traffic controllers directed the pilots to take evasive action. Since neither pilot filed a report, however, the incident is listed officially as a "pilot deviation," rather than a near collision.

"In the region's most notorious air disaster . . . on August 31, 1986, an Aeromexico jet collided with a four-seater Piper Archer II and crashed into the town of Cerritos," wrote Burton. "Eighty-two people died—all the crew and passengers on both airplanes and 15 people on the ground. After an 11-month investigation, the [National Transportation Safety Board] concluded that 'limitations' in the FAA's air traffic control system and safety regulations were to blame. The whole system, it said, was becoming inadequate for the increasingly crowded skies over Los Angeles." The same holds true for runways, too. On February 3, 1991, a USAir Boeing 737 jetliner crashed into a Sky West commuter flight at Los Angeles International, killing 34 people.

Trouble can be found even in relatively open skies. "Two jet airliners converging almost head-on missed colliding over North Carolina" on June 30, 1991, wrote Richard Witkin of the *New York Times*. "It was a close brush with disaster." The USAir and

Continental jetliners, flying at 33,000 feet, carried a total of 194 passengers and crew.

That there has been a boom in air travel is beyond doubt. Spurred by deregulation, the number of passengers boarding commercial airliners has zoomed upward from 243 million in 1977 to 455 million in 1989, meaning about 1.2 million people are now in the skies everyday. A statistician calculated that these passengers traveled the equivalent of 76 round trips to the planet Pluto.

The worst air-traffic delays historically occur at the three airports in New York City. Comparing 1989 to the prior year, delays were up 111 percent at LaGuardia and 52 percent at Kennedy. Airports in the New York metropolitan area have gotten busier over the years. Since 1957, Newark has had an 844 percent jump in usage, Kennedy was up 483 percent, and LaGuardia, 331 percent. Many passengers at these airports are traveling short distances. In 1988, about 56 percent of the combined aircraft departures at these three airports, and 82 percent of their travelers, were traveling to points less than 300 miles from New York.

"Chicago's O'Hare International Airport, the nation's busiest terminal, has more than 12 million hours of passenger delay per year—the equivalent of 1,400 people standing idle around the clock, all year," noted the Argonne Report. Between 1989 and 1996, the number of airports that rack up more than three million hours of passenger delay annually is expected to double, to 22.

"The cost of delay to the average passenger going through O'Hare has been calculated at about $10 a ticket," said Jay Franke, Chicago aviation commissioner. Seventeen airports in 1988 were

WINGLOCK!

classified as "seriously congested" because they handled 160 percent of the traffic for which they were designed. In 1989, air traffic control delays increased 16 percent over the prior year.

According to the FAA, the number of troubled airports could more than triple by the year 2000. The agency also predicts that as many as 722 million passengers will be flying by the turn of the century, with delays spreading to Raleigh-Durham, Cincinnati, and Las Vegas—airports that in the 1980s were free of serious congestion.

Only one large airport is under construction, and that is in Denver, with an opening scheduled for October 1993. Situated about 25 miles northeast of downtown, it will eventually have more than 200 gates sprawling over 53 square miles of high prairie and will be the world's biggest airfield.

"I think building 20 new airports at a cost of $3 to $4 billion—spending $100 billion for airports—is not out of the question," said Transportation Secretary Sam Skinner. But the costs could very well be higher. Hong Kong's new airport, due to open in 1997, will cost $4.5 billion, not counting costs of new access roads. Spending for new airfields in Seoul and Chicago will reach $5 billion each. By Skinner's thinking, new airports would result in a building project on the scale of the 43,000-mile interstate highway system. If the FAA had its way, it would spend more than that on airports.

Modernizing the air traffic control system also will be costly. FAA Administrator James B. Busey has admitted that the original $9 billion upgrading program has risen to $15.8 billion.

Aviation's all-out campaign to build more airports is to be expected; with so many expensive airplanes on order the industry will work to make sure that more runways are built rather than retrench. In 1989, American Airlines placed two aircraft orders totaling about $11.6 billion, Delta signed contracts for $10 billion in airplanes, and even financially strapped Continental Airlines found $4.5 billion to buy jetliners. In 1990, American said it will spend about $14 billion over the next five years for new aircraft while United Airlines announced a $22 billion order—the largest aircraft order in history.

Boeing, McDonnell Douglas, and Airbus Industrie of Europe are racing to meet the buying frenzy. As of early 1990, their combined order books were crammed with more than *$160 billion* worth of aircraft, with delivery dates stretched beyond the turn of the century. Domestic airlines alone had a record 2,000 plus new aircraft on order. Boeing's production of 737s rose from 14 per month in the late 1980s to 21 per month in 1991, more than one aircraft per work day. Airbus will quadruple its output from 45 aircraft annually to more than 200 aircraft a year by 1994, cranking them out as fast as they can.

The astonishing figures don't stop there. At the end of 1989, the world airlines' fleet totaled about 11,900 commercial jets and large turboprops. Through the year 2005, Boeing expects that nearly 10,000 more airplanes will be manufactured. Their total worth? About *$626 billion.*

Aviation experts say that approximately 3,000 of those will be needed to replace aging aircraft, which brings up the key point: 7,000 aircraft will be *added* to the system worldwide to meet travel growth making airport expansion essential.

The majority of the new aircraft will be the shorter-distance jetliners that are the lifeblood of the manufacturers. Through the turn of the century, Boeing estimates that the greatest number of units sold, at 7,347 aircraft, will be the Boeing 737, McDonnell Douglas MD-80 series, Airbus A320 aircraft—all short-range aircraft.

WINGLOCK!

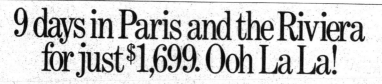

Pan Am advertised trains as the way to see Europe, as did American Airlines and Northwest Airlines, in 1990 promotions.

Supertrains are a direct threat to that short-range jetliner market and Boeing in particular fears any weakening in the market for such jetliners. Some aviation interests will fight for more airports and may openly oppose high-speed train service if that is what it takes. Already, in a 1989 transportation department hearing in Detroit, a Boeing spokesman discouraged ideas for Supertrains.

The aviation-aerospace lobby, even stronger than the fabled military-industrial complex or the influential highway lobby, is pressing for new airports. Boeing, McDonnell Douglas, and their suppliers, such as GE Aircraft Engines and United Technologies, are lined up to exert power, either individually or through industry associations. Additionally, the major airlines, American, Delta, Northwest, Southwest, United, and USAir may compete in their respective fields, but they're unified in asking for landing sites.

These companies have enormous clout with the government, as proved by Boeing in the aftermath of the 1989 riots in the Peoples Republic of China. There, in Beijing's Tiananmen Square, ruthless troops massacred countless unarmed pro-democracy demonstrators. Revulsion swept the world, and President Bush, citing human rights violations, imposed trade sanctions against that country. Among the items the State Department suspended for sale were the navigational systems in Boeing jets, which can have military applications.

Boeing, unhappy that federal sanctions held up delivery of 757s with a total value of about $150 million, appealed the suspension order. A mere 33 days later, Secretary of State James A. Baker III issued an exception, and Boeing's aircraft were delivered to China. As Congress debated China-related legislation well into the next year, Boeing's deliveries continued as if all were normal. Powerful? Some would say too powerful.

Persistent, too. In mid-1990, when Congress began considering elimination of "most favored nation" trade status with China, Boeing and other firms mobilized to help Chinese Premier Li Peng by deferring Congressional action. They won, again.

WINGLOCK!

Aviation benefits from a coalition of groups whose interest lies in building more airports, including the Air Transport Association, Air Line Pilots Association, and 30 other powerful organizations. A separate Washington-based group, the Aerospace Industries Association, with 54 major contractors as members, is a lobbying power looking out for the interests of the aircraft manufacturers. The muscle of the aviation-aerospace groups exceeds many times over the power wielded by the feared railroad robber-barons of the last century or the rail industry today.

——— ——— ———

Welcome to the "Great American Airport Revolt of the 1990s."

Despite its coercive capabilities, aviation is having trouble in its quest for more airports. In Chicago, for example, "airport" has become a dirty word. A metropolitan area divided over airport issues, it perhaps is the birthplace of the emerging airport revolt. Because of disagreement, and because of the *size* of Chicago's new airport, it may never be built. Gregory Furda, a Chicago zoning lawyer, told the *Chicago Tribune*: "Imagine the combined effect of 25 interstate highways connecting at one place. That's an international airport."

Chicago already has two major airports, O'Hare and Midway, both of which have been expanded and modernized in recent times. Nevertheless, O'Hare Airport is at the center of airline and city pressure for still more expansion, with citizens' groups in a fierce battle against such plans. A second wave of action focuses on the areas south of Chicago where many oppose locating a new super-airport.

Who thinks a new regional superairport is a good idea? Well,

Transportation Secretary Skinner, who also is a private pilot, for starters, as well as some Chicago city politicians and the FAA. Agreeing are elected officials in Du Page and northwest Cook County who are sick of O'Hare's noise, pollution, safety problems, and overcrowding. They campaign fiercely against plans to add runways at O'Hare and demand a third airport be put elsewhere. The new airport would be the largest public works project in Illinois history.

Five sites have been proposed for the new super-airport, three in Illinois—Kankakee, Peotone, or the southeastern part of Chicago. The fourth is a site east of Peotone called Bi-State, with the Illinois-Indiana border running right through the middle of it. Gary Municipal Airport, in downtrodden northwestern Indiana, is a fifth suggested site. Local officials want to turn that small airfield into a larger one, and Indiana Governor Evan Bayh has offered funding to help study the site.

Airlines that have a stranglehold on traffic at O'Hare, United and American, are opposed to the construction of any new airfield. They do not want to meet new competition nor shoulder the financial burden of operating out of still another site in the region. "O'Hare is capable of substantial additional expansion," said Jim Guyette, executive vice president of operations for United Airlines. "We must not let environmental considerations indefinitely halt expansion of our airports."

Environmental concerns are exactly the cause of the uproar. Residents near O'Hare oppose expansion plans that could result in more than one million flights a year taking off or landing there, up from about 800,000. "I can say that any effort to add more runways is going to create one hell of a battle," said Martin J. Butler, mayor of Park Ridge, a 125-year-old community that is close to O'Hare field. Butler is chairman of a coalition

WINGLOCK!

that represents some 300,000 residents. He points out that "there were 191,000 people living in nearby communities before the first jet plane flew. So we are not Johnny-come-latelies as we are attempted to be painted."

Roger Ginger, a Park Ridge resident who calls himself an "irate citizen," suggested placing a cap on O'Hare's capacity, saying, "I can't open a noisy gas station in front of my home. Other citizens wouldn't like it. I wouldn't do that to them, but the airlines insult me repeatedly and it's getting worse all the time, not better. I sit next to my wife and sometimes we can't hear one another talk."

Noise problems are so bad that 13 municipalities filed a class-action lawsuit against O'Hare on grounds of emotional and physical damage, and they are committed to carrying it to the United States Supreme Court. Congressman Henry Hyde of Illinois has advised school districts to sue the City of Chicago because soundproofing funds have never been provided to area schools.

Not one, but many citizens' groups are fighting O'Hare's congestion, pollution, and noise, with names that reflect their grassroots origins: CRAN (Citizens for Reduced Aircraft Noise), START (Save Trees And Residents Today), SORE (Save Our Residential Environment), We the People, IRATE (Initiative for Responsibility, Accountability and Tax Equity), SOS (Save Open Space), and the O'Hare Citizens Coalition. These groups plan to hold Governor Jim Edgar to his campaign pledge to oppose the construction of new runways.

City officials fear the loss of jobs, fees, and political strength if a new airport is built elsewhere. When competitors started pushing hard for their outlying sites, Chicago Mayor Richard M. Daley called for a new $5 billion airport on land formerly occupied by a steel mill on the southeast side of the city. The Daley plan would demolish 8,500 homes in an area nestled between Lake Calumet and the Indiana border, obliterating the Hegewisch neighborhood, move 47 businesses that employ 9,000 workers, and reroute the Calumet River.

Some Chambers of Commerce and land developers in Kankakee and Will countries, south of Chicago, want to see the proposed super-airport built there to boost the local economy. Construction could begin by 1995 with operations starting five years later on an airport 8,640 acres in size with a 40,000-acre buffer zone surrounding it. That's larger than O'Hare, which covers 7,000 acres.

So far, plans to build the super-airport have proceeded cautiously. No one is expecting protests as hostile as the Japanese opposition to expanding Tokyo's Narita International Airport. There, a 24-hour vigil by riot police, who patrol behind a series of steel barricades, barbed wire, and moats, protect the airport against attacks by student radicals and angry farmers. In the mid-1960s, and again in the late-1980s, protesters threw firebombs and clashed violently with police.

Illinois' citizens may be tamer, but trouble is still brewing as residents oppose airport proposals. Outrage has been expressed at public meetings, in letters and newspaper advertising, through roadside signs, and petition drives. Opponents have picketed in Chicago's Loop, carrying placards reading, "No Third Airport," "Stop the Rape of Prime Farmland," "Airport = Pollution, Taxes, Noise," and "Protect our Endangered Species—Farmers."

"I suggest we round up the politicians, deny them food, give them tainted water and stick their noses in the tail end of a jet fuselage," said Gloria Weidner, of Kankakee Area Research and

WINGLOCK!

Education (KARE), a non-profit corporation founded to oppose the new airport. She is not alone in her desire to stop the airport. Rockville Township Supervisor Gerald Benge said that "85 percent of the people here oppose this idea." The Farmers' Protective Organization and Will County Farm Bureau Board have joined the fray.

KARE's findings show that a new airport would bring more than just new jobs. With them would come more air pollution, creation of solid-waste disposal problems, injury to the area's wildlife, excessive noise levels, higher crime rates, pollution of the pristine Kankakee River, and increased taxes. The new airport would forever disrupt the lives of some farmers by forcing them to move, as well as destroying the quality of life for those who must remain.

"The O'Hare Citizens Coalition said the residents there should not have to sell their homes, period," said Weidner. "They insist that the solution is to build a new airport and tough luck for each and every resident and farmer who must leave home, family heritage, way of life, and livelihood. In other words, they don't want to leave their homes, but we are expected to sacrifice ours."

The first public assembly held on the topic, in Rockville Township, drew such an overwhelming turnout that the meeting room turned out to be too small and the crowd moved outdoors. Everett J. Quigley, KARE's first chairman, submitted 70 questions about the airport to planners. He has never received a response.

"You don't need to be a brain surgeon to foresee the new problems this huge airport would create," said Steve Granger of Bourbonnais, another rural community near Kankakee.

The citizen opposition brought results. "We have been ef-

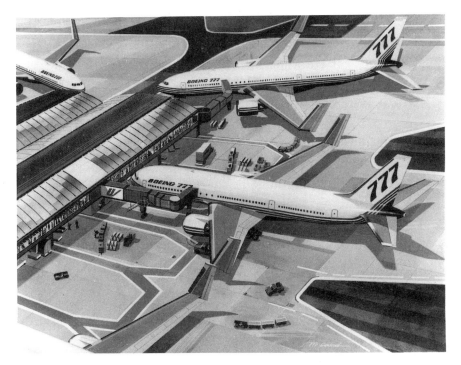

Taxpayers heavily subsidize commercial jetliners, including the new Boeing 777. The wide-body twinjet, to be delivered to airlines beginning in the first half of 1995, offers costly technological advances financed through several federal agencies. *(Boeing Commercial Airplanes)*

fective, so far, in stopping legislation to establish an airport authority in the Kankakee River Valley," said Weidner.

Helping the opponents was an Illinois Development Finance Authority study that questioned the need for a third airport. David Elsner of the *Chicago Tribune* wrote: "In addition to expressing concerns about projected air-travel demand, the report says economic benefits connected to the airport may have been exaggerated and costs underestimated." The study cast serious doubts on estimates that the airport would bring as much as $4.3 billion a year to the area's economy.

WINGLOCK!

The new Chicago-area airport won't be located near Peotone if the Residents United to Retain Agricultural Land (RURAL), headed by Carol Henrichs, have their say. At one forum, Jim Cavanaugh, a RURAL board member, said, "The issue is quality of life. I moved here because I love the serenity. If I wanted to live by an airport, I would have moved near O'Hare."

Sam Morris of the Plum Creek Animal Hospital brought an injured red-tailed hawk to a RURAL meeting to dramatize the need to protect endangered species from an airport. Charles and Arlene Moore from Grant Park showed a 12-minute film of the noise and commotion of takeoffs at O'Hare. After the runway scenes, their film closed with pastoral views that the audience recognized. "Scenes like these would be ended forever," he said.

Even the Peotone School Board got into the act by voting unanimously to oppose all nearby sites for the proposed airport. Superintendent Allen Hall said he could not see how a super-airport would benefit his school district in any way.

In the late 1980s, people who opposed highway or airport construction were said to be expressing the NIMBY syndrome, or "Not In My Back Yard." They were criticized for blindly opposing airports or highways in their neighborhoods with little or no consideration for the needs of the traveling public.

Anti-airport leaders like Gloria Weidner cannot be accused of that. They recognize that growing transport needs must be met and suggest that alternatives to airports—like Supertrains —be considered. Her thinking has spread to national environmental organizations. For example, the Sierra Club's Illinois chapter questions the need for another airport, instead suggesting a maglev network or "an efficient rail system such as those existing in France and Japan."

"High-tech rail or magnetic levitation would effectively fit into our transportation scheme," said Weidner. "The Illinois DOT, still in the Stone Age, has not included high-speed rail as part of the study process in solving Chicagoland's air and highway gridlock."

Her view was similar to that of Chicago's Anthony Haswell, who has argued for a network of Midwest high-speed trains. "At O'Hare, invariably if a fly lands on the runway it screws everything up," he said.

Probably not until 1993 will the site for a new airport be known, especially since additional thought is being given to turning Milwaukee's General Mitchell Field into a super-airport. Some residents there, however, oppose that plan, too.

Airports are considered to be a scourge elsewhere, and New York is a prime example. Officials have scoured the area for 30 years, looking for an acceptable site for a new airport. It's been said that the region will never build a new airport or even another runway.

The "Great American Airport Revolt" has spread to the South. In Atlanta's northern suburbs, groups have formed to oppose each of the three sites proposed for a new airport. In the placid Pacific northwest, two opposition groups have organized near the Seattle-Tacoma Airport—Citizens for Alternatives to Sea-Tac Expansion and the Seattle Noise Abatement Group. Partly because of such resistance, the FAA's administrator for the northwest region, Fred Isaac, said that he sees the possibility of only three new airports in the nation being built—Denver, Chicago, and Austin, Texas.

Even renovations have been resisted, as illustrated by the criticism heaped on a $600-million plan for Washington National Airport. "The new National will be more threatening environmentally and less safe," said Sherwin Landfield, a member of

Citizens Against Airport Noise. "More planes, wide-body turbulence, more night flights, and reverse thrust on landing guarantee it."

America could relieve airport congestion by building Supertrain lines as suggested by the engineers and economists at the Argonne National Laboratory. There, Larry Johnson says that savings in fuel, along with savings from abandoning airport construction plans, should be sufficient to pay for the cost of a 300-mph maglev system linking airports in many major cities from 100 to 600 miles apart.

— — —

Support for Supertrains by some aviation and airport officials and Argonne researchers does not mean the millennium has arrived. A few in aviation bitterly oppose construction of Supertrain systems: Southwest Airlines is the primary foe.

Southwest Airlines Chairman Herbert Kelleher is well liked by his employees and peers. Doug Carroll, writing in *USA Today*, said Southwest, a no-frills airline, painted one airplane to look like a killer whale. Kelleher, who keeps a closet full of costumes, has broken the ice with his crews by boarding aircraft dressed as the Easter bunny or a leprechaun.

Kelleher, however, could well don a Frankenstein costume when he discusses the Texas high-speed rail line proposed to link some of the cities his airline serves. "Everywhere I went, I had two lobbyists from Southwest Airlines following me, opposing everything I said," declared Pike Powers, an Austin lawyer who lobbied to create the Texas High Speed Rail Authority.

Kelleher once was an independent-minded David fighting the Goliath of entrenched aviation interests. He offered lower fares to travelers, and for that reason he's still a Texas-sized

THE AVIATION INDUSTRY'S GRAVY PLANE

Figures in billions of dollars

	Aviation taxes and user fees	Net general FAA spending	Taxpayer costs
1980	$1.874	$3.136	$1.262
1981	0.021	3.158	3.137
1982	0.133	3.134	3.001
1983	2.165	4.269	2.104
1984	2.499	4.651	2.152
1985	2.851	5.355	2.504
1986	2.736	4.872	2.136
1987	3.060	4.946	1.886
1988	3.189	5.191	2.002
1989	3.688	5.769	2.081
Total	$22.216	$44.481	$22.265

Source : Office of Management and Budget

Total FAA Outlays by Source, 1971-1988

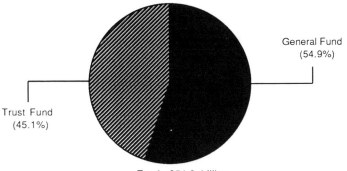

General Fund (54.9%)

Trust Fund (45.1%)

Total: $54.9 billion

Taxpayers have paid through the general fund nearly $22.3 billion of the FAA's spending over a nine-year period and another $22.2 billion in user fee taxes, according to the Office of Management and Budget. Another study by the Congressional Budget Office concluded that, over a 17-year period, direct subsidies paid 54.9 percent of the FAA's costs. Not included in either study are massive government handouts through aircraft research and development, pilot training, state aid, municipal backing for bond financing packages, and other programs vital to aviation. *(Congressional Budget Office)*

WINGLOCK!

hero to many. The airline has grown and offers up to 78 flights daily between Dallas and Houston. Southwest's success is partially due to the taxpayers since the Texas Aeronautics Commission went all the way to the United States Supreme Court to fight for the company's certificate.

"I can't tell you how many hours of employee time and travel and this sort of thing that went into that process," said C. A. "Clay" Wilkins, executive director of the Texas Department of Aviation. "There were hundreds and hundreds of hours that were spent during the hearing process, the regulatory process, to give them that authority."

Texas has done much more for the airlines than it has done for Supertrains. Despite that, Kelleher is behaving like the Goliath, ready to stomp on infant high-speed train proposals. His airline is now officially recognized as a "major," meaning its annual sales surpass $1 billion, and it has the means to delay Supertrain development.

Kelleher and his assistants called the Supertrain idea "ill-conceived" and said "we do not think the State of Texas should create a new transportation business, heavily subsidized with state tax monies, to compete with private enterprise." The airline questioned why passengers would desert air travel for high-speed rail, which it called an "untested and arguably *less safe* mode."

To claim that the Supertrains are less safe than flying is a mind-boggling inaccuracy. No means of travel on earth is as safe as the Japanese Bullet Trains and the French TGVs. Such trains, running for more than 25 years, have carried three billion riders and have *never* had a single passenger fatality. Every year, however, hundreds of airline passengers die in tragic accidents.

Southwest Airlines also has tried to obscure the merits of the steel-wheel Supertrain plan in Texas by arguing that it is "outdated" and should be delayed. Kelleher said a high-speed train would be a "Conestoga wagon with lights" and argued that Texas should wait and build a maglev system at some unknown future date. The statement was a clear attempt to split Texas' pro-Supertrain forces, but it failed.

"Our agency is charged with responding to critical transportation needs of the present, by comparing the costs and values of existing technology versus emerging technology," said Bob Neely, executive director of the Texas High Speed Rail Authority. "Our state does not wish to be an experimental proving ground for any technology; we want a successful operating system which can meet the critical transport needs of today."

Former Houston Metro Transit chairman Bob Lanier opposed the delay, saying, "If the private sector has a proposal that can be paid for and work today, let them go today. I wouldn't see not building a bank because they're going to have better banking 15 years from now."

When one argument failed to hold, Kelleher would try another. At one point, he threatened that if high-speed trains ever operate in Texas "the location of our corporate headquarters [in Dallas] would have to be reevaluated."

Like a barroom brawler picking a fight, the airline wouldn't stop with its arrogant accusations. It falsely claimed that "Commercial aviation is a self-supporting system" and it does not want to compete with "subsidized" high-speed trains.

That stance conveniently overlooked the massive free government handouts the airlines enjoy. If anything, the airlines seem to believe that the government owes them. In 1988, the powerful aviation lobby launched a two-year national lobbying campaign to persuade Congress to support big increases in tax-funded air-system improvements.

Conducted under the auspices of a group named the Partnership for Improved Air Travel, whose $10 million in funding comes from the big airlines and aircraft companies, the slick campaign ignores general-fund subsidies to aviation. In a 266-page "study" about the economic impact of aviation, the word "subsidy" is not mentioned once. A reader poring over data would never even get a hint about the billions in federal and state tax dollars the public shells out to aviation.

The chairman of this pro-aviation subsidy lobbying effort is none other than anti-Supertrain zealot Herb Kelleher of Southwest Airlines, who has served as the group's chief spokesman since 1988.

While the Partnership wants more aviation spending, it doesn't want higher taxes. Late in 1990, with public spending on airports increasing dramatically, with the nation's deficit at record levels, and with United States troops headed to the Persian Gulf, Kelleher opposed proposed increases in airline ticket and fuel taxes.

Those in favor of aviation subsidies know they have the upper hand in Washington. Remember that Congress treats airline ticket taxes as "trust fund dollars" to be spent only on aviation, while Congress never thought twice about putting railroad ticket taxes into the general fund, some of which went to new airports and other aviation programs.

Kelleher's group also wants the federal government to reduce the surplus in the aviation trust fund, but not everyone in the nation's capital agrees. W. David Montgomery of the

Congressional Budget Office (CBO) pointed out such arguments were not well founded. The trust fund surplus, said the CBO, is an illusion because "private-sector users of the aviation system, including airlines, have received more in capital and operating spending than they have paid in taxes."

Disregarding that statement from Congressional researchers, Kelleher wrote in the *New York Times* that "the squeaking of the aviation 'wheel' is going to get louder and louder."

The industry is quite prepared to make demands, especially after Kelleher and presidents of other major airlines met behind closed doors at 8:30 A.M. on April 12, 1988, at Washington's National Press Club. At a "mock press conference," they were coached on how to lobby for more aviation subsidies. The briefers were from Boeing and the public relations firm Burson-Marsteller, among others.

Right on cue—at a Partnership news conference held at 11:30 A.M. that same day—Kelleher complained that no new major airport had been built since Dallas-Fort Worth in 1974 and that existing runways are not being expanded fast enough.

Yet, when in Texas, Kelleher said just the opposite. To justify his opposition to Supertrains, Kelleher told Texans that airport capacity there was sufficient to carry more passengers. Those statements weren't true as illustrated by ample evidence in Dallas, Houston, and Austin.

In Kelleher's back yard, officials are trying to expand the Dallas-Fort Worth Airport, over community objections. "The developers of Dallas-Fort Worth International Airport (DFW) thought they had planned the airport of the future in 1974 when they located the facility in the middle of nowhere on more than twice the acreage of O'Hare," wrote Patricia M. Szymczak in the

Chicago Tribune. "But today, only 15 years later, several communities neighboring DFW are fighting the airport on the issue of expansion. They don't want two new runways built."

Apparently, Kelleher wasn't on the flight in March 1990 that carried Senator Harry Reid to Nevada. The senator's story: "I left Washington at five o'clock in the afternoon, arrived in Reno 15 hours later. Why? Because I flew into Dallas, landed on the airfield, and waited 3½ hours to get a gate. Weather? There wasn't a cloud in the sky. I don't know what the problem was, but we waited in that airplane for 3½ hours. We were told they had 35 gates for 120-some-odd airplanes. Well, air traffic congestion is not a figment of our imagination, those of us who travel the country—and those of us in the Senate do that—it's a real serious problem."

Increasingly, thousands of other travelers risk such inconvenience at the Dallas-Fort Worth Airport, which in 1989 served almost 47.6 million passengers, a 7.5 percent increase over the prior year. The growth was so dramatic that it caused the airport to leapfrog over Atlanta and Los Angeles to grab the distinction of being the second busiest airport in the world, next to O'Hare.

Patronage at DFW and Love Field in Dallas is expected to continually rise through 2005, and "the City of Dallas has already initiated discussion of building an additional air carrier airport," reported the Texas Department of Aviation in a planning document.

The Transportation Department in Washington has warned that delays to Houston's airport could exceed 20,000 hours a year by 1997. In Austin, a new airport is planned because the old one lacks sufficient capacity. All told, the story was the antithesis of Kelleher's statements at the staged Washington press conference.

Aviation's high-visibility "we want more money" campaign is a bit unusual for the industry, whose leaders prefer that budgets for highways or Amtrak be under the spotlight of public debate, not the bountiful aviation subsidies that come in many forms. Aviation's tactics also take nerve. Kelleher has complained that "peddlers" were trying to sell high-speed trains. "It's like Boeing came to Texas and said, 'Guys, we've got this great idea—you spend $6 billion building airports and we'll sell more planes.'" Kelleher won't admit it, but that's exactly what Boeing is doing through the Partnership for Improved Air Travel.

If Americans examine the economics of aviation, they will see that the airlines, along with aircraft builders, component manufacturers, and airport planners, all share a common benefactor —they flew to success on the wings of billions of dollars in taxpayers' subsidies. The airline-airport-aerospace industrial complex masquerades extremely well as private enterprise; however, the money from Washington and the states means that the nation has government-funded aviation infrastructure.

"The Federal Aviation Administration estimates that 85 percent of its expenditures are on behalf of private users and that the government and public interest share of its costs is 15 percent," said the CBO's David Montgomery.

If the airlines were required to pay the cost of the air traffic control system, just as Amtrak must pay *all* the costs of its Boston–Washington train traffic control system, the airline industry would operate at a *multi-billion dollar loss*. For example, in 1989, the federal taxpayer paid $3 billion in general revenues toward air traffic control, about three times more than the combined net profit of the industry.

Airline subsidies are irrefutable. Putting it simply—here is what the government does that helps the airlines and aircraft manufacturers:

It provides the complex FAA air traffic control system and personnel; it reduces infrastructure expenses and what would be horrific borrowing costs thanks to the aviation trust fund; it subsidizes the so-called Essential Air Service Program to allow flights to small towns; it pays for FAA and NASA research, which helps in designing jetliners; and it spends big on Department of Defense research that brings priceless spinoff technology for commercial jetliners.

There's more: The federal government pays to train thousands of military pilots annually, many of whom shift to airline employment, and it has issued subsidized loans to airlines buying new aircraft. Also, co-production of commercial and military aircraft on the same lines brings lower costs to the airlines buying jetliners.

The operators, promoters, or designers of passenger train systems have had these options closed to them. The one limited exception is the government's subsidy to Amtrak, which started a half-century later than aviation subsidies. The amounts to Amtrak pale in comparison to the billions flowing into aviation.

The government has been helping to shape aviation since 1920, when the United States Air Mail Service was started. The Air Mail Act of 1925 and the Commerce Act of 1926 broadened the federal role to that of a promoter of aviation. Payments to airmail carriers exceeded estimated airmail revenue in 1929 by nearly $7 million. In 1930 Congress passed the Waters Act that provided aviation's pioneers with liberalized compensation for carrying mail.

More help from Washington came in 1938 when the Civil Aeronautics Act set up two new institutions—an air traffic con-

Travelers are frustrated with ground, runway, and airspace congestion at airports. Delays getting into airfield parking lots are common, as well as passing through security, on takeoff, and also on landing. California's Angie Papadakis coined the term "winglock" to describe growing congestion at airports.

trol service, based in part on towers taken over from private operators during the 1930s, and the Civil Aeronautics Board to undertake economic and safety regulation.

Aviation's Kelleher, in his blind opposition to Texas Supertrains, ignores governmental subsidizing of aviation. When it came to spending for airports, he even went so far as to tell *Houston Post* reporter Ken Herman that "It is true that some airports have been financed with revenue bonds which are paid off by the airlines. But there is not a tax dollar that has ever gone into them."

That's quite a claim, considering that the Texas Department

WINGLOCK!

of Aviation has a program scheduled to last through 1995 to spend millions of tax dollars to improve the state's airports. More striking is that Washington has paid to develop airports since the end of World War II when many military airfields were declared surplus and turned over to local governments, with the federal government's continued financial assistance, of course. Several legislative acts set up and perpetuated taxpayer support, beginning with the Federal Airport Act of 1946. The resulting aid paid for nearly half the capital spending on airports between 1947 and 1969.

"We are sort of a sugar daddy to provide federal grants to stimulate the development of airports throughout the United States," said FAA official John Rodgers. That statement would startle President Eisenhower, who once declared, "The federal government did not build the terminals for either the railways or the buses; I see no reason for doing it for the air terminals."

An example of federal largess can be found in Orlando, Florida, where McCoy Air Force Base was converted to civil aviation use. Few vacationing families touching down on 12,000-foot parallel runways realize the facility originally was built for B-52s.

In the North, Stewart International Airport in Newburgh, New York, is making its transformation from an air force base, assisted by a $5 million "military airport grant" from DOT Secretary Skinner. In the West, a more contemporary example is Grant County Airport in Moses Lake, Washington, formerly Larson Air Force Base, which was developed by the government in 1948, deactivated by the Air Force in 1964, and may be turned into a new superairport late in the 1990s. As many as a dozen other air bases are candidates for conversion to commercial airports.

While combined federal and local funding was pouring into various kinds of airports, railroads were disadvantaged all across the nation as they paid heavy real estate taxes on their passenger terminals.

"In February 1957, the Pennsylvania Railroad's employee magazine groused that Washington National Airport had been built with $36 million in taxpayer support and since 1941 had accumulated an operating deficit of $4 million, yet paid no taxes itself," wrote Dan Cupper in *Trains* magazine. "By contrast, the railroad said, Union Station and its supporting facilities, built with private capital and valued at about $32 million, were assessed during the same period for more than $6.9 million in property and income taxes, paid to the District of Columbia and the federal government."

High-speed intercity HSST-300 can be used for shuttle service between outlying airports and cities. The "300" stands for kilometers per hour, and that translates to 186.4 mph. This technology is being considered to connect Los Angeles International Airport with a proposed superairport at Palmdale.

(HSST Corporation)

WINGLOCK!

The problem was more severe in other cities. The Pennsylvania Railroad modernized its Pittsburgh station in the 1950s, only to see the tax increased on its improved property. Then, the railroad complained, Allegheny County spent those taxes to improve the Greater Pittsburgh International Airport. It was estimated that, in 1955 alone, the railroads paid $92 million in taxes on passenger-related facilities, most of it in state and local property taxes. Over the years, railroads have paid billions in such taxes.

Costly federal handouts to aviation are America's most entrenched and systemic subsidies. The government programs, continued over decades, are spread through so many accounts that they are difficult to pin down; however, Warren T. Brookes, a Washington-based syndicated economics writer, took the trouble to calculate them. He found that since 1980, the FAA spent $44.5 billion for aviation projects of one sort or another, but that airlines and general aviation paid only $22.2 billion in taxes and user fees to the aviation trust fund. "The taxpayers paid the other $22.3 billion, slightly over half," wrote Brookes, "a gravy plane ride on the general taxpayers."

Newspapers often focus on the subsidy to Amtrak, but in 1990, for every dollar of expense, Amtrak covered 72 cents of it from revenues and 28 cents from the federal government. Aviation costs soak up a greater percentage of tax—50 cents on the dollar after taking into account fees paid into the aviation trust fund.

Subsidies to aviation have been exposed before. In 1978, the director of the California Department of Transportation, Adriana Gianturco, told Congress that "air travelers pay only one-third the cost of their transportation. If the United States were to remove its subsidies to the airlines, very quickly the airplane would be threatened as a means of travel."

Aviation subsidies could skyrocket. How much? Fasten your seat belt. The American Association of State Highway and Transportation Officials (AASHTO), in looking at public spending for aviation between 1991 and 2000, concluded that $116.9 billion would be needed, "although inflation and the costs for new hub airports could well increase this figure." AASHTO's researchers uncovered numerous government accounts, and their review was the first to combine all federal aviation efforts in one document.

The federal government's aviation spending in nine years could equal what it would spend on Amtrak for the next 195 years, at Amtrak's current levels. Putting it another way, the United States would spend more than 1½ times on aviation what *all European nations combined* would spend on their far-reaching web of international Supertrains, tracks, tunnels, signals, stations, and so forth. The Congressional Budget Office issued a report agreeing with AASHTO and economist Brookes.

Another example of tax support to aviation is the Essential Air Service Program, where service to rural communities with a tiny trickle of customers is subsidized by the federal government's general fund. While such a program might be justified in remote Alaska, it is not elsewhere.

For example, at Manitowoc, Wisconsin, an average of one person daily boards a flight. The fare is $89, but that traveler's trip is subsidized by $515, or an astounding 578.7 percent of the cost. Is Manitowoc a remote community? Hardly—it's a mere 39 miles from Green Bay, which in itself is a small airline hub. Similar circumstances can be cited in Moultrie, Georgia; Kokomo, Indiana; and dozens of other communities.

"The Essential Air Services program is one of the better pieces of pork-barrel legislation in Washington and, despite the deficit problem, few in Congress are likely to vote it out of busi-

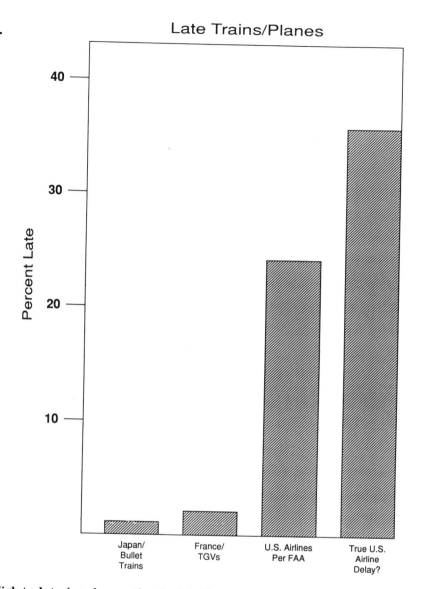

Late Trains/Planes

Percent Late

| Japan/ Bullet Trains | France/ TGVs | U.S. Airlines Per FAA | True U.S. Airline Delay? |

High-tech trains observe the clock. This graph compares late Supertrains in Japan and France with United States airline performance. The FAA data is deceptive, however, because it fails to count as late any flights that are delayed by mechanical problems, about 23,000 per month. Also, a portion of flights that are shown as "late" really were cancelled outright, which happens 4,700 times every month. In contrast, in 1990, when a Bullet Train was late, it was late an average of *90 seconds.*

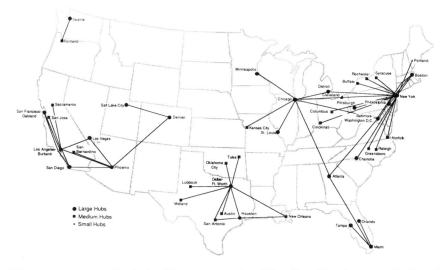

These are the top 50 air traffic routes under 600 miles. The Argonne National Laboratory, in a 1989 report, recommended that maglev Supertrain networks be built to handle part of this traffic. *(Argonne National Laboratory)*

ness," said Kathryn B. Creedy, owner of Global Airline Enterprises. Indeed, the Bush Administration has proposed an increase in the program.

This type of direct subsidy to airlines—$25 million in 1989—is nothing new and it contributed to the decline in rail service. The chairman of the Interstate Commerce Commission, in Senate testimony in 1963, said the effect of such subsidies was "devastating" to the New Haven Railroad where it competed against Allegheny Airlines (now USAir).

In 1963, the airline received $6 million, or 24 percent of its revenue, in direct subsidies from the federal government. How many passengers did it carry to earn that subsidy? Only 1.1 million. In that year, the New Haven, with no comparable public help, carried more than 25 million passengers. Small wonder that the New Haven Railroad went bankrupt.

WINGLOCK!

The airlines have had government help in purchasing aircraft. In the 1960s the Civil Aeronautics Board guaranteed loans of as much as $5 million to buy aircraft for local air service. A vestige of the program remains in the 1990 budget to allow the Treasury to cover the costs of aircraft loan defaults.

Aviation's spending spree with taxpayers' dollars will continue. President Bush's 1990 budget called for a 14 percent increase in funding the FAA's day-to-day operations, to a record $3.9 billion, and a 45 percent jump in funding for FAA facilities and equipment. The agency became one of the fastest growing accounts in the Federal budget.

Money also pours out of state coffers to help aviation. Texas, the stronghold for Kelleher's Southwest Airlines, has spent about $1.3 billion in public funds annually on airports. "All the money for aviation development has come from the general fund," said Clay Wilkins of the state's aviation department. "We have no aircraft licensing, no airport licensing, no aircrew licensing, no aviation fuels tax." Texas is the only state without any type of aviation fuels tax. Like most states, however, Texas doesn't spend a dime to improve rail passenger service.

— — —

The United States gives lavish help to its aircraft builders under many guises. Generous subsidies exist for aircraft research and development, the biggest beneficiary of which is also the world's biggest maker of commercial jetliners—Boeing. It manufactures more aircraft than McDonnell Douglas and Airbus combined. The hump-backed silhouette of the Boeing 747 is known throughout the world, and the workhorses for many airlines are the company's narrow-body 727s, 737s, and 757s, and wide-body 767s.

Even if all planned capacity improvements are made, 33 airports are forecast to exceed 20,000 hours of annual delays to aircraft in 1997. Multiplied by the number of passengers waiting aboard airplanes and in terminals, delays could run into millions of person-hours annually. *(Federal Aviation Administration)*

Now comes the Boeing 777, a new jetliner. The Boeing 777 will be a twin-aisle twinjet, with a range of seating from six to 10 abreast. The wide-body aircraft, scheduled for delivery by 1995, could carry as many as 400 passengers. Boeing needs it to compete with the Airbus A-330 twinjet and the McDonnell Douglas MD-11 trijet.

A significant amount of Boeing money will go into that program, but so will government money. Boeing is building the largest structural parts ever made from composite materials for the high-tech B-2, a $75-billion aircraft program. "We've made some very important advances in aircraft technology that could be used for commercial aircraft," Dale G. Shellhorn, Boeing's B-2 project manager told *Aviation Week*. "There is talk about making the entire tail section of the 777 from composites."

Overall, how much of the Boeing 777 development costs will be paid by the shareholders and how much by the federal government? It's impossible to say, unless the government commissions a special investigation—an action that may be warranted, considering the many hidden subsidies Boeing receives.

Alleged violations of international trade agreements have caused Airbus, a European consortium, to complain that United States taxpayers help pay jetliner development costs. In 1988, Airbus completed a study alleging that "over the past ten years, the United States government has provided approximately $23 billion in identifiable direct and indirect financial support of a subsidy nature to Boeing and McDonnell Douglas."

Trying to defend its domestic companies, the United States government shot back that Airbus has enjoyed $15.3 billion in aid over a 20-year period from European governments, or $25.9 billion if interest is included. In reality, it wasn't a debate of free enterprise versus subsidies, but rather a case of who gets the bigger subsidies.

Defense contracts helped give birth to existing civilian aircraft. A look at only two of Boeing's products is instructive.

Boeing 747: Airbus points out that "the same teams who worked on the design for the Air Force's giant C-5 transport devoted their talents to jumbo commercial jets like the Boeing 747."

Boeing 707: "The Boeing 707 was the first successful United States jet transport," according to *Aviation Week*. "Its development was aided by work done by Boeing on the KC-135 tanker for the United States Air Force."

Such underwriting by Defense budgets of the costs of developing aviation technology for eventual commercial use continues unabated today, as this example published by *Aviation Week* early in 1990 clearly shows: "The V-22 tilt-rotor aircraft will be dead as a commercial vehicle if the Defense Department drops it,

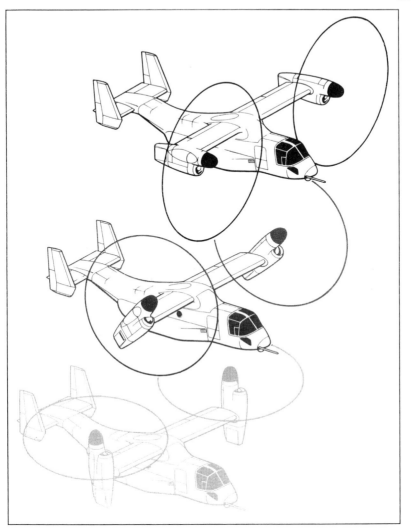

This tilt-rotor aircraft is destined to fail commercially unless propped up with tax dollars. Defense Secretary Richard B. Cheney wants to kill the V-22, also known as the Osprey, a $28 billion program. Congressional friends of aerospace interests say defense dollars should be spent to develop it anyway, even though most benefits will go to aircraft manufacturers and airlines. The FAA and NASA also pay into V-22 research and development, a wasteful effort. If presented with a choice, most passengers would avoid the tilt-rotor with its small seats and helicopter-like ride in favor of fixed-wing aircraft or Supertrains.

(Federal Aviation Administration)

WINGLOCK!

according to FAA Administrator Busey. He said the V-22 could expand capacity in short-haul markets, 'but it won't happen unless the Defense Department develops and proves the technology.' "

The V-22, also known as the *Osprey*, is a Marine Corps aircraft that can take off vertically, like a helicopter, then swing its rotor blades downward into horizontal position to serve as propellers for forward flight. The process is reversed on landing, permitting a helicopter-style descent. Although advertised as "affordable" by aerospace companies, taxpayers would pay $28 billion for 650 Ospreys.

Even the Pentagon found it excessive and wanted out. In 1989 Defense Secretary Richard B. Cheney began pleading with Congress to allow him to drop the V-22 as part of proposed cuts. Despite the repeated outcries about wasting money, Congressman James L. Oberstar, the chairman of the House Public Works and Transportation Aviation subcommittee, said, "We ought to just take defense dollars and admit that the principal benefit of the tilt-rotor is for civilian use."

Despite generous defense spending, other government aid supports the V-22 coast to coast. The FAA studies special tilt-rotor air traffic control systems in its Atlantic City Research Center while it finances a study of V-22 marketability in California. Also, NASA provides research into the V-22's aerodynamics, which are unstable. In New Castle, Delaware, on June 11, 1991, a V-22 hovering about 15 feet off the ground tipped to one side and crashed.

Defense contracts also help keep costs down on production lines when military and commercial jetliners are built together. The 707, still built today in a version for Airborne Warning And Control Systems (AWACS) and the joint Air Force-Army Joint STARS program, is assembled on the same line in Renton, Wash-

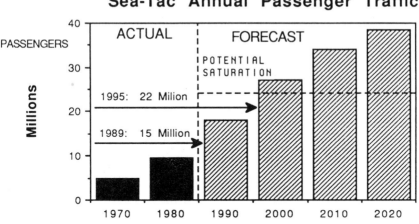

Sea-Tac Annual Passenger Traffic

The forecast for Seattle-Tacoma International Airport shows traffic rapidly nearing the saturation point. This is typical of the capacity constraints facing America's largest airports. *(State of Washington House of Representatives)*

ington, as Boeing's other narrow-body aircraft, helping to lower price tags for the company's 737s and 757s.

Military and NASA programs continually develop costly technology that finds its way into commercial aircraft. Breakthroughs worth billions of dollars have included landing gear, complex cockpit and electronics systems, streamlined aerodynamic shapes, new metals and composite materials, advanced gyroscopes, new fuels and engines, fail-proof alert systems, and more.

"Ever since the Wright brothers got off the ground, the military potential of the airplane has been obvious, and military aircraft continue to lead the way in developing advanced capabilities," wrote *Aviation Week*'s Breck W. Henderson. "Aerospace engineers who want to work at the leading edge of their profession have few choices other than military aircraft programs."

Federal contributions to the art and science of aircraft build-

WINGLOCK!

ing are huge, which explains why most of the $41.5 billion defense research and development budget in 1990—*one year alone*—went to aircraft and aerospace companies.

Boeing and McDonnell Douglas are working for NASA on a new 1,850-mph supersonic vehicle, named the High-Speed Civil Transport. Developing one working aircraft could cost up to $15 billion, enough to build several fully complete Supertrain systems. In a different effort, the Congress has appropriated $574 million in research for the National Aerospace Plane, also known as the X-30. Aviation, however, would not see these as any form of subsidy; and whatever the merits of these aircraft, they will do nothing to untangle domestic gridlock or winglock.

Critics of Amtrak fail to recognize that Amtrak buys locomotives and cars from companies that have received no government funding for research and development. In effect, airlines buy subsidized products; Amtrak doesn't have that option.

Taxpayers help aviation in still one other major way: most commercial aircraft pilots are trained by the Air Force, Navy, Marines, or Army. "In 1988, 69 percent of the hires at major airlines were ex-military pilots," said Wendell H. Ford, chairman of the Senate aviation committee. Government-financed training has been a windfall worth several billion dollars to all airlines.

"Aviation is proof that given the will, we have the capacity to achieve the impossible," said Eddie Rickenbacker, World War I hero and founder of Eastern Airlines. He could have said, more accurately: "Aviation is proof that given *limitless subsidies*, we have the capacity to achieve the impossible." The aviation system is not paying its way, period. Too bad more taxpayers are not aware of that fact.

Think of the train network the United States might enjoy today had the federal government lavished money and attention

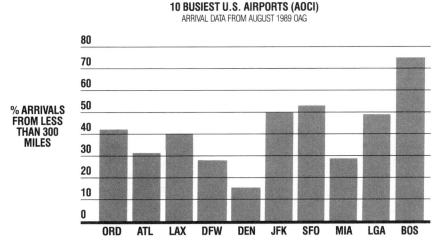

LOTS OF AIRPLANES . . . DON'T GO VERY FAR!

10 BUSIEST U.S. AIRPORTS (AOCI)
ARRIVAL DATA FROM AUGUST 1989 OAG

% ARRIVALS FROM LESS THAN 300 MILES

ORD ATL LAX DFW DEN JFK SFO MIA LGA BOS

Many airplanes don't go very far. This shows the percentage of arrivals from points less than 300 miles away to the 10 busiest airports in the United States during just one month, August 1989. Diversion of traffic to Supertrains can reduce the pressure, particularly during critical peak hours when airports are less safe. *(Data from* Official Airline Guide*)*

on Supertrains as it has, decade after decade, on aviation. Far-reaching programs would have brought intense research into high-speed equipment, construction of hundreds of high-technology trains per year, new stations and high-speed tracks, all perhaps superior to France's TGV trains or Japan's maglev technologies.

Is it any wonder that in the last half century aircraft rose to new technological heights while American trains stayed about the same? Is it startling that in early 1991 Boeing alone had a $102-billion order backlog for nearly 1,800 commercial airliners while not a single United States-owned passenger railcar manufacturer remained in business? With subsidies pouring into aviation from every direction, is it surprising that people shifted

WINGLOCK!

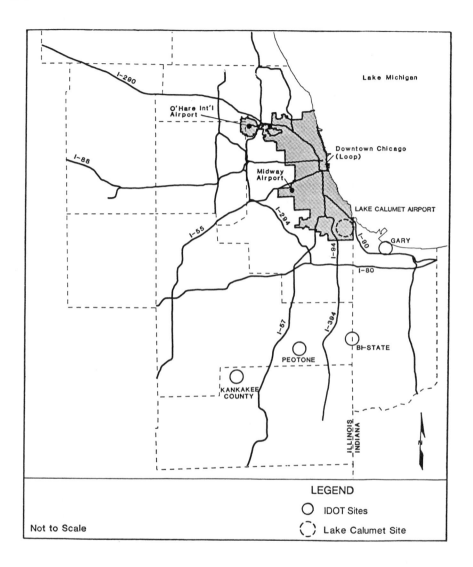

LEGEND

○ IDOT Sites

⊙ Lake Calumet Site

Not to Scale

The Great American Airport Revolt of the '90s has started in Chicago, where there's opposition to expansion of O'Hare International and to proposed new superairports. Numerous groups are decrying the proposed displacement of residents and disruption of the environment. Three sites are in Illinois, in Kankakee, Peotone, and the southeastern part of Chicago. The fourth, Bi-State, is on the Illinois-Indiana border, while the fifth is Gary Municipal Airport. The new airport, if built, would not be completed until 2020. About 42 percent of all flights at O'Hare travel to points less than 300 miles away—the ideal market for Supertrains. A Supertrain network would greatly diminish the need for a new airport. *(Lake Calumet Airport Feasibility Study)*

to air travel—even in short-distance, crowded corridors where trains will always make more sense?

American aviation can no longer ignore the growing drumbeat of the "Great American Airport Revolt" and the growing public interest in Supertrains. Boeing's overseas competitor takes an open minded approach to high-speed trains: "Airbus Industrie's view is that improved train services do not necessarily compete with air travel but in many cases complement it," wrote Arthur Reed in *Air Transport World*. He went on to report that Jan Carlzon, president of Scandinavian Airlines, took a similar view, saying, "I am generally in favor of a high-speed train network for Europe." In mid-1991, Air Canada Chairman Claude Taylor said his company and CP rail will jointly examine the possibility of operating Supertrains on Canada's busy Quebec-Ontario corridor.

Aviation in the United States has to make up its mind. Will it follow Southwest Airlines' Herb Kelleher and fight Supertrains in a knee-jerk fashion? Or will the industry listen to its own experts, people like USAir's Edwin Colodny, Lufthansa's Joseph Zucker, and former FAA administrator Lynn Helms who all say trains are the answer to airport congestion?

WINGLOCK!

TRAINS: SPARING ENVIRONMENTAL HARM

"If ever there were a time to suggest that Ohio needs an electrically-powered high-speed rail system, that time is now. Once again we find that the mobility of our citizens is threatened by the unpredictable political developments of a distant unstable region."
—Ohio State Senator Robert J. Boggs, speaking six days after Iraq invaded Kuwait

THE NATION SHOULD BE LOOKING FOR A WAY TO move travelers between its largest cities by energy-efficient Supertrains, minimizing consumption of gasoline and jet fuel. America's insatiable appetite for petroleum is shocking. The United States has only two percent of the world's population, but consumes a quarter of the world's oil. The nation, which uses more oil than any other, blew a colossal $1.1 trillion of its wealth on oil imports between 1970 and 1989.

Overdependence on gas-guzzling automobiles and fuel-gulping jetliners leaves America open to the threat of fuel shortages that could devastate the economy. The country remains painfully vulnerable to disruptions in supplies from the Middle East,

where undependable or even hostile powers control oil wells. Many Arab states remain as unstable in the 1990s as they were during the two energy crisis periods of the 1970s.

In August 1990, Iraqi President Saddam Hussein ordered a massive invasion force to take control of Kuwait, which he later annexed. Soon after, the United Nations Security Council's worldwide embargo on trade with Iraq and Kuwait removed about 4.5 million barrels of oil from the world's daily supply. The United States worried that gasoline supplies would be disrupted by the embargo and the outbreak of war.

Even though the quantity of oil was cut only marginally, the world's refinery capacity was reduced when Kuwait's sizable, sophisticated gasoline refineries were shut down.

At the time of the invasion, America was continuing to use oil extravagantly, not having learned from previous lessons. Twice in the 1970s the United States suffered an energy crisis that sent shock waves through the world economy. The first resulted from the outbreak of the Arab-Israeli War in October 1973, when members of the Organization of Petroleum Exporting Countries (OPEC) imposed an oil embargo against the western countries and cut back production. Prices on the world market tripled, from around $4 per barrel to more than $12 per barrel.

The second crisis resulted from unrest in Iran that halted as much as 6 million barrels of that country's average daily production from November 1978 through April 1979. This short-fall, by mid-1980, caused prices to more than double from $14 to over $30 per barrel.

In both cases, the result was a mad rush away from gas pumps and toward public transportation. People flocked to transit for local commuting and to Amtrak trains for intercity trips. Even though Amtrak does not run Supertrains, events sparked intense ridership gains on every train, short-distance or long-distance, during both of the 1970s energy crises.

Lines of autos formed at filling stations, gasoline prices skyrocketed, states instituted odd-even rules for gasoline purchases determined by the last number on the license plate, and intercity drivers worried about where to find the next open gas station. Evidence of the public's accelerated use of train service includes California, where demand in the late 1970s smashed railroad records set during World War II. Desperate for equipment to meet the traffic, Amtrak rehabilitated cars that had been built as long ago as 1948 and pressed them into service. For months on end, the railroad's reservation agents received almost 1.4 million telephone calls per week, more than four times the normal amount. "Many of the persons flooding Amtrak with calls don't even ask the price," said Amtrak spokesman Arthur Lloyd. "They just ask what time the train leaves." To reduce the intense demand, Amtrak cancelled its advertising.

If America had had Supertrains running then, the meteoric rise in patronage would have been even more spectacular. The crisis caused France, Germany, and Japan to put their plans for electrically powered Supertrains in high gear. Why didn't Washington do likewise? One answer is that the federal government has been unable to make up its mind whether there would be another energy crisis.

The Department of Energy can't provide a decent forecast, although in March 1987 it issued a weak report that said "beyond 1995, it is likely that the United States and other countries will continue to be highly dependent on potentially insecure oil supplies." In that report, issued almost four years prior to the Persian Gulf War, the Energy Department admitted that this dependency remains a threat to national security.

PERSONAL TRANSPORTATION ENERGY USE
1987 Data in trillion BTU

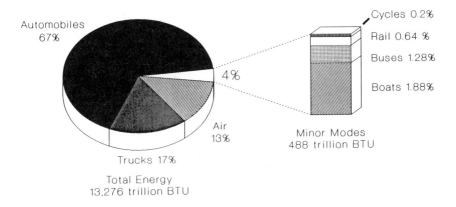

Automobiles
67%

Cycles 0.2%

Rail 0.64 %

Buses 1.28%

4%

Boats 1.88%

Air
13%

Minor Modes
488 trillion BTU

Trucks 17%

Total Energy
13,276 trillion BTU

United States transportation alone uses more oil each year than the nation produces. For personal transportation, the above shows how we use fuel. America must reduce petroleum use by building energy-efficient train systems. Trains powered by electricity would do more to cut oil imports than any other single act Washington could take. Little has changed since this data was released in 1987, indicating that the nation continues on its disastrous oil course. *(Richard E. Gibbs, New York Department of Environmental Conservation)*

The United States did little to lessen its oil dependency. In fact, the Reagan Administration built more roads, loosened auto fuel economy standards, raised the speed limit, and slashed funding for Amtrak and transit systems—all of which demolished conservation programs and helped oil imports soar once again.

"When Iraq's tanks rumbled into Kuwait in August 1990, the world suffered its third oil shock in just 17 years," wrote Christopher Flavin and Nicholas Lenssen of the Worldwatch

Institute. "The invasion . . . caused a 170-percent increase in oil prices in three months and led to near panic in world financial markets." Within one week the cost of gasoline across the United States surged by as much as 30 cents a gallon.

Fears of gasoline shortages were rekindled. In a *Washington Post* story by Cindy Skrzycki and Mark Potts, just two days after the Iraqi invasion, they warned against panic buying by motorists: "Experts say that prices could continue to spiral if consumers don't show restraint. If motorists begin topping off their tanks, they say real shortages and gas lines might not be far behind."

Worry spread that the oil price increases would kick the United States economy, already moribund, into a recession. Oil prices reached new highs, at one point topping $40 a barrel. Radio talk-show hosts urged their listeners to drive less. Saudi Arabia's oil production shot 57 percent above what it was before the Iraqi invasion. President Bush authorized oil imports from Iran, a former adversary, dipped into the Strategic Petroleum Reserve, and urged motorists to save gas by keeping their tires properly inflated, a puny conservation measure that was ridiculed by environmentalists.

The airline industry was shocked by the steep, swift rise in fuel prices. United Airlines, for example, could see as much as a $400 million increase in the $1.35 billion fuel bill it had in the previous year. Soon after the invasion, most airline fares rose 10 percent simply as a result of oil embargo-induced price rises.

Amtrak's energy efficiency helped it survive. Fuel represents only three percent of Amtrak's total cost of operations, compared to approximately 15–20 percent in the airline industry. Amtrak officials worried about accommodating thousands of additional passengers with its small fleet. After its experiences with two energy crisis-induced ridership surges, it had requested capital funds to increase capacity, but Washington did little.

In contrast, Tokyo had acted decisively over a number of years. Although it is the world's second largest economy, and even though the embargo of oil from Iraq and Kuwait cut its supply by an eighth, Japan experienced less turmoil than the United States. That was rather astonishing. After all, Japan's economy is more than twice as large as it was during the last energy crisis, yet its oil demands have barely grown.

How did they manage that?

Among other things, Japan has continued to expand its energy efficient Supertrain system and rail transit lines that depend upon stable supplies of domestically produced electricity. Those trains need no foreign oil. That simple message has been lost in America.

Regardless of the Iraqi crisis, other predictions about oil shortages are explicit and pessimistic. Deborah Lynn Bleviss, executive director of the Washington-based International Institute for Energy Conservation, wrote in her 1988 book *The New Oil Crisis and Fuel Economy Technologies* that by the year 2000, the world could again be gripped by a major oil crisis. She wrote that oil use in the Third World could mushroom by nearly 60 percent and the world was not prepared to meet such a strong increase in demand.

The gloomy view is shared by others. According to Andrew Kimbrell, policy director of the Greenhouse Crisis Foundation, "When commercial vehicles are included, almost a half billion motor vehicles are being driven on the world's roads, a ten-fold increase since 1950. And more are on the way. Current automobile production is at a record 38 million units per year, and is expected to rise to about 60 million by the year 2000."

TRAINS: SPARING ENVIRONMENTAL HARM

PER CAPITA GASOLINE CONSUMPTION
Comparisons Among Various Cities

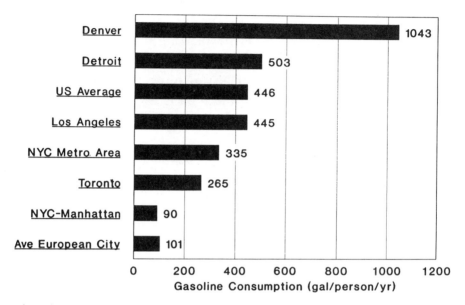

City	Gasoline Consumption (gal/person/yr)
Denver	1043
Detroit	503
US Average	446
Los Angeles	445
NYC Metro Area	335
Toronto	265
NYC-Manhattan	90
Ave European City	101

Americans use much more gasoline than their counterparts in the average European city where transit and intercity trains offer options superior to driving automobiles.

(Richard E. Gibbs, New York Department of Environmental Conservation)

Population is part of the equation, too. During the next 10 years, the world's population is expected to grow by 959 million, the largest increment ever for a single decade, according to Lester R. Brown in the Worldwatch Institute's *State of the World.* That means 88 million more people—equal to the combined populations of the United Kingdom, Belgium, Denmark, Ireland, Norway, and Sweden—*every year*, all of whom will need energy for heating, transportation, food production, and industrial processes.

Transportation accounts for nearly two-thirds of all oil use in the United States, with most of it going to autos. Even if all other sectors of the economy could switch to non-petroleum fuels, the nation would still have to import oil because transportation alone uses more petroleum each year than the nation produces.

It's a far cry from the 1950s when America was a major oil exporter. Experts agree that the nation is past its peak as an oil producer. Although oil imports in 1989 were the highest in 10 years, they may double by the year 2010.

"Our public fails to understand that America's Achilles' Heel is our overdependence on foreign oil," said former Lieutenant Governor Paul Leonard of Ohio, in a speech promoting Supertrains for the Buckeye state. He wants to see Americans riding in trains powered by electricity, not riding in cars powered by the Mideast oil cartel. Congressman Michael A. Andrews of Houston, in a speech just weeks before the embargo of Iraqi oil, supported Supertrains for Texas, saying, "The less we rely on oil products, the less susceptible we will be to oil embargoes."

According to the Federal Highway Administration, California led the nation in 1988 in total gasoline use for highway travel by devouring more than 12.5 billion gallons. Texas ranked second, consuming nearly 8.5 billion gallons, while Florida took third place, burning more than 5.7 billion gallons of gasoline.

Here again is where Supertrains come in—and in a big way. These very states are in the forefront of Supertrain planning, and any shifts from auto to train travel will reduce foreign oil imports. The energy savings, as well as reduced pollution, on just one route will be substantial. Look at the Los Angeles–Las Vegas Supertrain:

"Over a million interstate travelers and between 1½ million and 2½ million commuters would leave their cars to ride this new, fast, quiet, non-polluting system," said Richard Katz, for-

TRAINS: SPARING ENVIRONMENTAL HARM

World Crude Oil Reserves
(700 Billion Barrels)

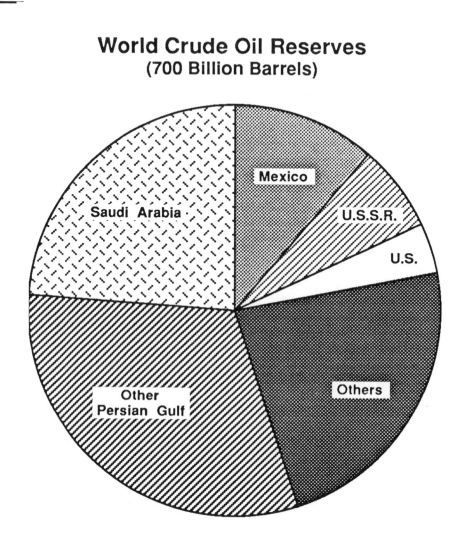

The United States needs to lessen oil use. Compared to the rest of the world, the nation's petroleum reserves are small. Failure to reduce oil dependency only places the nation at the mercy of oil-rich countries. There have been about 15 oil supply interruptions since 1950, and all of the major oil shortfalls occurred as a result of political events in the Middle East.

(Department of Energy)

mer chairman of the California-Nevada Super Speed Train Commission. "Approximately 70 million vehicle-miles would be trimmed from the region's trips each year, resulting in reduced tailpipe pollutants by hundreds of tons and saving millions of gallons of fuel. In fact, estimates just in the Las Vegas to southern California corridor alone are a fuel reduction of 17 percent."

Florida's Tim Lynch pointed out that Supertrains powered by electricity in his state would result in a reduction of as much as 20 million gallons of expensive imported oil for 1999 alone. "The shifts from auto and air travel to high-speed trains offer prospects of annual foreign debt reductions exceeding $50 million by the year 2020," said Lynch.

Despite this state-inspired bonanza for the federal government, despite this benefit to Americans in every part of the nation, not one Supertrain proposal has originated in Washington. Instead, Uncle Sam continues to build more facilities for autos and jetliners, helping intensify dependence on the *least* fuel-efficient vehicles.

Some are angry about Washington's dilatory attitude. Early in 1991, Jan C. Lundberg, president of the Fossil Fuels Action Institute in Fredericksburg, Virginia, called for a "national moratorium on paving." He said no new roads or parking lots should be built until the nation graduates from its overdependence on petroleum.

The Senate's maglev advisory committee report confirmed that new magnetic-levitation Supertrains are far more efficient than autos and airplanes: "In a petroleum-based transport economy, it is twice as efficient as autos and four times as efficient as airplanes, in terms of gross energy used."

Supertrains like the French TGVs are fuel-stingy, too. Their per-passenger energy consumption is so low that the Paris–Lyon TGVs use about one-sixth as much energy per mile as a modern narrow-body aircraft, according to Louis S. Thompson, railway advisor to the World Bank, and the new *Atlantique* is even more efficient. Clearly, the French TGVs help minimize France's oil imports, whereas airplanes in the United States have a voracious demand for fuel, using about 16 billion gallons annually, much of it wasted on short-hop flights better served by Supertrains. Substituting trains for planes in selected areas will bring about enormous energy savings.

Trains are quite efficient because a steel wheel rolling on a steel rail encounters remarkably little resistance, which was illustrated in 1930 when the Timken Roller Bearing Company hired four young women to pull Northern Pacific locomotive *No. 1111*, built by the American Locomotive Company. Pull it they did, despite the locomotive's weight of 355.7 tons. The publicity stunt has been repeated over the years, sometimes with just one muscle-bound weight lifter.

An example of concern over energy can be found in Germany. Peter Haefner, director of the international department at the *Deutsche Bundesbahn*, the German Federal Railway, explained: "We want major independence from oil, especially from imported oil. The electric train is the only means capable of using all kinds of energy and at the same time has the lowest specific energy consumption of all modes. This is why our government believes it's sensible to interfere and steer investments into rail."

When it comes to wise use of energy, the United States can learn from several of its industrialized competitors—Japan, France, and Germany.

—— —— ——

One environmental worry about Supertrains is that they are powered by electricity and could increase demand on power plants. That increased electrical usage, however, doesn't mean more pollution.

"High-speed trains use electrical power, but they would reduce the demand for other, less acceptable types of energy consumption—the burning of gasoline in automobiles and kerosene in jet airliners," explained F. K. Plous Jr., a Chicago writer. "In other words, high-speed trains represent a *good* energy tradeoff. There would be more centrally generated electricity, a form of energy in which environmental intrusion is relatively easy to control, in return for less combustion at the vehicle level, where environmental impact is widely dispersed and very hard to control."

Added electrical output need not necessarily mean more pollution at power plants, either. Since 1973, electric companies have reduced emissions by 21 percent, even though the use of coal to generate electricity has jumped by 88 percent. The Edison Electric Institute stated that the industry is employing new technologies that will enable it to increase efficiency and reduce pollution even more.

Again, superconductivity will help. James B. Birk of the Electric Power Research Institute reports that a superconducting magnetic energy storage plant is under development that can store electricity virtually without losses, expanding the supply of power without increasing generating capacity. Kevin D. Ott of the Council on Superconductivity reports that "in the utility sector, the use of new superconductors in large current energy applications offers the opportunity for an overall 25 percent savings in electricity."

TRAINS: SPARING ENVIRONMENTAL HARM

The question of nuclear power is usually considered separate from transportation-related concerns. However, American researchers continue to make progress on developing a fusion reactor, a clean alternative that uses seawater for fuel and creates less harmful radioactive waste than today's fission plants. Experts say the fusion process, which does not present meltdown fears, might be achieved early in the 21st century. Dale M. Meade of the Plasma Physics Research Laboratory in Princeton, New Jersey, said the Tokamak fusion reactor program holds great promise.

"High-speed rail is as environmentally clean a transportation project as man has yet been able to design," said Minnesota Transportation Commissioner John Riley.

Gilbert Carmichael, Administrator of the Federal Railroad Administration, said it differently: "Since my perspectives on transportation began to crystallize during the oil embargo of the early 1970s, I have settled on a notion that I describe as 'ethical' transportation. People tell me that this is a strange term to apply to transportation . . . but my use of the term 'ethical' is a deliberate choice of wording.

"An ethical transportation system conserves resources. It makes wise use of energy. It makes wise use of increasingly valuable land. Teddy Roosevelt, I believe, would have been very comfortable with this concept, as fitting into the classic definition of resource conservation," Carmichael said. "An ethical transportation system contributes to improving environmental quality, rather than contributing to its degradation."

As outspoken an environmentalist as can be found anywhere is Alfred Runte of Seattle. Runte, a former park naturalist, has written books about the parks, such as *National Parks: The American Experience* and *Yosemite: The Embattled Wilderness*, as well as a history of the partnership between passenger trains and America's national parks, *Trains of Discovery*. In lectures and in Congressional testimony, Runte is blunt.

"I grew up with the automobile; I grew up necking in the back seat, and I think the automobile stinks," said Runte, a critic of the policies of the Carter and Reagan administrations. Runte likes the idea of Supertrains taking travelers off the roads and out of the airports, but sees where some fellow environmentalists might be unhappy:

"Some people are worried about high-speed trains because they will cause development in new places, more dispersion of the population. But we already have that problem, caused mostly by the automobile. The problem isn't the trains, it's the lack of effective planning that's killing us. We need to channel the growth, put it in the right places. The trains can help do that."

He pointed out that some might question the need for high speeds. "We keep getting faster and faster, but the world isn't getting any larger," he said. "What is the speed for? The answer is that Americans have loved speed. The world loves speed. We like going fast and we don't go backwards in transportation, we go forward.

"Look at what Europe did. After World War II, Europe was in ruins. This was the perfect time to build all *autobahns*, but what the Europeans said was, 'No, we're a compact mass of people, and we don't have the fuel to waste.' They didn't have Texas pumping oil for them, and they rebuilt their railroads," said Runte. "Now that much of the population in the United States is in cities strung along corridors, and now that Texas pumps less oil for us than the Mideast does, it's time for us to follow Europe's example."

When environmentalists, business interests, and belea-

TRAINS: SPARING ENVIRONMENTAL HARM

Passenger Energy Intensities
BTU to Move Passenger One Mile

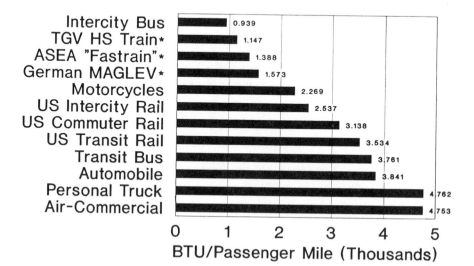

	BTU/Passenger Mile (Thousands)
Intercity Bus	0.939
TGV HS Train*	1.147
ASEA "Fastrain"*	1.388
German MAGLEV*	1.573
Motorcycles	2.269
US Intercity Rail	2.537
US Commuter Rail	3.138
US Transit Rail	3.534
Transit Bus	3.761
Automobile	3.841
Personal Truck	4.762
Air-Commercial	4.753

Self-explanatory illustration of the most and least efficient ways to move people. *(Richard E. Gibbs, New York Department of Environmental Conservation)*

guered travelers all start speaking positively about Supertrains, then it's only a matter of time before they'll all be riding them together.

A true aficionado of rail travel will insist that "trains are the way to go." Increasingly, informed environmentalists are saying, "Trains are the *cleanest* way to go."

"Imagine stepping onto a train in downtown San Francisco, relaxing as you speed down the length of California, then stepping off a few hours later in downtown Los Angeles, breathing in cool, clean Los Angeles air, and wandering down a lightly-trafficked street to your destination." That vision is being promoted by the Sacramento-based Planning and Conservation

League, an alliance of more than 100 groups pushing to improve the state's environmental laws.

Today, this image is just a dream, but it could be closer to reality as more financing packages come together and new California laws take effect. According to the League: "We can begin to build a network of trains to provide clean, fast transportation without fouling our air, clogging our cities, or destroying our environment. Trains are the technology of the future."

The voters have been listening. In June 1990, the California electorate voted in favor of nearly $3 billion in bond issues for rail projects, as well as a gasoline tax increase that in part will help fund additional transit and rail improvements. The measures were promoted by the League and the Train Riders' Association of California.

Why are the environmentalists so active in promoting trains? Let's face it—when a tree dies, it isn't because a train killed it. When ozone stings our eyes or carbon monoxide burns our lungs, it isn't because a train emitted it. When petroleum runs short, it isn't because a train guzzled it, and when a brown cloud hovers over our city, it isn't because a train put it there.

America's conservationists have some new allies. Pehr G. Gyllenhammer, president of Sweden's biggest automaker, Volvo, said cars should be banned from big cities to curb air pollution and traffic congestion and save populated areas from "choking." The Dutch environmental ministry is considering banning private autos in big cities, and encourages people to use trains for trips between cities. Smog kills an estimated six people a day in Athens, Greece, and that city has restricted the number of cars entering its central core.

In the United States, John DeVillars, Massachusetts secretary of environmental affairs, has considered making mass

TRAINS: SPARING ENVIRONMENTAL HARM

transit free to riders when smog levels edge up to the unhealthful zone. George Haikalis, chairman of the Auto-Free New York Committee, wants the city to "explore the upper limit of devehicularization."

The Supertrain movement will grow as people start to understand that hordes of autos moving *between* cities spread almost as much environmental damage as auto use *within* cities. An overwhelming 83 percent of intercity travelers go by car— all the planes, trains, and buses combined handle a mere 17 percent.

"As a nation, we must greatly increase our investment in clean, energy efficient alternatives to the private automobile," wrote T Allan Comp in *Blueprint for the Environment*, noting that most urbanized areas have little or no room left for more highways. Environmental groups have banded into a pro-transit and pro-train coalition whose members include Environmental Action, Friends of the Earth, the National Audubon Society, the National Wildlife Federation, the Sierra Club, and others.

One of the greatest sins of motor vehicles is that they are the single largest source of poisonous exhausts, treating the atmosphere as if it were an open sewer. Under the Clean Air Act of 1970, the Environmental Protection Agency (EPA) sets health-based limits on the amount of certain pollutants allowed in the air. Many cities fail the test for the two pollutants most closely associated with motor vehicle emissions—ozone and carbon monoxide.

Highway vehicles alone contribute about 40 to 45 percent of the total ozone in our skies. While ozone in the upper atmosphere shields the earth from harmful ultraviolet radiation given off by the sun, ozone at ground level presents a major health concern, destroying lung tissue almost as thoroughly as do some chemical weapons, according to the United States Center for Disease Control.

"The ozone standard was violated 60 percent more often in 1988 than 1983, and violators included 26 new cities and two rural areas," wrote *Washington Post* reporter Michael Weisskopf. The EPA and the National Park Service have blamed southern California smog for obscuring summer views in the Grand Canyon, 550 miles away.

"Nineteen eighty-eight was a public health disaster," Thomas Godar, president of the American Lung Association, told Congress, "unless you're interested in pernicious population control." Air pollution from motor vehicles, he said, causes $40 billion to $50 billion in annual health-care expenditures and as many as 120,000 unnecessary or premature deaths.

About 60 percent of southern California's smog is caused by automobiles. The EPA said that to attain federal clean air standards in southern California by 1993 would destroy the local economy by imposing rules so draconian as to completely reshape the patterns of daily life there. The EPA won't go that far because it can't wreck the regional economy. As a result, carbon monoxide and ozone levels are expected to exceed the federal health standard through the start of the next century.

Congressman Henry Waxman of California, along with Senator Frank Lautenberg of New Jersey, has been fighting an uphill battle for tougher tailpipe emissions standards. Environmental Action, a Washington-based group, says the 1990 revisions to the long-debated Clean Air Act will not solve the problem because the rules have been watered down at the insistence of automakers.

Thus, while more than 200 United States cities now exceed the maximum permissible smog levels at some point each year,

TRAINS: SPARING ENVIRONMENTAL HARM

pollution will only get worse through at least 1994. While some advances continue to be made in pollution controls, gains in air quality are offset by growth in auto travel, which means that, to be effective, any clean air plan must encourage people to shift to trains and transit. "If the largest single source of air pollution in this country is vehicle emissions, does it make any sense to design a federal clean air policy with no effort to entice people out of their cars?" asks David R. Boldt, editorial page editor of the *Philadelphia Inquirer*.

"Air pollution in our state comes largely from automobiles. . . . We look to high-speed rail as a unique opportunity for trying to reduce the drastic impacts on our air resources," said Victoria Tschinkel, former secretary of the Florida Department of Environmental Regulation.

Other countries know that Supertrains reduce motor vehicle use. "In Germany, one-third of our precious forest is sick," said Peter Haefner of the German Federal Railway. "What we want is clean air and water, healthy forests, unpolluted soil, a space-saving infrastructure, and above all, safer transportation."

The Germans have decided to improve their rail system everywhere, including construction of Supertrain lines, as the best weapon against further environmental damage. Haefner added: "Our government has come to a complete change in its infrastructure investment policy. In the past 10 years, $9 billion has been invested in rail but $12 billion in the road system. In the coming 10 years, there will be $11 billion for rail and $8 billion for roads." That's quite a switch.

The United States, by relying on environmentally friendly trains, can begin to curb ecological damage. Every trip taken on an existing transit system instead of by car cuts smog-producing hydrocarbon emissions by 90 percent, carbon monoxide by more than 75 percent, and nitrogen oxides by a range of 15 to 75 percent, according to the American Public Transit Association.

"Congress should begin to look at transportation funding as a pollution control strategy," said Robert E. Yuhnke, a lawyer with the Environmental Defense Fund. "To severely polluted cities, such as Los Angeles, Chicago, New York, Houston, that are going to come to Congress and demand long periods to meet air quality standards, Congress should say, 'Ok, then federal transportation dollars will be spent in your cities to build transportation systems that will provide alternatives to the automobile.' Congress must begin to shift transportation investments."

The Senate's maglev technology advisory committee said: "Electrically powered vehicles do not emit any pollutants, nor does the guideway. . . . To a small degree, maglev operation does produce some pollution, since power plants do emit pollutants. However, these are much less than equivalent auto, truck, and airplane emissions. Moreover, they are usually emitted in rural areas, where pollution is much less of a problem." Steel-wheel Supertrains like Japan's Bullet Trains, France's TGV, and Germany's ICE offer benefits that are virtually identical.

Florida looked at what both maglev and steel-wheel Supertrains could contribute to cleaner air. Tim Lynch, an economist with that state's high-speed rail commission, said, "I'm not suggesting these trains as the only solution to air pollution, but they certainly can make a major contribution to clean air if implemented on a large scale—and that's irrefutable."

Lynch ticks off the benefits by 1999 of Florida's super-speed trains: Carbon monoxide reduced by as much as 5,417 tons per year, carbon dioxide down by 62, 805 tons annually, and nitrogen oxides down by as much 1,350 tons every year.

Another concern is global warming, the greenhouse effect.

Evidence suggests that rising carbon dioxide levels in the atmosphere could trigger rapid warming of the Earth's climate, with potentially devastating consequences. Of course, the best way to reduce gas emissions that cause the greenhouse effect is to burn less fuel. Supertrains issue only one-fourth as much harmful gas as airplanes, and about one-half as much as autos. Any switch to Supertrains will help retard the soaring levels of carbon dioxide.

Another environmental issue is the growing question of how land is used. America's cities have been split into pieces by superhighways. An area the size of West Virginia is covered with asphalt and concrete. Do we really want more of that?

Savvy experts overseas have long appreciated that only a narrow right-of-way is required to build high-capacity Supertrain systems. The space required for railway right-of-way is comparable to that for a road of minor importance, according to the French National Railways. The entire Paris–Lyon TGV system uses less land than de Gaulle Airport near Paris.

The Senate advisory committee said that, in general, a maglev Supertrain requiring only 50 feet of right-of-way can carry the volume of approximately 10 lanes of highway traffic. Furthermore, this can be accomplished on existing rights-of-way. Building additional highways to handle such a volume of traffic would require new rights-of-way hundreds of feet wide.

A report by the Bechtel Corporation confirmed that the Transrapid maglev requires far less land and creates fewer permanent environmental impacts on a route it studied. The required clearance width of the maglev Supertrain to Las Vegas is only 36 feet while the section of I-15 from the Nevada state line to Barstow is about 300 feet wide. Of course, the interstates get much wider the closer they get to Los Angeles.

"The environmentalists out here like the train," said Paul Taylor of the California-Nevada Super Train Commission.

While it would be devastating to build bigger highways in our urban areas, they can also damage even undeveloped areas such as California's Mojave Desert. There, the Wilderness Society and others want to cordon off new areas to help save the fragile ecosystem. They would create a 1.5-million acre national park east of Barstow to help prevent the loss of habitat, which is the greatest threat to wildlife.

The French TGV planners incorporated wildlife passages under their lines, allowing easy animal movements. Their system is totally protected with fences, and wildlife kills by France's Supertrains are virtually unknown. Maglev Supertrains can be built on an elevated track, with pylons resting on small "footprints" in the Mojave Desert. The designers of the Transrapid maglev use an elevated test track in Germany, and directly underneath cows graze and crops are grown.

People living near major airports have another concern —noise pollution so pervasive that it disrupts their daily lives. If Supertrains somehow were to replace all airplane travel, quiet would descend on communities throughout the land. So noiseless are Transrapid trains that the people in the fields don't even look up when one passes overhead. The scene was peaceful before the maglev track came, and it remains peaceful today.

Should America build Supertrains or more superhighways through the Mojave Desert? Over Florida's delicate wetlands? In Pennsylvania's forests? Within the cities of Texas and Ohio? Clearly, the choice should be trains.

— — —

TRAINS: SPARING ENVIRONMENTAL HARM

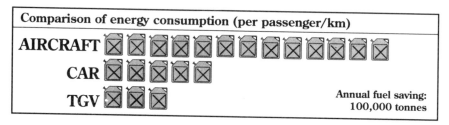

Comparison of energy consumption (per passenger/km)	
AIRCRAFT ⊠⊠⊠⊠⊠⊠⊠⊠⊠⊠⊠⊠⊠	
CAR ⊠⊠⊠⊠⊠	
TGV ⊠⊠⊠	**Annual fuel saving:** 100,000 tonnes

The French TGV wins the energy consumption race.

(French National Railways)

Gridlock is killing freedom.

For years, our automobiles gave us the feeling of freedom. Even the most run-down, rattletrap junker allowed us to ignore limitations. As drivers, we were our own masters. We moved about on a whim, more easily than any other people in the history of the world.

But that freedom has become an illusion. As each day brings more motorists and autos, the result is less and less freedom—in other words, gridlock. During rush hours, or on holiday weekends, or after fender-benders, traffic backups make prisoners of millions of Americans. Missed appointments, overheated engines, high blood pressure—even fatal shootings on California's freeways—are the prices we pay on highways today.

Gridlock is getting worse as the number of cars multiplies twice as fast as the nation's population. *Time* magazine, in a 1988 cover story on gridlock, said: "Today's average motorist will spend an estimated six months of his lifetime waiting for red lights to change, according to a study by Priority Management Pittsburgh, a time-management consulting firm."

Drivers slogging along congested highways will find no comfort in the latest figures on highway congestion. "Statisticians try to make the astronomical numbers more comprehensible by expressing them in terms of trips to the moon, although no interstate goes there," wrote Matthew L. Wald of the *New York Times*. "Thus, in 1970, vehicle-miles traveled in the United States came to about two million round trips to the moon. Now cars do about three million round trips annually."

The Federal Highway Administration estimates that vehicle delays due to freeway congestion will increase by an awesome 400 percent in urban areas from 1985 to 2005. "A typical commuter will spend a total of over five years of life just stuck in traffic," reported Douglas I. Foy, executive director of The Conservation Law Foundation of New England. Wasn't the auto supposed to *save* us time?

"Across the nation, public opinion surveys reveal that traffic congestion has superseded crime, housing, and unemployment as the primary concern of voters," said a report by New York State's Commission on Critical Transportation Choices, led by Senator Norman J. Levy and Assemblyman Michael J. Bragman. In the San Francisco Bay Area, traffic has been cited as the top priority issue eight years in a row. Transportation led all other problems by a wide margin.

"The Europeans are close to being light-years ahead of us," said Robert Kiley, former chairman of New York's Metropolitan Transportation Authority. "We keep kidding ourselves into thinking that we have the number-one transportation system in the world. Well, that's a joke."

Highway congestion hits America's pocketbooks, and hard. According to the American Association of State Highway and Transportation Officials, the estimated yearly drain to the economy in lost time, productivity, and other costs such as fuel consumption and accidents will reach $40 billion in the year 2005.

Yet, the federal government is planning to spend billions

TRAINS: SPARING ENVIRONMENTAL HARM

more on highways. The 42,798-mile network of interstates is almost complete and the price tag should reach $122 billion—three times its original cost estimate—by the time the last mile is paved. America's interstate program is the largest public works project in the history of the planet, but mobility does not increase despite the large expenditures.

In many cases, highway cost overruns have ruined whatever cost-benefit ratios were calculated. Suburban Detroit's I-696, for example, projected to cost $76 million, actually had a final price tag of $675 million.

"In the 34-year history of the national interstate highway network, few roads have been as long in coming or were as hotly contested as Interstate 696," wrote *New York Times* reporter William E. Schmidt. "Construction on the 28.2-mile freeway began in 1961. The last link, the 9.1-mile stretch that cuts across Pleasant Ridge and seven other suburbs, was caught up in nearly two decades of bitter fighting."

"I spent 20 years of my life fighting that highway," Mary Chambers, leader of highway foes, told the *Times*. "It was a bad idea when the Eisenhower Administration came up with it, and it's still a bad idea today."

Many highways were stopped in New York, Memphis, and Washington, D.C., and anti-highway activity persists elsewhere. In the West, a group called the Citizens United To Save South Pasadena is opposing construction of a 6.2-mile section of the Long Beach Freeway that would cut their community in half.

"To even consider demolishing houses and forcing their estimated 6,000 residents to relocate during the present housing and community crises gripping Los Angeles is madness, pure and simple," wrote Sam Hall Kaplan in the *Los Angeles Times*.

America's interstate highway system is nearly complete. As traffic continues to grow, it will be impossible to expand it further in urban areas.

(Federal Highway Administration)

"The effect on lives, families, friends, local schools and businesses, and community spirit, would be devastating."

Nevertheless, some still believe in building such highways. The former administrator of the Federal Highway Administration, Francis C. Turner, in a startling 1989 lecture to highway engineers, said that America needs "more miles and lanes of both the interstate system and its feeder and distributor arterials, most of which are in or adjacent to urban areas." In building them, officials must be "ready to accept the harsh criticisms leveled by the individual Mr. and Mrs. Citizen, U.S.A., whose sidewalk and front porch we will be having to take away from

TRAINS: SPARING ENVIRONMENTAL HARM

them, for the larger public's benefit." Turner's insensitivity goes far to explain why environmentalists have had so many bitter disputes with highway officials.

Turner should stay away from Michigan. There, when officials planning I-696 asked for an additional nine feet of right-of-way in Pleasant Ridge, the community refused. If highways can't be made wider, how about higher? Los Angeles has long thought about double-decking its freeways. However, the fatal collapse of the double-decked portion of I-880, the Nimitz Freeway's Cypress Street viaduct in Oakland, during the *Lomo Prieta* earthquake late in 1989, has changed thinking about layered highways.

Although the earthquake was centered in the Santa Cruz Mountains 60 miles southeast of San Francisco, it cut a wide path of destruction through the region, crippling major portions of the highway system. In all, 68 road structures were damaged and 11 were closed. "I'll make you a bet," said William J. Hall, a structural engineer at the University of Illinois, after the earthquake, "a lot of highway officials around the country are going to be doing some obvious thinking about double- or triple-decking their highway structures, no matter where they live."

"In Los Angeles County, Supervisor Kenneth Hahn has already called for an end to the Harbor Freeway double-decking program, and it is difficult to see how similar two-deck proposals for the Santa Ana Freeway and Highway 80 will survive," reported *California Rail News*.

Reconstruction of I-880 may never happen. At a Caltrans public hearing, residents of West Oakland vociferously opposed putting the highway back in. "We're willing to stand in front, lay in front of bulldozers" to stop the freeway, said City Councilman Wilson Riles, Jr., in rhetoric reminiscent of the anti-highway fights of the 1960s. This leg of the interstate system is the first in history to be ripped up and not replaced, which means the interstates will finally have something in common with canals and railroads—a portion has been abandoned forever.

Finances play a role, too, and Supertrains can help save tax dollars. The California Department of Transportation has plans for adding two lanes of highway between Barstow and Victorville, based on traffic forecasts. The Los Angeles–Las Vegas Supertrains, however, may negate the need for the state's costly plan.

According to Florida's Tim Lynch, an analysis indicates a "diversion of perhaps $1 billion in foregone investments in highway construction as a result of implementation of high-speed rail" in that state alone.

Where rail passenger service is well developed, the evidence is strong that it reduces the burden on highways. Studies report that more than 50 percent of the 1.7 million riders on the Los Angeles–San Diego Amtrak route would have driven their automobiles if rail service were not provided. Supertrains will divert many more than even Amtrak does.

Washington should be thinking about how Supertrains could help ease congestion by shifting millions of city-to-city travelers off the roads. New highways, no matter how modern, between large cities will still allow a top speed of only 65 mph. A Supertrain system can be built at less cost and move passengers at 300 mph.

— — —

In many aspects of life we preach "Safety First." In transportation planning, it's always been "Safety Last." The traffic death toll has worsened just about every year since 1899 when

TRAINS: SPARING ENVIRONMENTAL HARM

Mr. H. H. Bliss, a New Yorker alighting from a trolley car, was killed by a horseless carriage—America's first recorded death by auto.

"In the United States, the automobile had cost its first million dead by 1952, its second million by 1975, and the third million is likely by 1994," wrote environmentalist Andrew Kimbrell. "Along the way, some 90 million Americans have sustained disabling injuries in auto accidents. In all, the more than 2.5 million Americans who have died violent deaths on our highways represent more than four times the 641,691 Americans killed in World War I, World War II, Korea and Vietnam combined."

Science fiction author Ray Bradbury may be the only resident of Los Angeles who doesn't drive an automobile, telling Jeffrey A. Frank of the *Washington Post* that it stems from car-wreck scenes he witnessed as a child. "I saw five people killed right in front of me, decapitated, that sort of thing," Bradbury said.

"So I don't think you ever get over that," he continued, "it's like being in a war, isn't it, eh?" Bradbury also asked: "Where are the parades, where are the marchers for the 100,000 people killed in the last two years in cars? Why aren't there demonstrations?"

Deaths on the road will continue to escalate. If current accident rates continue through the year 2020, with projected travel volumes of twice today's amounts, about 100,000 people will die each year on our nation's highways. That figure is nearly equal to the entire population of Bakersfield, California.

"The National Safety Council is appalled that Americans got bent out of shape about such headline-grabbing events as two Chilean table grapes allegedly tainted by cyanide [causing a brief nationwide embargo on grape imports] but somehow either overlook 49,000 fatalities on our highways every year or else accept those statistics as the price of progress," said Robert W. O'Brien, the group's director of public relations.

According to the Coalition for Consumer Health and Safety, motor-vehicle crashes are the leading killer of Americans under the age of 35, and the leading cause of head injuries, epilepsy, quadriplegia, paraplegia, and facial injuries, as well as a significant cause of blindness. Each year, 1.8 million people suffer disabling injuries resulting from such accidents. When the vehicular wreckage is towed away, the human wreckage is left behind.

Still another group, the Insurance Institute for Highway Safety, reported that motor-vehicle accidents in the United States cause one motor-vehicle death every 11 minutes and an injury every 18 seconds.

How about diverting people to trains, removing thousands of people permanently from the highways? Throughout the world, Supertrains have no equal whatsoever because they have *never* had a passenger fatality. Considering the staggering national economic cost of motor vehicle accidents—an estimated $70.2 billion in 1988 alone—the savings from a reduced accident rate could be directly correlated to the trains.

"What will it be?" asks environmentalist Al Runte. "Supertrains or super slaughter?" There is a choice. In one case, at the California-Nevada Super Speed Train Commission, planners looked at the number of lives that could be saved if drivers were lured to trains. Most traffic attracted to Las Vegas–Los Angeles super-speed trains will be diverted from autos, and that could amount to 1.5 million fewer cars using I-15 by the year 2000.

"Travel between Las Vegas and southern California is about 80 percent by highway, and we predict with the implementation

German officials cite protection of the environment from more highways and air pollution as reasons to build the ICE train network. *(German Rail)*

TRAINS: SPARING ENVIRONMENTAL HARM

of the super-speed train the highway mode would drop to about 50 percent," said Paul Taylor of the Supertrain commission.

In the first year of the system, the big switch to trains is expected to prevent more than 270 accidents, 140 injuries and 15 fatalities on or near I-15. These savings in life and limb would grow in future years as the Supertrains develop a deeper market penetration. American planners did not estimate the savings in highway accident costs attributable to the Supertrains. The Australians, however, calculated total savings at about $77 million annually as their proposed Sydney–Melbourne VFT Supertrains reduce road traffic.

"The perfect safety record of high-speed trains is the result of careful design," said Pennsylvania Assemblyman Richard Geist. "For one, they generally operate at their highest speed only on trackage dedicated to passenger trains exclusively. Second, sophisticated computer controls provide a crucial backup to the train's human operators."

Senator Moynihan asked during hearings if United States-designed maglev Supertrains would be safe. At the witness table was Carl H. Rosner, chairman of Intermagnetics General Corporation, who said, "This system can be made virtually fail-safe. . . . I believe it can be in fact made foolproof." At Rosner's side was Richard Gran of Grumman Corporation, who said if a maglev train breaks down "that can be sensed and the whole system can be brought to a halt."

William Meeker of the National Transportation Safety Board has examined America's safety record. His conclusion: it should be part of our national ethic, part of a life-saving mission, part of our government's policy, to divert people from dangerous highway travel to super-safe Supertrains.

French leaders call for additional TGV lines, pointing out that high-capacity transportation results while taking no more land than would be required by a "road of minor importance." *(French National Railways)*

TRAINS: SPARING ENVIRONMENTAL HARM

Transrapid maglev trains occupy only small "footprints" as they pass overhead. The capacity of such Supertrain lines is equal to a 10-lane freeway.

(Transrapid International)

However, despite the costs endured and the hazards faced by motorists, the automobile and highway travel are firmly a part of American culture, more than in any other place in the world, and we spent money by the truckload to make it that way.

The highway trust fund institutionalized the automobile in America more than any other single factor. The fund also has proven to be more important than any supposed economic superiority of the auto. Thus, as long as federal officials make money available for highways, and not Supertrains, many state and local officials will opt for more highways.

The first question asked of planners bringing Supertrain projects to their state legislatures is, "How many federal dollars will this project bring to the state?" Most often, the answer is, "zero." The federal government will match funds for highway programs, but such grants are non-existent or puny for rail programs. Thus, the federal bias toward highways fosters a state bias toward highways.

California's State Transportation Director, Robert Best, has urged the federal government to do away with the disparity in matching funds. He told Don Phillips of the *Washington Post* that "if you want a freeway, you get public money, but if you want a rail system, you're on your own."

At a personal level, Americans also have a bias toward the automobile. We're virtually brainwashed into thinking we must have one. Some estimates have shown that American automakers, over time, have spent well in excess of $40 billion to advertise their products. In 1989, according to the Television Bureau of Advertising, car and truck advertisers spent $2.84 billion on broadcast television alone. The result: we are a people moving around in 144 million automobiles, sharing crowded roads with 40 million trucks, and we hear daily sales pitches to put more of our money into more of the same.

The American penchant to build roads originated in 1806 when the federal government began work on the National Pike, which by 1819 extended 131 miles from Cumberland, Maryland, to Wheeling, West Virginia, but it turned out to be a unique venture when Washington ultimately decided that states and local communities should build roads. To help in the development of turnpikes, which made profits by charging tolls, some states invested in securities of those private companies.

TRAINS: SPARING ENVIRONMENTAL HARM

Gridlock and pollution are too much a part of daily urban life.

The coming of the railroads also allowed government to postpone developing highways. Attitudes changed, however, with the beginning of the auto age. Federal interest in bringing about a true national highway network dates to the construction of the first transcontinental road, the Lincoln Highway, in 1913.

Federal funds were first given to the states by the 1916 Rural Post Roads Act, which required states to establish highway departments. The act paid half the cost of building roads used to deliver the mails. At that time only about one-tenth of the roads were paved, and only about 4 million autos were registered, or about one for every 30 people. From 1920 through the 1950s, rural and urban highways proliferated, aided by $1.5 billion in funding from the Federal Highway Act of 1944.

Although President Dwight D. Eisenhower is credited with the Interstate Highway program, it was first proposed by President Franklin D. Roosevelt in 1939. Congress, sensing benefits to commerce after World War II, authorized construction of a national interstate highway system in 1944.

"In 1947 the federal government and the states agreed on the location of 37,700 miles of the system," according to Daniel Patrick Moynihan, in a 1960 article in the *Reporter*, 16 years before his election to the United States Senate. "But no special funds were appropriated to build them; only regular federal highway-aid funds were made available, on the standard 50-50 matching basis. . . . The result was that the interstate mileage didn't get built."

Trying to prod the states to lay concrete, the federal share was increased to 60 percent. Nevertheless, by 1952 less than 1 percent had been completed. The message from the states was clear that if Washington wanted interstate highways, Washington would have to pay for them. A precedent existed in that President Franklin Roosevelt in 1938 had given Pennsylvania a grant of $29.25 million, with no repayment expected and none received, as well as purchasing $40.8 million in bonds, to help that state build its interstate-style toll turnpike.

President Eisenhower offered to raise most of the $40 billion needed to pay for the new roads, setting in motion construction of a National Interstate and Defense Highway System. The action also set off the biggest boom in road building that the world has ever seen. These limited-access superhighways were planned to connect 90 percent of all cities with populations of more than 50,000 and carry 20 percent of the nation's traffic.

Under Eisenhower's plan, the interstates would be financed on the basis of 90 percent federal funds and 10 percent state funding. That financial clout meant Washington would control the highway program; ironically Republicans would take away one of the few areas of significant government initiative that still resided with the states after Roosevelt's New Deal.

The states had no real freedom of action. "The basic decision to build the system has been made for them," wrote Moynihan, adding, "the enormous 'bargain' of the 90-10 money makes it politically impossible to do anything but take the money as fast as possible and try to match it."

The plan went awry. "In Eisenhower's vision, the super-highways were not supposed to have gone *into* the cities, but only *around* them, as in Europe," wrote Stephen E. Ambrose in his biography *Eisenhower*. In 1959, while *en route* to Camp David, the president was appalled to see a deep freeway construction gash near Washington. He ordered a White House study of the interstates, only to learn that nothing could be done to stop their construction into the cities. Instead of massive highways, Eisenhower thought the nation's capital needed a subway.

According to the Congressional Budget Office, various levels of government in this century have spent $1 trillion (in 1982 dollars) to build highways—approximately $400 billion from federal budgets and about $600 billion from the states and localities. Today, a big need exists to repair the middle-aged interstates and other roads, fix bridges, and replace traffic signals. That could cost as much as $3.2 trillion, a sum roughly equal to this country's annual gross national product and well in excess of the current national debt.

The figures are enough to unmask the word "freeway" as one of the greatest public relations ploys of all times. There's nothing free about them. Barry Batemen, director of the Milwaukee Airport, questioned the wisdom of highway programs:

"Probably the last big one done was the interstate highway system, and that was before a lot of the environmental laws were adopted. Certainly it was done before the cost-benefit ratio accountants got involved. If we had to do a cost-benefit ratio of the interstate highway system, it wouldn't have been built."

Clearly, America is in the midst of a highway finance crisis. Who will pay? More importantly, who should pay? According to Colorado Senator William Armstrong, now retired, "Roughly speaking, the roads are paid for by the users through fuel taxes." The problem with the statement is, it's flat-out wrong. It's a fairy tale that the Highway Trust Fund pays for our roads and like most fairy tales it's told over and over. In 1989 alone, the Federal Highway Administration reports that all levels of government spent a record-smashing $71.2 billion on highways.

Where did the money come from? About $44.3 billion came from the user fees such as gasoline taxes, vehicle taxes, and tolls. About $26.9 billion, however, came from other sources: federal and state income taxes, sales taxes, property taxes, bond issue proceeds, and other miscellaneous taxes and fees.

Worldwatch Institute researchers, taking into account air pollution and other harmful environmental effects of the highway system, estimated that every automobile is subsidized at about $2,400 annually. The group said if subsidies were ended and gas prices were jacked up to pay the true costs of auto usage, the price of a gallon of gas would be at least $4.50.

"We spend more on our automobiles than we do on groceries," pointed out former New York transit chief Robert Kiley. "We spend more on automobiles than on health. We spend almost as much on automobiles as we do on education. I mean, come on, something's gone wrong."

TRAINS: SPARING ENVIRONMENTAL HARM

More and more, highways are busting budgets across America. The costs are mind-boggling: through the year 2005, Phoenix wants to spend $5.9 billion for 232 miles of highway construction. That's more, for one city alone, than the cost to build the entire Las Vegas–Anaheim Supertrain system.

The most extreme price tag is found in Boston's Central Artery project, the largest remaining section of the interstate highway system to be built. It is 7.5 miles long, which includes 3.7 miles of tunnel and 2.3 miles of bridges. By the time the contractors are finished pouring concrete in 1998, the roadway will cost $4.4 billion. If Boston's residents were to vote on highway projects as they do on transit bond issues, and in essence tax themselves for the road, how many would agree to pay more than $586 million *per mile* for the new highway? Also, how many would have voted with leaders who have called for a rail connection along the Central Artery route? Ironically, the Conservation Law Foundation of New England, which represents major financial and legal interests in Boston, said the Central Artery project will do little to relieve traffic congestion unless officials improve mass transit and discourage commuting by car.

Perhaps a way to put these costs in perspective is to compare them to an alternative—urban transit. Gerald H. Meral, executive director of California's Planning and Conservation League, has tried to highlight transit's cost-effectiveness. "The entire Sacramento light-rail system was built for less than the cost of a single proposed freeway interchange in Walnut Creek," he said.

One reason the United States is so automobile oriented is that the auto industry and its supporters sometimes took direct measures to eliminate rail transit systems. The disappearance of the nation's trolley systems in the 1950s was caused by automobile interests acting secretly. General Motors, Firestone

Tire, Mack Truck, and Standard Oil formed a holding company named the National City Lines that from 1936 to 1945 conspired to buy and dismantle street car lines in 45 cities. In each city, steel-wheel transit systems were replaced with General Motors buses. The Justice Department brought suit against the companies and the conspirators eventually were found guilty.

"The impact may have been greatest for Los Angeles," said *Environmental Action* magazine. "In 1935 that city was noted for palm trees, orange groves, and clean air and was served by one of the largest inter-urban electric railway systems in the world." Now it's known for its traffic-snarled freeways and thick smog.

That may be history, but the considerable influence of the highway lobby in Washington and in each of the 50 state capitals is one reason why governments continue to spend big money on highways. The highway lobby has four components; most visible are the automobile manufacturers and the steel, glass, and rubber industries they contract with. Also powerful are highway builders, their suppliers of concrete, sand, and other materials, and excavation equipment businesses. Third, oil companies push road projects; and fourth, real estate interests also lobby for additional highways, but more often at the state and local levels.

The pro-highway interests have many influential Washington-based organizations, such as the Highway Users Federation, American Automobile Association, American Road and Transportation Builder's Association, National Automobile Dealers Association, American Trucking Associations, and others. These groups want more roads, including more in crowded urban areas.

The propriety of earmarking funds for highways still is debated. Many argue that every tax dollar ought to go into the general fund, to be divvied up according to public needs. After

TRAINS: SPARING ENVIRONMENTAL HARM

Supertrains like these Bullet Trains are the safest form of transportation ever devised, having carried three billion passengers without ever having had a fatality. *(Japanese Railways Group)*

TRAINS: SPARING ENVIRONMENTAL HARM

all, the government doesn't dedicate taxes collected on liquor for the benefit of more and better whiskey. At least, say critics, turn the highway trust fund into a total transportation trust fund. Some monies already are diverted from the trust fund. Revenues from 1½ cents of the federal 19-cent per-gallon motor-fuel tax support urban transit programs.

If a gas tax can be used to shift drivers to transit *within* cities, isn't it equally logical to use those funds to shift auto travelers to environmentally clean and safe trains between cities? California's voters think so, voting to allow portions of the gas tax to be used to finance improvements to Amtrak.

An epic change in public financing of transportation is coming. The 1991 Moynihan provision to allow states to spend a portion of highway funds on Supertrains was strongly supported on a bipartisan basis by senators Quentin N. Burdick, North Dakota; Steve Symms, Idaho; Frank Lautenberg, New Jersey, and John H. Chafee, Rhode Island. In the House of Representatives, four of the country's most influential congressmen agreed with Senator Moynihan: Public Works and Transportation Committee Chairman Robert A. Roe of New Jersey, as well as committee members Norman Y. Mineta of California, John Paul Hammerschmidt of Arkansas, and Bud Shuster of Pennsylvania. The Moynihan approach also received the critical approval of other powerful representatives, such as House Ways and Means Committee Chairman Dan Rostenkowski, House Budget Committee Chairman Leon E. Panetta, and Speaker of the House Thomas S. Foley.

The Bush Administration lacks interest in helping finance working high-speed train systems. The president's background may be part of the reason. Daniel Yergin's 1991 best-selling book about the oil industry, *The Prize*, notes that Bush is "the oil man who became President." Oil men like highways. Just weeks after the end of the Persian Gulf War, which many called an "oil-war," the Department of Transportation shamelessly urged a no-growth policy for transit while calling for a highway program that would cost $87 billion. Half, or $43.5 billion, would establish "a new 150,000-mile network of highways that includes both the Interstate Highway System and a vast new network of other major highways," wrote John H. Cushman, Jr., in the *New York Times*. "Jack Gilstrap, executive vice-president of the American Public Transit Association, called the proposal 'a recipe for more traffic jams, air pollution, and wasted energy.' "

Does America need its highways? Yes, we long ago reached the point where we simply can't get along without them. Can America handle *more* highways in urban areas? Clearly, no. Our most populated corridors must be spared more environmental wreckage. A new superhighway connecting Boston with Washington, or between Miami and Tampa, would be madness.

"We cannot go on widening existing roads, creating 10-and 12-lane monsters," said Congressman Thomas A. Luken of Ohio. "There has to be a point at which the traffic simply becomes unmanageable. . . . It is the existence of problems like these—the environmental, the energy, and the traffic problems—that convince me that high-speed rail is inevitable."

TRAINS: SPARING ENVIRONMENTAL HARM

THE INEVITABLE DEBUT

"This is not a quantum leap into the future;
this is a quantum leap into the present."
—Senator Mike Patrick,
Washington State Legislature

"WE ARE GOING TO PUT A MAN ON THE MOON BY THE
end of the decade." With those words, President John F. Kennedy
galvanized the nation into action. Filled with ambition and zeal,
America in the early 1960s began shaping its space effort, the
Apollo Program. Congress granted the funds; engineers toiled
over their drafting tables, and astronauts began their training.
By July of 1969, Americans had explored the moon.

The president made his declaration when no one was certain
about how to reach the moon, nor was the technology available.
Another element missing in the Apollo project was economic
justification. The program had to be carried out for the better-
ment of the world and for the prestige to the country, but it never
could be defended on economic grounds. Overriding the whole
effort was a major risk: could the astronauts be brought back
safely to Earth?

Yet, despite these problems, the United States went forward anyway, astonishing the world in the process.

More than a century earlier, the federal government fostered another pioneering effort—the settlement of the American West. The tool used to achieve that expansion was the railroad. Unlike the situation with the space program, the federal government did have enough information about how to achieve the goal. The proper technology was available to anyone who could read a book about railroads. The proper industrial prowess existed, because manufacturers for 35 years had been turning out locomotives, rails, telegraphic devices—all the equipment needed to build a working railroad.

It was difficult for private investors alone to push the first rail lines toward the Pacific. The government, seeing potential growth in vast unsettled lands, gave the railroad companies an economic incentive to head west by establishing the land grant program.

The point of these two stories is that leadership in Washington has sparked major advances in America, even when the government had to take economic, technological, and political risks. In the past it seems that federal leadership has been capable of vision, and of the far-reaching action necessary to achieve visionary goals.

America has all the knowledge, ability, and resources needed to build Supertrains, but has failed to build even one line anywhere in the country. Washington questions, and blindly questions some more. The federal government has stumbled around, too timid to make a commitment to help build Supertrains, and that's why the states have been the leaders.

One reason is that history views the railroads as abusing the privilege of westward expansion, and virtually every school-

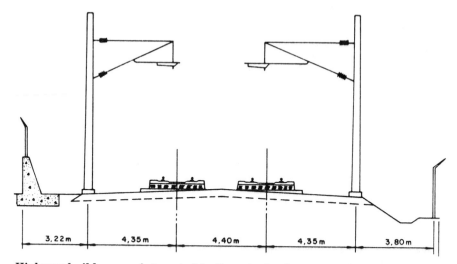

| 3.22 m | 4.35 m | 4.40 m | 4.35 m | 3.80 m |

Highway builders are interested in Supertrains because equipment used for grading and bridge building can be used in constructing new rail lines.

(Texas FasTrac Inc.)

child in America learns about the misconduct of the robber barons. As travelers, we still pay for those past sins. America's "let's not help the railroads" philosophy stems from the strong anti-railroad sentiment generated during the agrarian Populist and Progressive eras. However, we should not take our ancestors' attitudes about greedy railroad barons of the last century as justification to impede the visionaries today who would build super-speed, high-tech trains.

Yet, look at the record. The United States has had 10 secretaries of transportation, and only one has clearly stated that Supertrains might do this country some good. That was John A. Volpe, in President Richard Nixon's first term. Volpe had been a road builder and had served under Eisenhower as the nation's first Federal Highway Administrator, and he said high-speed trains might be an effective way to link the city centers of Los

Angeles and Washington, D.C., with new outlying airports. Others have said that Supertrains are worth discussion and some research.

Discussion and research? Yawn.

How about building them—now?

While other nations design and build super-speed trains, Washington has tended to do no more than issue reports, often inaccurate and misleading reports. The nation's capital has been the worst place to go for information about trains. Although that may be changing as the new decade unfolds, through the 1970s and 1980s congressmen were badly informed because of poor research done on Capitol Hill. In particular, the Congress relied upon a pathetic study done on Supertrains issued in December 1983 by the Congressional Office of Technology Assessment (OTA).

The sins of the report were many: it presented an untrue financial picture of the overseas Supertrains; it overlooked the critical importance such trains can play in helping to overcome some of the nation's most intractable problems—traffic gridlock, for one, and downtown decay, for another; it completely ignored the clear safety benefits of super-speed trains.

Making a bad situation worse, the publicists for the report ignored the few positive facts that Congressional researchers had identified. Americans would never know, by reading their newspapers, that the study identified four routes where Supertrains stood a chance of capturing profitable levels of traffic from airlines and highways, the Philadelphia–Pittsburgh, Los Angeles–San Diego, Chicago–Detroit, and Boston–Washington Corridors.

The Federal Railroad Administration and high-speed train commissions in several state capitals had better information

THE INEVITABLE DEBUT

about Supertrains, but, because of slipshod work in Washington, their views were lost in the shuffle.

None of this sat well with Chicago journalist F. K. Plous Jr., who has been writing about railroads since preparing a high school research paper in the late 1950s. The High Speed Rail Association, a group whose ire was raised by the Congressional OTA report, pressed Plous to pen a critique. He was anything but gentle:

"The study is a less than honest evaluation of America's high-speed rail options. It is appropriate to ask why the study, in spite of all the fanfare preceding it, turned out to be so superficial. Was there a deliberate effort on the part of OTA not to examine the real, substantive benefits of high-speed rail? If so, what interests are served by such a timid approach?"

Indeed, it was puzzling why OTA neglected one of the most important aspects of the domestic Supertrain scene—the willingness of states and even private entrepreneurs, rather than the national government, to finance and operate the new lines.

"In view of the Reagan administration's popular policy of returning all possible decision-making power to the states or the private sector, it is curious that this novel, 'Made in U.S.A.' approach to high-speed rail was ignored by OTA," wrote Plous. "OTA cannot be expected to act as a cheerleader for projects or to adopt certain technologies as pets. Neither, however, is the agency supposed to poison the potential for a new technology through suppression of favorable data, refusal to bring up pertinent issues, or biased presentation of those data selected for inclusion."

The report was bungled, pure and simple. Americans were cheated out of an understanding of how Supertrains could substantially ease a number of pressing problems. "The OTA approach to high-speed rail only postpones the hour at which those problems are solved and raises the eventual cost of solving them," stated Plous, who pinpointed the root problem behind OTA's flawed reporting:

"A lack of information cannot justify the negative tone of the OTA study. A similar lack of information existed prior to the development of the nation's existing transportation systems. Nevertheless, the Interstate Highway System and the Federal Airways System were built anyway. No one 'proved' in advance that they could be 'profitable' in a conventional, commercial sense—and no subsequent cost-benefit study has since shown that they are profitable in this sense. The simple fact that high-speed rail is attracting private venture capital suggests that the technology has a built-in superiority to its competition."

Furthermore, Plous added, "Travelers make their decisions based on the 'Mount Everest Theory of Transportation'—they choose to go by a given mode 'because it is there.' If there are good trains, people ride them. If there are good planes and convenient airports, people fly. If there are fast, safe expressways, people drive."

Exactly the same brand of federal pessimism toward a state initiative prevailed in the 1930s, when Pennsylvania was attempting to build its turnpike, the nation's first superhighway. The federal Bureau of Public Roads (BPR), forerunner of the Federal Highway Administration, believed two-lane intercity highways were adequate and scoffed at the idea of four-lane, limited-access, grade-separated toll roads.

But Pennsylvania pressed ahead, catching the attention of President Franklin Roosevelt, who in 1938 backed the revolutionary concept with a $29.25 million grant and the purchase of $40.8 million in turnpike bonds. To great fanfare, the first stretch of 160 miles opened October 1, 1940. The Bureau of Public Roads in the meantime had issued a report, *Toll Roads and Free Roads*, that "predicted" the turnpike would carry a mere 715 cars daily.

But as author Phil Patton noted in his 1986 book *Open Road*, "The BPR had no notion that the construction of new super-highways, like the introduction of such inventions as the telephone and the auto itself, might create its own demand. Within a year after *Toll Roads and Free Roads* was issued, the Pennsylvania Turnpike had already destroyed the bureau's assumptions of traffic flow. The superhighway the BPR predicted would carry only 715 cars a day was carrying nearly ten thousand." Over the years the turnpike expanded, and 270,000 autos a day would cruise the superhighway by 1990.

The OTA's report in the 1980s about Supertrains mirrors the same inaccurate, fact-starved, narrow approach as that of the federal highway bureaucracy of the 1930s. The parallels between Washington's early view of superhighways and its early view of Supertrains is uncanny.

It isn't just Congressional researchers who have done a bad job. Studies out of the Administration also fall short of the mark. Take for example the Department of Energy's March 1987 study, which was supposed to be a review of how the nation produces and uses energy. The document was absurd for what it *didn't* say. Despite a chapter titled "Energy Efficiency: Getting the Most from the Energy We Have," it utterly failed to deal with America's grossly excessive dependence on petroleum-based highway and aviation systems, and failed to offer one word about the good energy efficiency of Supertrains.

The inside cover of the report acknowledged help from 13 government agencies, with the Department of Transportation conspicuously absent. That was strange, considering that transportation is one of the nation's biggest users of energy. One wonders whether President Reagan's energy secretary, John S. Herrington, was on speaking terms with the transportation secretary at the time, James H. Burnley, or his immediate predecessor, Elizabeth Dole.

Despite all this nonsense, Supertrains are as inevitable as was the Wright Brothers' second flight.

Washington has binged on aviation and highways for so long, is so steeped in the postwar auto and aviation mentality, that it cannot see a transportation revolution taking place before its eyes. If it could, would it have budgeted $16.1 billion in its fiscal year 1991 budget for energy inefficient highways—the highest annual level of federal highway funding in the nation's history—while spending next to nothing on energy efficient Supertrains?

The capital city's inability to come to terms with the future is something relatively new and ominous in transportation. Historically, Americans have always enjoyed a reputation as successful inventors of new transport technologies, and as daring exploiters of breakthroughs developed elsewhere.

"Only about a decade of debate and turf disputing was necessary before the decision was made to build the Erie Canal," stated author Plous. "Only five years separated the opening of the first public steam railway in England and its first imitator in the United States. Seven years elapsed between Henry Ford's establishment of mass auto production and the pouring of the first slab of concrete highway near Detroit. Only Depression and war retarded the steady development of the United States highway infrastructure thereafter."

America's tradition of innovative transportation has changed. The French set a new world's record operating a passenger train at 206 mph during a test run in 1955, but the United States pretended not to notice. In 1964 the Japanese launched Bullet Train service. In the ensuing years the United States has failed to respond, has failed to either import or duplicate the advanced technologies, and has not laid a single mile of super-speed track.

The government often makes policies based on its reports, even when the reports are badly done. Perhaps that's why when President George Bush unveiled a clean-air plan, it ignored trains, which are the least polluting form of transportation.

With great fanfare, on March 8, 1990, Transportation Secretary Sam Skinner released a National Transportation Policy. The report, the front cover of which featured the walkway that connects terminals at Chicago's O'Hare International Airport, called for more private-sector involvement in transportation, including high-speed rail. That was followed by a February 1991 National Energy Strategy that briefly stated the federal government will pursue high-speed rail and maglev technologies as alternatives for auto travel and short-distance air travel.

Again Plous was unimpressed: "Now, every kind of report that comes out has a perfunctory paragraph about high-speed trains. They say, 'and planners should continue to examine the possibility of high-speed rail.' Then they walk away. They don't say how it should be funded or where it should be built. They don't develop the ideas for high-speed rail; they don't propose any money. They just sort of cite it, but they don't explain how it's important."

New York Times columnist Tom Wicker was even more blunt: "On the one hand the president cites the need for high-speed rail systems for trips of 100 to 500 miles. On the other, in his so-called new federal transportation 'policy,' no federal funds, except for research, are provided for high-speed systems. Meanwhile, numerous states, including Texas, Florida, California, Ohio, and Nevada, already are moving ahead with their own plans for these modern rail lines—no thanks to the man living in the White House."

The Administration's priorities came into question when President Bush inappropriately called for a "blueprint for a new national highway system" in the 1991 State of the Union address that focused on the Persian Gulf War. In the Democratic response, Senate Majority Leader George J. Mitchell asked, "If we can build a high-speed Patriot missile, can't we build a high-speed train? I believe we can."

One reason, perhaps, that Washington has not pushed harder for trains is that many of its technological programs are out of control. The cost of running the nation's premier high-technology agency, NASA, threatens to level the Treasury. Its $14.3 billion budget for 1991 makes it one of the fastest growing in government, but future spending is headed toward outer space. For instance, "America's planned space station, sold to Congress in 1984 as an $8 billion project, will actually cost at least $120 billion when operating and other expenses are counted," reported William J. Broad in the *New York Times*. The manned exploration of Mars by the year 2019 will cost as much as $500 billion; NASA's $25 billion space shuttle fleet has been grounded many times because of safety problems and fuel leaks, and its $1.6 billion Hubble Space Telescope satellite doesn't work properly because one of its mirrors was made in the wrong shape.

On a more down-to-earth level, the government did issue two reports in 1989 favorable to Supertrains—the Senate's maglev advisory committee report and the Argonne National Laboratory study—but, interestingly, both were produced by experts located outside of Washington.

In mid-1990, two additional reports were issued. In one, the Federal Railroad Administration concluded that maglev Supertrains are technically feasible in the United States. Finally, Washington was making some progress. But the report also concluded that the trains may be economically feasible in only a limited number of markets. It found that a range of only 850 miles to 2,600 miles of high-speed maglev lines could cover all operating and capital costs exclusive of right-of-way acquisition. The study effort was based on the premise that Supertrains would have to be unsubsidized even when competing with heavily subsidized aviation and highway systems.

In the other study, the Army Corps of Engineers said maglev trains had benefits such as reduced dependence on petroleum and reduced air pollution, then presented a long-term plan to design a United States maglev technology.

Both reports contained accurate information. The FRA confirmed that maglev Supertrains can reduce the need for some public spending for additional airport and highway capacity, and conceded that "public expenditures for maglev systems may be justified by these broad economic benefits."

The studies were getting somewhat better, but both recommended still more studies.

"I must question the Administration's commitment to providing the federal leadership that this field requires," said then-Congressman Doug Walgren of Pittsburgh. "Both the reports offer recommendations for federal action that I feel are far too timid and rely too heavily on the initiative of state and local governments and private industry."

Change is difficult. Historians often like to quote Niccolo Machiavelli, an Italian philosopher, who observed more than four centuries ago that "there is nothing more difficult to plan, more doubtful of success, nor more dangerous to manage than the creation of a new system. For the initiator has the enmity of all who would profit by the preservation of the old institutions and merely lukewarm defenders in those who would gain by the new ones. The hesitation of the latter arises in part from the fear of their adversaries, who have the laws on their side, and in part from the general skepticism of mankind which does not really believe in an innovation until experience proves its value." He could have been talking about Supertrains.

There are many more people who would travel by train, if only better trains were available. A Gallup poll in 1989 found that 44 percent of airline passengers think flying is dangerous, compared to only 10 percent in a decade-old poll conducted by an aircraft manufacturer. That's one potential market. Those who are beleaguered behind the steering wheel and want to give up driving automobiles represent another group of tens of millions. Then, there are America's existing train travelers who are convinced that Washington has discriminated against them. They would ride more trains if only more trains were available.

The Germans, the French, the Italians, the Spanish, the Japanese—all enjoy premier train service thanks to their central governments. What has happened in this country to make us so inept?

Why doesn't our government officially admit that the Supertrain technologies in Europe and Japan are practical and would work here? Why do we ignore the fact that thousands of scientists, engineers, mechanics, and executives overseas know *exactly* how the systems work and what the trains can accom-

THE INEVITABLE DEBUT

plish? Is our national pride so blind that we can't admit we can learn from others?

In earlier eras, we used the British-born steam locomotive to conquer time and distance; we copied Italian architecture in planning some of our biggest train stations; we studied French aerodynamic theories in developing our airplanes; and we modified German rocket designs in our space program. Why shouldn't we take advantage of foreign technology now to conquer pollution and gridlock?

Some Congressmen do not want foreign trains to operate in the United States, fearing the potential erosion of domestic technology expertise and jobs. Such fears are unfounded. If a Supertrain system were to be built, for instance, in the Pittsburgh–Philadelphia corridor, the overwhelming majority of jobs would be American, indeed, would be created right in the state, even if a foreign-design technology were used. But what if Pennsylvania fails to build that Supertrain line? What kind of jobs would be created?

If airlines were to purchase more airplanes to serve the route, chances are high that the orders would go to Boeing. But that company's products have a high level of foreign content as it routinely subcontracts major components to companies located overseas. Boeing proudly states, especially when seeking orders from Air France, that it subcontracts more work in France than its Airbus competitor, whose primary manufacturing plant is located in that country. McDonnell Douglas, too, has big subcontractors abroad, including in the Peoples Republic of China. Thus, airplane orders create many jobs—many overseas jobs.

Suppose Pennsylvania doesn't build that Supertrain line and instead builds another highway or turnpike. Americans will buy automobiles to drive over that road, and where will those vehicles come from? Experience says many will come from Japan, Germany, France, Korea, Yugoslavia, Italy, and other countries. Again, jobs are created overseas.

Cooperative ventures to build trains here in America could do more to create jobs at home than further expansions in jetliner or automobile fleets. If the United States wants to create work within its borders, it will accelerate plans to build Supertrain systems. If Pennsylvania wants to create jobs, it should accelerate efforts to link Philadelphia with Pittsburgh by Supertrains.

Americans should ask more questions, like, when will government officials place a higher value on saving lives by providing Supertrains that are much safer than driving or flying? When will the government start to provide better train service as an alternative to gridlock?

Frustrated travelers have the right to relief today, without interminable studies. Washington's contributions to space exploration and highway building happened because of effective leadership and action, not because every single puny question was answered in detail by a horde of dilatory bureaucrats. Travelers have the right to expect Supertrain systems to be built now.

What is clear is that the federal government cannot be the enemy, nor can it be the savior, to those wanting Supertrains in America. Washington has to be a partner in whatever progress lies ahead. Political leaders need to recognize that the new trains have public support. When Paul Taylor of the California-Nevada Super Speed Train Commission was asked, "Who's against your project?" he had to pause and think. Then he answered: "The 'againsts' are mostly skeptics. They're people who don't believe the train will ever be built. That's really it. This is a hard thing to be against."

THE INEVITABLE DEBUT

Washington needs to help in a number of ways. It could help build systems, instead of limiting its aid to financing research into an American-style maglev technology.

Why should the federal establishment refuse to help Florida build a Supertrain system while federal officials agree to finance more Florida highways? The entire nation will benefit as Florida's rail system helps reduce the country's oil imports. More Florida highways won't help, so why continue the imbalance?

Why should Washington refuse to help build a Chicago–Milwaukee–Minneapolis Supertrain line while it will help pay for a new Chicago airport? The train line will reduce air pollution, while a new airport will increase it. So why is the clean train system left in the poorhouse while the dirty airport benefits from free flowing cash?

Will Congress take the right steps?

Will the president?

The top echelon in the White House, pampered when traveling on *Air Force One* or other military jets, is out of touch with the needs of America's business and pleasure travelers. How unlike our heritage.

Republicans in the White House have in the past helped bring about new transport facilities that allowed America to grow. Abraham Lincoln, in an 1832 campaign for the Illinois General Assembly, was in favor of "the opening of good roads" as well as navigable streams. Theodore Roosevelt built the Panama Canal. Dwight Eisenhower brought the interstate highway system to reality.

The Democrats have helped mobility, too. In the Great Depression of the 1930s, President Franklin Roosevelt developed programs to put workers to the tasks of building roads, and, as already noted, helped pay to build the Pennsylvania Turnpike, predecessor to the interstate highway system. Lyndon B. Johnson signed legislation to rebuild part of the Boston–Washington rail corridor, a small but important program. President Kennedy launched the Apollo program, a project with technological spin-offs that have helped aerospace and aviation prosper.

When will the United States elect a president of either party who can provide the leadership needed to untangle our clogged roads and crowded skies? Will this country ever have a president like François Mitterrand, who has encouraged Supertrain development throughout France? Where is the visionary American who, when elected president, will finally declare—for the first time in our nation's history—that *"America will have a passenger train network second to none."*

Until then, Americans will have to depend on leadership from the states. Fortunately, there's plenty of it. Bit by bit, a consensus has grown in the states that Supertrains are the way to go, and the states are not just talking, they're doing. It's been difficult, because the state's coffers are not flush with money, as they have shouldered increased burdens passed on by a program-cutting federal government. Investments in super-speed trains started as a trickle, but every indication shows it spreading further, with small investments becoming larger as confidence grows that people will ride the Supertrains. Says Plous: "If Americans invest in high-speed trains, Americans will ride them."

The convergence of events means that today's equivalents to Dwight Eisenhower and John Kennedy are not in Washington; rather, they're in dozens of state and city governments. The "can-do" spirit is alive in grass roots America, where a mixture of synergism and serendipity is contributing to dramatic progress.

THE INEVITABLE DEBUT

An action plan for Washington might include these objectives:

1. **Fund transportation more realistically.**
2. **Start building super-speed train systems now.**
3. **Enact a federal law to permit Supertrains to use highway rights-of-way.**
4. **Eliminate useless Interstate Commerce Commission regulation.**
5. **Conduct research on high-speed ground transportation systems.**
6. **Modernize key Amtrak lines and give Amtrak a stable funding source.**

Let's take a brief look at these recommendations.

Fund transportation on a more realistic basis. One approach is to create a single federal transportation trust fund, with the best system built to serve the particular public need. Supertrain advocate Robert J. Casey has suggested that the Aviation Trust Fund be used to build maglev systems that serve airports.

"If new maglev systems could relieve even one-third of our airport delays, more than $30 billion in congestion costs would have been saved. That's enough to build a 2,000-mile maglev system, as the Argonne study says. So, I say let's not build more runways; let's not have more screeching airplanes over people's rooftops. Let's instead spend that money on high-speed trains."

A different approach was suggested by John Riley, former head of the Federal Railroad Administration: "I think we need to seriously consider the use of highway funds, not to build the high-speed rail systems, but to build the grade separations that are going to be required to make any speed rail system work. That maintains the basic principle of using highway funds only to build highways, but does it in a way that also promotes high-speed rail." Indeed, the start of a grade-crossing elimination program has been discussed in the Federal Highway Administration, with pro-road insiders admitting that a $1.2 billion program is justified.

The government can also improve laws relating to tax-exempt bond financing and loan-guarantee programs to ease the entry of private capital into Supertrain projects. If private interests in England and France can build a $14 billion cross-channel tunnel, surely the United States has the ability to be able to emulate their program.

Those are sensible recommendations. After all, by what logic is it acceptable for taxpayers to fund capacity in the form of a new highway, but not to fund capacity in the form of a new track? Why is it acceptable for public agencies to help build a new airport, which is environmentally destructive of the very area it is intended to serve, and not to fund environmentally benign high-speed trains?

There is no logic—if there were, the nation would have a unified transportation trust fund building systems that are easier on the environment, that save energy, and are more appropriate to travelers' needs.

Start building now. Ample justification exists for the federal government to begin construction of an advanced Amtrak line between Boston and New York and to help fund selected demonstration projects around the nation. People are stuck in traffic today. They want solutions today.

Enact a federal law to permit Supertrains to use highway rights-of-way. State laws are a hodgepodge of confusion regarding the right of Supertrain systems to use highway rights-of-way. According to Francis Francois of the American Association of State Highway and Transportation Officials, a survey showed that California law would permit Supertrains on highway property; New York would not. Michigan would permit highway land to be used, but only if Supertrains were built with public funds. A private system between Detroit and Chicago would be classified as a "commercial activity" and would be prohibited. One clear federal law needs to be passed to permit Supertrain developers to use highway rights-of-way at little or no cost.

The federal preemption would help; just as Congress aided interstate commerce by simplifying laws relating to waterways, railroads, highways, aviation, and telecommunications, so must Washington now set fair standards and rules for Supertrains to share space with highways.

Eliminate useless Interstate Commerce Commission Regulation. Why must the California-Nevada Super Speed Train Commission endure the costs of hiring lawyers to obtain a federal "certificate of service" to operate between Anaheim and Las Vegas when all the airlines have been freed of such unnecessary, constraining, bureaucratic regulatory obligations?

Conduct research on high-speed ground transportation systems. Long-term, the United States should refuse to surrender the market for high-technology trains to overseas interests. The United States can have domestically designed and manufactured steel-wheel and magnetic levitation Supertrains, but the government will have to help that industry similarly to the manner in which it helps aircraft manufacturers.

Such assistance should be aimed at numerous ventures. For example, Pittsburgh's Maglev Incorporated could Americanize the Transrapid for deployment in the United States, helping the city establish itself as a maglev manufacturing center. In San Francisco, Ernst Knolle's maglev design is a candidate for government research. In Essington, Pennsylvania, near Philadelphia, helicopter pioneer Frank Piasecki and his son John are

FEDERAL OUTLAYS FOR TRANSPORTATION ($ BILLIONS)

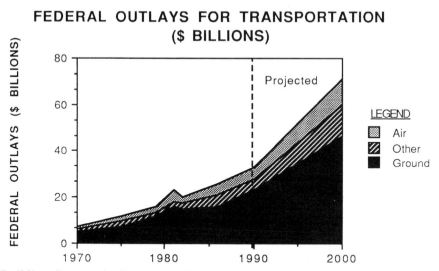

Building Supertrain lines, some Americans think, will only increase public expenditures for transportation. That is not a valid conclusion. Often overlooked is that all projections show the nation needs to spend more to insure future mobility. The question then becomes which modes the government will favor with funding.   *(Department of Transportation)*

working on a vehicle named Airtrain that hangs from trolleys and is driven by propellers. Elsewhere, others are pioneering trains where steel wheels run sideways on special rails; Raymond Lashley of Lashley Advanced Bi-Rail Systems in Syracuse, Utah, is designing a 200-mph version, while Stuart Resor, an architect in Cardiff By The Sea, California, is working on a 300-mph model named Railplane. Both trains look like an airplane fuselage, but with wheels instead of wings on the sides.

Modernize key Amtrak lines and give Amtrak a stable funding source. The federal government must help upgrade Amtrak routes that cross many state borders and constitute interstate commerce. The Boston–New York corridor is a prime example. Financing via a penny a gallon from the gasoline tax would be one way to put some rationality into the Amtrak funding process.

THE INEVITABLE DEBUT

The High Speed Rail Association is working for many of these goals in Washington, and has emerged as the single most effective force behind the Supertrain movement in the United States. The group is growing fast, helping the befuddled government focus its efforts, and building support by working on a friendly basis with other groups.

The result was that by April 1991, Washington was witnessing a flurry of legislative proposals to help Supertrains. Florida Senator Bob Graham met with the association. The brainstorming of ideas included establishing a federally aided High Speed Rail Venture Corporation to assist the states and consortiums with their projects.

The roll call of others introducing measures represented a geographic cross section of the country: Senate sponsors from the sunbelt included John H. Breaux, Louisiana; Richard H. Bryan and Harry Reid, Nevada; and Ernest F. Hollings, South Carolina. Support also came from Senators J. James Exon, Nebraska, and Paul Simon of Illinois, as well as Barbara A. Mikulski and Paul S. Sarbanes, both of Maryland. "It is almost criminal that we have not yet meaningfully exploited this technology," said Congressman Don Ritter of Pennsylvania as he, along with Al Swift of Washington, introduced a Supertrain bill in the House of Representatives. Even the Office of Technology Assessment yielded to the flood of developments and began to modify its views. In a 1991 report on train technologies, the agency finally recognized that Supertrains are technically feasible and could warrant federal support.

One Supertrain advocate, Paul Bartlett of Fresno, California, in urging a pro-train audience to be vocal, employed a timeless quote: "If the trumpeter gives forth an uncertain sound, who will hasten to the battle?"

One trumpeter is a television personality in Pittsburgh, Al Julius of KDKA. In a commentary early in 1990, he made the case for Supertrains in that city:

"This country is going to go back to trains and forward to high-speed trains. And we, here in western Pennsylvania, have the high-tech expertise plus the heavy industry experience to know exactly how to do it. If it takes seed money, *let's do it*. If it takes giving them right-of-way, *let's do it*. If it takes cooperating with the Japanese, *let's do it*. If we want to surpass what we were—whiz right by at 250 miles per hour what we were—right into the 21st century—hey, *let's do it*!"

Applauding was Robert J. Casey, who said, "This is not just a fad—it's going to happen. High-speed rail is not just a downgraded airplane, not just an upgraded train. It's a new form of transportation that continues to develop a special constituency."

Casey, when named to head Ohio's high-speed body in 1979, became the nation's first employee dedicated full time to Supertrains. After more than a dozen years in the business, he predicted: "The popularity of these trains will take off fast, similar to the early days of the interstate highways. There'll be many thousands of miles of high-speed train service in this country in the next 25 years. Thirty years from now, they'll be looking at new kinds of trains that we can't even imagine now."

Public consciousness on the topic has become widespread. Jay Leno, on the "Tonight Show," held up a clipping with the headline, "High Speed Train Could Reach Valley in Five Years." Leno, pointing to the Palmdale *Antelope Valley Press* story, quipped, "Gee, how early do I have to get up to catch that?" When jokes about Supertrains are told on a network entertainment show, that means the issue has reached mainstream America.

THE INEVITABLE DEBUT

EPILOGUE: A 21ST CENTURY RIDE

"Gimme a ticket for a fast train.
Ain't got time for an aeroplane."
—Possible lyrics to a future
hit compact disk recording

SAN FRANCISCO, MAY 7, 2005—THE EXCITEMENT OF launching north-south Supertrain service in California today rivals a Presidential inauguration. Bands compete to play patriotic marches, bunting surrounds a speakers' platform, and politicians boast of starting another new era of train travel.

"It used to be said that Californians had a love affair with the automobile," says the governor, who has worked for legislation that helped bring about the train service. "Maybe that was because there were no other lovers around. Today, it is clear that the object of your affection is the Supertrain."

Thousands of people surround the new Supertrains when, exactly at 7:00 A.M., the white and blue speedster slides out of the station *en route* to Los Angeles on its charter trip. Its passengers include the governor, as well as members of Congress, Hollywood stars, and reporters.

Crowding the station are people boarding the first train to carry paying passengers, scheduled to depart five minutes after

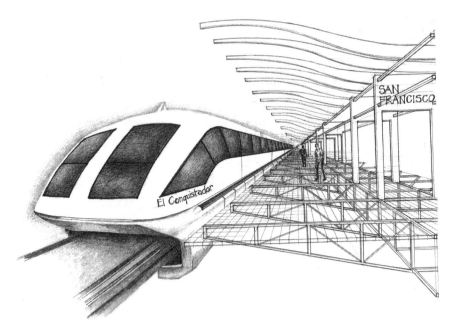

(*Jean Marie O'Toole*)

the inaugural special. *El Conquistador*, fully booked months in advance, will carry executives, artists, entrepreneurs, computer experts, lawyers, and families with small children.

Other Supertrains—their sleek aerodynamic shapes suggesting that they are poised to run a race—are ready to leave on schedules that call for departures every five minutes at this time of day.

After the special carrying the dignitaries departs, attention turns to *El Conquistador*. It looks like a jet about to take off, with three major exceptions—the train has no wings; it's quiet, and it has oversized window panes.

When the gates open, the crowd moves briskly, as the shiny

EPILOGUE: A 21ST CENTURY RIDE

windows reflect images of approaching passengers. They notice what appears to be an airline pilot, but turns out to be a smartly dressed train engineer heading toward *El Conquistador's* control cabin.

Travelers pass through pressurized plug doors that slide silently shut, similar to those on aircraft. Rubber seals insure uniform air pressure throughout the trip, even through tunnels, so there will be no bothersome ear-popping.

The train's interior is fully carpeted and outfitted with roomy storage space above the seats. Oversized padded armrests, individual reading lights, a fold-down tray, and curtained windows promise comfort. Most importantly, after many flights in four-abreast jetliner seating, passengers are thrilled to find no more than two seats side-by-side, plush, wide and offering ample legroom. Some passengers, when settling in, grope for a seat belt that isn't there.

Most passengers speak in hushed tones, almost whispering. "It's the mood," explains the conductor. "People aren't elbowing each other to get their packages on the overhead racks as they do on airplanes. Also, we have no rule to stay in your seat on 'takeoff.' This trip is meant to be enjoyed."

A few seconds before departure, a chime sounds to warn that the doors are closing. The train glides out of the station so smoothly that the acceleration is imperceptible.

Facing each seat, a flat electrical panel allows business travelers to plug in their portable computers, place phone calls via the train's telecommunications center, and transmit documents to virtually anywhere in the world. Passengers can flip a switch to reveal a television monitor that shows 52 channels, featuring everything from cartoons to cooking shows, soap operas to soccer.

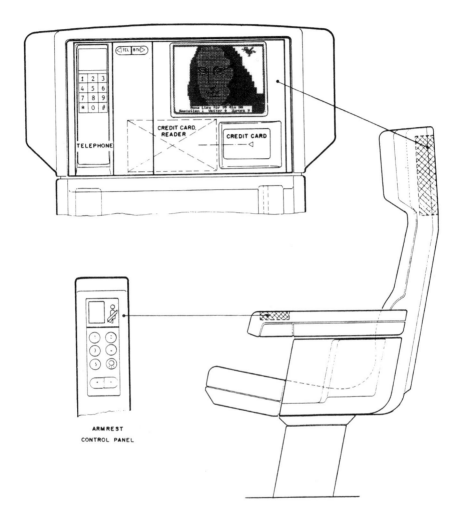

Communications system for train seats.

(Texas FasTrac Inc.)

EPILOGUE: A 21ST CENTURY RIDE

Few passengers do so today, however, being caught up in the excitement.

As the Supertrain moves at an easy pace through the suburbs, passengers begin to circulate through the train. The ride is so smooth that no one appears to have any difficulty walking. Elderly travelers appreciate how easy it is to move through the train, as there are no access doors between cars.

Those who explore the length of *El Conquistador* are entertained by the different types of cars. A catering car offers a "bistro" snack section, as well as a restaurant with more substantial fare. Meals are delivered to passengers at their seats, but many want to stretch their legs and get their own.

Another Supertrain car contains a conference room, where eight executives are already deep in work. The elegant wood-paneled room offers all the necessities—a speaker phone, photocopier, computer jacks, videocassette player, and telefax machine. Coffee steams on the hot plate. Adjacent to the conference room, the conductor's office includes a panel that displays the status of all connecting trains at Los Angeles.

Further forward, the luxurious first-class section offers even more roomy two-and-one seating with tinted glass partitions for semi-privacy. Another car is a double-decker called the "family compartment car." Some children gather around toys in the play area while others gaze, transfixed at the windows by the passing scenes. No babies cry, although one is being fed in the nursery by its relaxed parents.

Of all the surprises, perhaps the most pleasant is the variety of interior color schemes, which makes it easier for passengers to remember which car is theirs. Even the small water fountains in each car match the surrounding colors and design.

(ABB Traction Inc.)

El Conquistador, far from urban areas by now, glides along at 300 mph. Even at that speed it is quiet. The only train-related noise is a faint hiss of air moving through the coach. Some passengers doze while the train whizzes by cars and trucks on parallel highways.

Two trains follow, each serving intermediate stations on a "skip stop" pattern. The 7:10, for example, stops at the San Jose International Airport, Fresno, and Bakersfield, while the 7:15 serves Redwood City, Stockton, Merced, and the new Palmdale International Airport. The 7:20 is another nonstop express.

A mere two hours after leaving San Francisco's city center,

EPILOGUE: A 21ST CENTURY RIDE

El Conquistador pulls into Los Angeles Union Passenger Terminal—on time—while the politicians from the inaugural train are already being interviewed on live television news shows. The grand Los Angeles terminal, an example of Mission Spanish and Mediterranean architecture, is filled with crowds celebrating the arrival of the first Supertrains from the Bay Area.

Each Supertrain is greeted by leaders of environmental organizations who hail the train's energy efficiency and low pollution rate. Such groups have pushed the idea for years as a way to reduce oil imports and as an alternative to more airports and highways in crowded areas.

Most trains continue past Union Station to Los Angeles International Airport. The integration of Supertrains with so many air terminals illustrates how trains have become a vital part of the air system. Also, virtually every Supertrain connects at Union Station with a parade of other advanced super-speed trains destined for San Diego, Las Vegas, Palm Springs, Phoenix, and Tucson. The station is a bustling hub for local light-rail lines as well, a rapid transit system, and scores of commuter trains to Orange, Riverside, and Ventura county population centers.

This newest of the Supertrain lines was sparked by the 1990s initiation of Supertrains elsewhere, which were a hit with the public the day they began running. Indeed, other parts of the country beat the Los Angeles–San Francisco route in getting super-speed trains up and running. Dallas and Houston were connected by Supertrains several years ago. In the Northeast, fast trains blaze between Boston and New York, while several lines operate in the flatlands of Florida.

There are major differences in the trains. *El Conquistador*, for example, is a magnetic levitation train, while some lines have

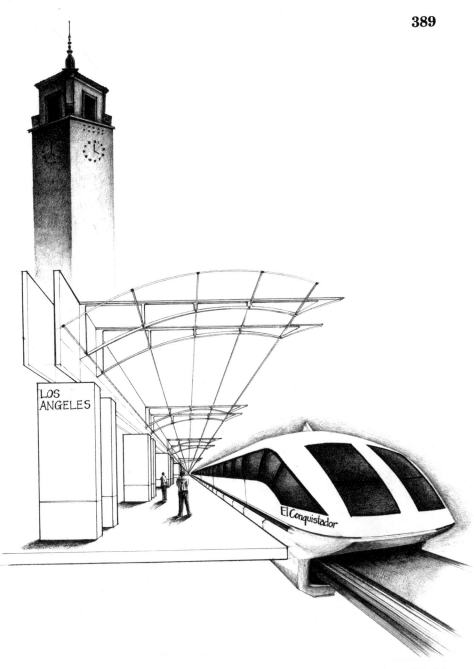

LOS
ANGELES

El Conquistador

(Jean Marie O'Toole)

EPILOGUE: A 21ST CENTURY RIDE

LINEAR MOTOR CAR MAGLEV

RAILWAY TECHNICAL RESEARCH INSTITUTE

(Japan Railway Technical Research Institute)

advanced steel-wheel systems. Yet, passengers who have ridden both say the experience is virtually identical.

Both train types offer superior ride quality and comfort, and both are faster than air travel on the short- to intermediate-distance routes they serve. Regardless of the mechanical apparatus involved, the new technologies are so alluring that they have quickly converted tens of millions of people to train travel. Experts are calling it a transportation revolution as Supertrains make travel quicker, safer, more dependable, and less susceptible to weather.

With Supertrains, commuters can work in cities that previously were too distant to reach by auto. Some are taking Supertrains as a less expensive option to avoid new pollution-related auto taxes, higher gasoline taxes, and exorbitant parking fees.

Airlines are catering to Supertrain travelers. For example, passengers still fly Los Angeles to Dallas, but most prefer taking the Supertrain on the continuing segments to places like Houston and San Antonio. Most airlines will include those Supertrain trips in their frequent-flyer plans.

New Supertrain industries have sprouted, and old companies have adapted to changing times. A Pittsburgh enterprise manufactures high-speed trains, while a Colorado supplier of jetliner seats now builds a wider model for trains. Highway contractors are working on new Supertrain links between Cleveland and Cincinnati, from Pittsburgh to Philadelphia, on a routing from Atlanta to a new super-airport, and on a network centered in Chicago that will reach Minneapolis, Detroit, St. Louis, and Indianapolis.

Cities are competing for Supertrains. Beaumont officials demand that the Texas system be extended eastward though their city to New Orleans, while the Louisiana communities of Shreveport and Baton Rouge want to see it routed their way.

The nation's attention today, however, is on California. The consensus aboard *El Conquistador* and other Supertrains could be summed up in these few words: "We should have done this sooner."

FURTHER READING

GOVERNMENT AGENCIES AND PRIVATE CONSORTIUMS have issued dozens of Supertrain-related studies and reports in recent years. A listing of such documents would quickly be outdated. It will prove more helpful to present names of organizations that are sources for data about high-speed trains in North America:

Amtrak, Washington, D.C.

Argonne National Laboratory, Argonne, Illinois.

California-Nevada Super Speed Train Commission, Las Vegas.

Caltrans, Los Angeles-Bay Area High Speed Rail Study Group, Sacramento.

Carnegie Mellon High Speed Ground Transportation Center, Pittsburgh.

Florida High Speed Rail Transportation Commission, Tallahassee.

Georgia Department of Transportation, Atlanta.

High Speed Rail Association, Pittsburgh.

Illinois Department of Transportation, Springfield.

Michigan Department of Transportation, Lansing.

Minnesota Department of Transportation, St. Paul.

New Mexico Department of Transportation, Santa Fe.

New York Department of Transportation, Albany.

Ohio High Speed Rail Authority, Columbus.

Ontario-Quebec High Speed Rail Task Force, Toronto.

Pennsylvania Department of Commerce, Harrisburg.

Queen's University, Canadian Institute of Guided Ground Transport. Kingston, Ontario.

Texas High Speed Rail Authority, Austin.

United States Army Corps of Engineers, Washington, D.C.

United States Federal Railroad Administration, Washington, D.C.
United States Senate Maglev Technology Advisory Committee, Washington, D.C.
Washington Department of Transportation, Olympia.
Wisconsin Department of Transportation, Madison.

BOOKS OF INTEREST

Allen, Geoffrey Freeman. *Railways of the Twentieth Century*. New York: W. W. Norton, 1983.

Cohen, Linda R. and Roger G. Noll. *The Technology Pork Barrel*. Washington, D.C.: Brookings Institute, September 1990.

Cupper, Dan. *The Pennsylvania Turnpike—A History*. Lebanon, Pa.: Applied Arts Publishers, 1990.

Hughes, Murray. *Rail 300: The World High Speed Train Race*. North Pomfret, Vt.: David & Charles Inc., 1988.

Itzkoff, Donald M. *Off The Track: The Decline of the Intercity Passenger Train in the United States*. Westport, Conn.: Greenwood Press, 1985.

Lyon, Peter. *To Hell in a Day Coach*. New York: J. B. Lippincott, 1968.

Pell, Claiborne. *Megalopolis Unbound: The Supercity and the Transportation of Tomorrow*. New York: Frederick A. Praeger, Inc., 1966.

Renner, Michael. *Rethinking the Role of the Automobile*. Washington, D.C.: Worldwatch, 1989.

Runte, Alfred. *Trains of Discovery*. Niwot, Colo.: Roberts Rinehart, Inc., 1990.

Southerland, Jr., Thomas C. and William McCleery. *The Way to Go: The Coming Revival of United States Rail Passenger Service*. New York: Simon and Schuster, 1973.

ACKNOWLEDGMENTS

WRITING A BOOK IS A DAUNTING TASK, LIGHTENED by the feeling of being helped by so many people. I owe special thanks to novelist Tom Clancy, who rides the trains of today, for offering to write the Foreword to this book.

I'm thankful and indebted to many who gave so generously of their time. I've been privileged to interview experts from around the world—scientists, engineers, business leaders, railroaders, airline management, aircraft manufacturers, anti-airport environmentalists, highway builders, professors, lawyers, federal and state officials, congressmen, and, of course, manufacturers of super-speed train equipment.

Information has come into my office from more than 300 sources in 19 countries.

I am specially indebted to Robert J. Casey of the High Speed Rail Association for spending many hours over many months responding to my inquires.

My work has benefitted greatly from the help and advice of Dan Cupper of Precision Editing, Harrisburg, Pennsylvania, who possesses an expert knowledge of transportation issues. I'm also thankful that Jim Fitzgerald, my editor at St. Martin's Press, shares my enthusiasm for trains as well as for this book, and to Mel Berger at the William Morris Agency.

I appreciate the assistance of many others: Paul Arneson, a Washington, D.C., attorney; Claire Austin, Arne J. Bang, and Jim McQueen of the Federal Railroad Administration; Bob Banks, of R. L. Banks and Associates, Incorporated; Don Deer, Capital Ideas; Ross Capon, National Association of Railroad Passengers; Mark Dysart, Transportation & Communications

Union; Hermann Eisele, Texas High Speed Rail Corporation; Mike Fite; Edward A. Greene, United States Army Corps of Engineers; Sean P. Hankinson and David S. Glass, University of Pittsburgh at Johnstown; Gigi Jantos, Pennsylvania General Assembly; Milton G. Jaques, National News Speakers Bureau.

Also, Richann Johnson, California-Nevada Super Speed Train Commission; Sandy Jones, Grumman Corporation; Donald L. Lindsey, Brotherhood of Locomotive Engineers; Dina Levinsky, K-III Press, Incorporated; Frank Maggio, HSST Corporation; Stephen J. McKnight, High Speed Rail Association; Kevin McKinney, *Passenger Train Journal*; Luther Miller, *Railway Age*; Jean Marie O'Toole, Catholic University; Joan Turkaly Patchett; Larry Salci, Jeanine Ipsen, and Mary Anne Kowalski, Bombardier Corporation; Henry C. Schrader, URS Consultants; Victor Shafarenko, Gross & Janes Company; Joseph S. Silien, ABB Traction Incorporated; Donald M. Itzkoff, Daniel K. Steen, and Meg Stevens, all of Reed Smith Shaw & McClay; Jennifer Blei Stockman, Stockman & Associates; David Tittsworth, House Committee on Energy and Commerce; John Baesch, Bruce Heard, and Sue Martin, all of Amtrak; Dan Lovegren, Matt Paul, and Rich Tolmach, all of Caltrans.

Although I've been helped by many friends and colleagues through this effort, the work is mine and I alone am responsible for its contents.

INDEX

Numbers in italics refer to illustration captions

McKay, Brian, 165
McLane, Louis, 21
Madison (WI), 195
Madrid–Seville line, 54
Maechel, Jean Francois, 170
Maglev Incorporated, *129*, 134, 187, 378
Maglev Mid-Atlantic Working Group, 210–11
Maglev Technology Advisory Committee, 120–21, 127
Maglev Transit, 103, 142, 221
Maglev 2000, 131
Maglev USA, 200
Magnetic levitation trains (maglevs), xii, 6–7, 8, 15, 18–19, *20*, 86–137, *140*, 180, 182–83, 186, 196, 200–1, 204–5, 209, *303*, 333, 335, *348*, 370; repulsive vs. attractive, 90, *95*, 109, 135
Maine, 254
Malone, Larry, 195
Manry, Daniel, 143
Martin, James G., 211
Martin, John R., 262
Martinez, Bob, 142
Massachusetts Institute of Technology (MIT), 116
Mathieu, Albert, 44
Mathieu, Gerard, 28, 31, 36, 37, 68, 69
M-Bahn systems, 90, 105, 136
MBB, 59, 98, 100
Meade, Dale M., 326
Meeker, William, 346
Menden, Werner, 100
Meral, Gerald H., 354
Messina Straits bridge, 63
Metroliner, xi, 91, 123, 197, *232*, 237, *239*, 243–45, 248
Miami (FL), *70*, 139; –Orlando–Tampa line, 146–55
Michigan, 193, 194, 340, 378
Midwest, 189–96
Midwest High-Speed Rail Transit Conference (1967), 192–93
Mikita, Makoto, 136
Mikulski, Barbara A., 137, 200, 380
Mills, James, 253
Milrite Council, 184
Milwaukee (WI), 189, 195, 237, 374
Mineta, Norman Y., 358
Minneapolis (MN), 189, 195, 374
Mitchell, George J., 369
Mitre Corporation, 115
Mitsubishi, 109, 124–25, 136
Mitterrand, François, 26, 44, 212, 375

Miyazaki, Japan, 109, 111, 112
ML-500, 109
MLU-002, *98*, 109, 110–11, *114*, *118*
Molitoris, Jolene, 173, 193
Montgomery, Larry, 171
Montgomery, W. David, 292, 295
Montreal, Canada, 192, 200–1, 254
Moore, Clifton A., 159, 271
Moore, Kate L., 240
Morgan Stanley, 219–20
Morton, Alastair, 48
Moscow, 112–13
Moynihan, Daniel P., 94, 119–22, 125, 127, 130, 135, 346, 351, 352, 358
Mrazek, Bob, 122–24, 125
Munich, 104

Nakasone, Prime Minister, 108
NASA, 121, 125, 296, *307*, 308, 309, 310, 369
National Airport, 199, 287–88, 298
National Association of Railroad Passengers, 185, 228, 243
National City Lines, 355
National Governors' Association, 17
National Highway Committee, 104
National Interstate and Defense Highway System, 104
National Maglev Initiative, 131
National Mediation Board, 5
National Pike, 349
National Science Foundation, 116
Natural Resources Defense Council, 161
Neely, Bob, 170, 291
Neerhout, John, 48
Nelson, Bryce, 171
Nelson, James, 216
Netherlands, 16, 26, 42
Neue Bahn, 65
Nevada, 109, 139, 187
Newark Airport, 275
New Haven (CT), 246, 249, 252
New Haven Railroad, 303
New Jersey, 198
New Mexico, 206
New Orleans (LA), 213
New York Central Railroad, 23, 226
New York City, 97, 105, 127, 192, 196–97, 199, 200, 220–21, 244, 248, 258, 262, 287, 333; –Boston line, *247*, 249–52; –Buffalo line, 237; –Chicago line, 23, 98, 226; –Montreal line, 200–1; –Washington line, 91, 200, 237, 243–44, 248; Westside Connection, 244. *See*

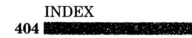